Code Crafting

Code Crafting no. 4

The Language Stack: From Silicon to Semantics

Second edition

Set Lonnert
with AI Coöperation

Cover illustration in: Rudbeck, Olof the Younger. c. 1693–1710. The Book of Birds (also known as Entomologia et Ornithologia). Watercolour manuscript. Uppsala University Library. *An illustration of the woodlark.*
http://urn.kb.se/resolve?urn=urn:nbn:se:alvin:portal:record-103375
The work is marked with Public Domain Mark 1.0 Universal

Second edition.
Author: © 2026 Set Lonnert
AI Support: Multiple large language models
Publisher: BoD · Books on Demand, Östermalmstorg 1, 114 42 Stockholm, Sweden, bod@bod.se
Print: Libri Plureos GmbH, Friedensallee 273, 22763 Hamburg, Germany
ISBN: 978-91-8134-438-7

Contents

Foreword i

Introduction 1

I The Machine 9

1 Instruction Sets and Memory 11
1.1 The Fetch-Decode-Execute Loop . . . 12
1.2 Stack Machines and Register Machines . . . 13
1.3 The 6502: A Minimal ISA . . . 14
1.4 RISC-V: A Compiler-Friendly Design . . . 16
1.5 Memory Models . . . 17
1.6 The Embedded Constraint as a Clarity Instrument . . . 19
1.7 Exercises . . . 20

2 A Virtual Machine in Software 21
2.1 Why Virtual Machines? . . . 22
2.2 A Stack Machine in Two Hundred Lines . . . 23
2.3 The Register Machine Variant . . . 27
2.4 Dispatch Strategies . . . 30
2.5 Bytecode as a Language . . . 32
2.6 Counting the Cost . . . 35
2.7 Exercises . . . 36

II From Text to Structure 39

3 Lexical Analysis 41
3.1 The Scanner's Contract . . . 41

3.2 A Model for Tokens: Finite Automata . . . 44
3.3 What Regular Languages Cannot Do . . . 46
3.4 Building Lark's Scanner . . . 47
3.5 Reporting Lexical Errors . . . 55
3.6 Exercises . . . 56

4 Parsing **59**
4.1 Context-Free Grammars . . . 60
4.2 Recursive Descent . . . 61
4.3 LL(1): Making Recursive Descent Formal . . . 64
4.4 Bottom-Up Parsing . . . 66
4.5 Choosing a Strategy . . . 67
4.6 Abstract Syntax Trees . . . 68
4.7 Error Handling . . . 72
4.8 Exercises . . . 74

III Meaning **77**

5 Names, Scope, and Types **79**
5.1 Names and the Symbol Table . . . 79
5.2 Scope . . . 82
5.3 Types as Ontology . . . 83
5.4 The Simply Typed Lambda Calculus . . . 84
5.5 Hindley-Milner Type Inference . . . 85
5.6 Algebraic Data Types and Pattern Matching . . . 89
5.7 Affine Types and Ownership . . . 93
5.8 Traits . . . 96
5.9 Type Errors as Design . . . 99
5.10 Exercises . . . 101

6 A Working Interpreter **105**
6.1 Tree-Walking Evaluation . . . 105
6.2 Environments and Closures . . . 107
6.3 Attribute Grammars . . . 109
6.4 Tail Calls and the CEK Machine . . . 110
6.5 The Ceiling of the Interpreter . . . 117
6.6 Exercises . . . 118

IV Compilation **121**

7 Intermediate Representations **123**
7.1 The Case for an Intermediate Representation 124
7.2 Three-Address Code 125
7.3 Control-Flow Graphs 128
7.4 Static Single Assignment 129
7.5 Common Subexpressions and the DAG 130
7.6 Lowering Lark to TAC 131
7.7 Running the Intermediate Representation 136
7.8 Exercises 139

8 Optimization **143**
8.1 What Optimization Is 143
8.2 Constant Folding and Propagation 144
8.3 Dead Code Elimination and Reachability 145
8.4 Expression Simplification 147
8.5 Loop-Invariant Code Motion 147
8.6 The Diminishing Returns of Optimization 148
8.7 Exercises 149

9 Code Generation **153**
9.1 From Intermediate Representation to Instructions 153
9.2 Instruction Selection 154
9.3 Register Allocation 155
9.4 Targeting RISC-V 157
9.5 The 6502 as Contrast 159
9.6 Tail-Call Elimination in Generated Code 159
9.7 The Program on Silicon 161
9.8 Exercises 162

First Interlude: One Program, All the Way Down **165**

Second Interlude: One Theorem, All the Way Down **169**

V Foundations **173**

10 Abstract Machines and Operational Semantics **175**
10.1 What an Abstract Machine Is 176
10.2 The SECD Machine 176
10.3 The CEK Machine 177

10.4 Machines as Operational Semantics 178
10.5 The Warren Abstract Machine 179
10.6 A Miniature Prolog 179
10.7 What Abstract Machines Teach 180
10.8 Exercises 181

11 Correctness **183**
11.1 What "Correct" Means 183
11.2 Hoare Logic 184
11.3 Type Safety: Progress and Preservation 185
11.4 Formal Specification 187
11.5 Testing a Compiler 188
11.6 Trusting Code You Did Not Write 188
11.7 Affine Types: Correctness the Checker Enforces 189
11.8 Exercises 190

12 Types as Proofs **193**
12.1 Curry–Howard Made Exact 194
12.2 What Dependent Types Add 196
12.3 The Proof Kernel `lcore` 196
12.4 Lark's Soundness Proof, Read 198
12.5 The Road From Lark 200
12.6 The Limit 201
12.7 Exercises 201

13 The Adversary **205**
13.1 Making the Language Attackable 206
13.2 Manufacturing Adversaries 207
13.3 Validating the Validator 209
13.4 The Certificate 211
13.5 The Hole in the Affine Wall 212
13.6 Who Checks the Checker 214
13.7 What the Adversary Leaves Standing 217
13.8 Exercises 218

Conclusion **221**

A The Lark Language **225**
A.1 What Lark is 225
A.2 What Lark is not 226
A.3 The language at a glance 227
A.4 Grammar 228

A.5 Quick reference 230

B The Decision Record **233**
B.1 Phase 0 — Language design and the lexer (`lark/01`) 233
B.2 Phase 2 — The parser (`lark/02`) 234
B.3 Phase 3 — The type checker (`lark/03`) 235
B.4 Phase 4 — The interpreter: the CEK machine (`lark/04`) 235
B.5 Phase 5 — The compiler and its analyses (`lark/05`) 236
B.6 Phase 6 — Hardening (`lark/06`) 237
B.7 Phase 7 — Native runtime and REPL (`lark/07`) 237
B.8 Phase 8 — Rigour: exhaustiveness, totality, defined `Int` (`lark/08`) 238
B.9 Phase 9 — The adversary: generation, certificates, discharge (`lark/09`) 239

C Reading the Formalism **241**
C.1 A Judgement Is a Question 241
C.2 An Inference Rule Is a Clause of a Recursive Function 242
C.3 A Proof by Induction Is a Recursive Function 244
C.4 The Symbols, in One Table 245
C.5 How to Read a Formal Statement 245

Bibliography **250**

Index **251**

CONTENTS

Foreword

This is a book about building one small programming language—Lark—all the way down: from the instruction set of a real processor to a machine-checked proof that the language's meaning is sound, with no level left as a black box. It is a continuous construction, treating the hardware, the theory, and the proof as parts of one argument rather than separate subjects.

Companion code. Everything in this book exists twice: once as prose, once as running code. The repository at `https://github.com/Feyerabend/stack` contains two directory trees.

`lark/` holds Lark itself as a sequence of sealed build-phase snapshots; each folder is self-contained and runnable. The root holds per-chapter companion code, worked examples, alternative implementations in `/ch01/` to `/ch13/`.

Lark build phases. Each `lark/0N/` folder is a snapshot sealed at the end of the corresponding phase. Phase numbers skip from 0 to 2 because Phase 1 (a machine-checked type-soundness proof) was completed between Phases 4 and 5 and lives in `lark/formal/proof/` rather than a numbered snapshot.

Folder `lark/`	Ph.	Content	Ch.
01/	0	Language design: grammar, lexer, acceptance tests	3
02/	2	Frontend: LL(1) parser, AST	4
03/	3	Type checker: Algorithm W, affine tracking	5
04/	4	CEK interpreter: pattern matching, IO	6
05/	5	Compiler: TAC IR, RV32I backend, Pico 2/2W	7, 9
06/	6	Hardening: differential tests, formal spec	8, 11
07/	7	C CEK native runtime, REPL, sample programs	10
08/	8	Rigour: exhaustiveness, totality, defined `Int`	13
09/	9	Adversary: typed-program fuzzing, certified regalloc	13
`formal/proof/`	1	Machine-checked soundness proof, `lcore` kernel	11–13

Appendix A, *The Lark Language*, is a standalone reference to the language—what it is, what it is not, and its full grammar. The design decisions taken at each phase—and the alternatives weighed against them—are collected in Appendix B, *The Decision Record*.

Code from my book *From Code to Computation* [Lonnert, 2026] reappears throughout this repository.

Introduction

Why Build a Language?

There is a fair objection to a book like this, and it belongs first. It is 2026. A large language model can generate a lexer, a type checker, and a working bytecode compiler from a description of the language, in seconds, on request. So why spend the months it takes to learn to build these things by hand?

The book concedes the premise. A capable model can produce most of the code in these pages, and produce it quickly; pretending otherwise is the one claim the book is least entitled to make. *The value was never in the typing.* It is in a kind of reasoning that the construction forces—and that turns out to be exactly what using such a tool well requires.

The Question Under the Objection

The objection proves too much. A surgeon who understands anatomy reasons differently from one who does not, even when a robot makes the incision; a structural engineer who understands load paths thinks differently about a building, even when the stress calculations are automated. The question is never whether the tool exists. It is what understanding the practitioner brings to directing it, and to judging what it hands back.

Language implementation is where that understanding lives in its most concentrated form. A type system is a formal claim about what programs mean; a register allocator is a constraint-satisfaction problem with a cost model; a calling convention is a contract between independently compiled modules. A generated artifact is an *assertion*, and an assertion you cannot evaluate is not knowledge—it is a hope with good syntax. If you do not understand the answer, you have not outsourced the task; you have abandoned the position from which it could be checked.

So the real question is not *how do I build a compiler?* It is *what kind of thinking does a language embody, and how does that thinking propagate from hardware to syntax to type system?* Language design is not a solved engineering problem; it is, in part, a philosophical one. What should a type system be able to say? When is a constraint a safety property and when is it a limitation? What is it that ownership owns? These questions have no algorithmic answers, but they have precise ones, and finding them requires the reasoning compilers reward: close attention to definitions, the ability to hold a hierarchy of abstractions in mind at once, and comfort with the fact that a choice at the type-theory level reaches all the way down to the register allocator.

That last kind of reasoning—*propagative* reasoning, following a decision through the levels it constrains—is precisely where current models are weakest. They are strong at producing working code from familiar patterns and much weaker when the pattern does not fit: when a type-system decision creates a downstream constraint in the code generator, or an assumption baked into an intermediate representation turns out wrong for the target. This book is a sustained exercise in that reasoning, and it returns to the LLM question once more in the Conclusion—now that the reader has the machinery to see the answer rather than be told it.

How to Use a Tool You Could Be Used By

It would be evasive to raise the LLM question and offer only a defense of understanding in the abstract. The book also teaches—as compiler engineering, because that is what it is—the concrete discipline for working with generated code. A model asked confidently enough will produce a constant-folding pass that is unsound on floating point, a copy-propagation that silently breaks a variable assigned on two branches, or a claim that a control-flow graph has a back edge where it has only a call. These are not hypothetical; they are among the mistakes made and caught while this book was written. Catching them is not a matter of trust but of having an *oracle*.

Lark's runtime interpreter *defines* what a program means, so any compiled back end that disagrees with it has a bug, and a differential-testing harness will say which one (Chapter 11). The type-safety theorem says what a correct transformation may never do—turn a well-typed program into a stuck one—so it bounds what any generated pass is allowed to be. These tools let you accept or reject what a model produces on evidence rather than faith, and the book builds them in the open. Lark itself was built with the assistance of large language models; the reasoning behind every design decision is in the book and the repository, not hidden inside a generation process. Tool-assisted construction, human-owned understanding—that is the intended model for what this kind of technical work looks like now.

The Books That Already Exist

This book does not replace the standard texts; it exists because none of them quite asks this question. *Crafting Interpreters* [Nystrom, 2021] is exceptional on its own terms—Nystrom writes with unusual clarity, and the tree-walker-then-bytecode-VM strategy is pedagogically sound—but it stops, by design, before the territory becomes formally interesting: no type system worth the name, no ownership semantics, no abstract machines in the sense that connects to operational semantics. The language that emerges is a pleasant scripting language, and that is the intent.

Appel's *Modern Compiler Implementation* [Appel, 1998] has the right instinct—one example language, Tiger, built from the first chapter—but it is a quarter century old, its ML/C/Java editions feel like three incomplete versions of one idea, and its type system is not the one interesting languages now have. *Engineering a Compiler* [Cooper and Torczon, 2022] is the most accurate and organized of the four, and the hardest to use as a first encounter: it is organized the way a compiler is, not the way understanding develops. The Dragon Book [Aho et al., 2006] is comprehensive, authoritative, and by design a reference—a reader meeting it first is trying to understand a cathedral from the maintenance manual.

Each is a good book. None carries one language from a real instruction set to a machine-checked proof that its meaning is sound, treating the hardware, the theory, and the proof as parts of a single argument. That is the gap this book is for.

What This Book Does Differently

Four commitments, taken seriously, define the book's direction.

Hardware is not abstracted away. Real instruction sets—the 6502 as a historical lens, RISC-V as the modern target—appear as working systems with costs you can measure. Register allocation means something different with thirty-two registers than with three. The 6502 is not nostalgia; it is a clarity instrument, making invisible costs visible. By the end, Lark programs run as native machine code on a Raspberry Pi Pico 2/2W. The target is real.

Theory is earned, not assumed. The type-theory content—Hindley–Milner inference, affine types, trait bounds—appears when the implementation needs it, after the reader has seen what the implementation does without it. This ordering is not a simplification; it is the correct epistemological sequence, and the book holds to it even into the formal chapters.

One language, start to finish. Every chapter advances Lark—the Lambda Affine Resource Kernel—a small, purely functional language with Hindley–

Milner inference, affine ownership, and RISC-V as its compilation target. The reader ends with something working, not a collection of fragments. What Lark is, what it deliberately is *not*, and its full grammar are set out in their own right in Appendix A, which can be read first as a map or kept open alongside the chapters.

The safety argument is structural. Lark takes Rust's central insight seriously: ownership can be enforced by the type system rather than by a garbage collector. Affine types make memory safety the salient case of a more general discipline—any resource that must not be used twice, from a heap allocation to a file handle—and they enter in Chapter 5 and shape every later decision—through the code generator in Chapter 9 and into the machine-checked proof in Chapter 11. The connection to Rust is named and precise (Lark is not Rust, and the differences matter), as is the lineage of functional languages—Clean, Cogent, and especially Alms [Tov and Pucella, 2011], OCaml extended with affine types—that have treated ownership as a type-theoretic property rather than a runtime mechanism. Lark is approximately Alms, made compilable, with traits in place of OCaml's module system.

How the Book Is Built

The book is one continuous construction in five parts, each a layer the next stands on.

Part I, The Machine, starts at the bottom: instruction sets, memory, and the costs a processor actually charges (Chapter 1), then a virtual machine in software (Chapter 2). Everything above is built to run here.

Part II, From Text to Structure, turns characters into meaning-bearing form: lexical analysis (Chapter 3) and parsing (Chapter 4), where the regular and context-free hierarchies decide what can be said at all.

Part III, Meaning, gives the tree a semantics: names, scope, and the type system—including affine ownership and traits (Chapter 5)—and then a working interpreter that drives the reader from a naive tree-walker to the CEK machine the tail-call wall forces (Chapter 6).

Part IV, Compilation, lowers meaning to a machine: an intermediate representation (Chapter 7), optimization (Chapter 8), and code generation that reaches genuine silicon (Chapter 9).

Part V, Foundations, turns back to ask what was built: abstract machines as operational semantics (Chapter 10), the correctness proof that the type system is sound (Chapter 11), the dependent-type proof checker that did the proving—types as proofs, the idea that ran under everything, made exact (Chapter 12)—and finally the adversarial coda (Chapter 13), in which the finished construction is attacked with manufactured programs and planted bugs, compiler, tests, and proof kernel alike, until every guard has a guard. A short Conclusion then steps back from the whole.

A reader is not obliged to go straight through, and it is worth naming the two paths explicitly. The *builder's path* is Parts I through IV, Chapters 1 to 9: everything needed to build, run, and extend the working compiler, from silicon to silicon. It is the book's practical core, and a reader who stops there has a complete language and a complete education in how one is made. The *full path* continues into Part V, where what was built is proved sound and then attacked, and it is the steeper half: Chapters 11 through 13 use inference-rule notation and machine-checked proof in earnest. Neither path assumes mathematics the book does not supply. Appendix C is a short decoder that translates every piece of the book's formal notation—the judgements, the horizontal bars, the induction—into the Python the reader will by then have already seen; the steep chapters point to it at the moment the notation arrives, and the builder can read it as an epilogue or not at all. Within either path, the hardware chapters can be skimmed by someone who knows assembly, and the formal sections of Chapter 5 taken at half speed on first pass. But the spine is deliberate—each part is a constraint on the parts above it, and reading in order is reading the propagation in the direction it actually runs (Figure 1).

One honesty is worth stating before the book begins rather than discovering chapter by chapter. A book that explains language implementation must teach more than any one small language uses: to understand why Lark allocates registers by linear scan, you should know what graph colouring is and why it was not chosen. So a good deal of what follows is explained without being built into Lark, and a few things are built only to be taught. This is deliberate curation, not drift, and Table 1 draws the line explicitly—what is part of Lark's real pipeline, what is partly realised, what exists only as an illustration, and what is surveyed so the reader can read other compilers. The honesty about that distinction is, throughout, treated as a strength: a working language is as much defined by what it declines to do as by what it does.

Who This Book Is For, and Where It Ends

The reader this book assumes is a technically literate programmer who wants to understand what is under their language. It is not a first programming book: it assumes familiarity with Python or C, preferably both, and with basic data structures. It suits advanced undergraduates, graduate students, and practitioners who have always meant to understand how compilers work and never found the right entry point.

The book ends at a defined place on the type-theory ladder. Lark sits at Hindley–Milner inference plus affine types plus trait-bounded polymorphism;

Table 1: What the book teaches and what Lark does. *Built*: in Lark's pipeline. *Partial*: partly realised. *Illustrative*: built only to teach. *Surveyed*: explained, not built.

Topic	In Lark	Where
Stack & register bytecode VMs	Illustrative	Ch. 2
Garbage collection	Surveyed (bump arena)	Ch. 1
Lexer (finite automata)	Built	Ch. 3
Recursive-descent parser	Built	Ch. 4
LL(1), LR, Earley, combinators	Surveyed	Ch. 4
Hindley–Milner inference	Built	Ch. 5
Affine types	Built	Ch. 5
Traits (dynamic dispatch)	Built	Ch. 5
Trait-bound enforcement	Surveyed	Ch. 5, 11
ADTs & pattern matching	Built	Ch. 4–7
Exhaustiveness checking	Built (static, witness)	Ch. 5, 13
Totality checking (opt-in)	Built	Ch. 13
Tree-walking interpreter	Illustrative	Ch. 6
CEK machine	Built	Ch. 6
Three-address code & CFG	Built	Ch. 7
TAC virtual machine (oracle)	Built	Ch. 7
SSA form	Surveyed	Ch. 7
Value-numbering DAG / CSE	Surveyed	Ch. 7
Constant folding & propagation	Surveyed	Ch. 8
Dead-code elimination	Partial	Ch. 8
Loop-invariant code motion	Surveyed	Ch. 8
Instruction selection (1-to-1)	Built	Ch. 9
Linear-scan allocation	Built	Ch. 9
Graph-colouring allocation	Surveyed	Ch. 9
Move coalescing	Built	Ch. 9
Tail-call optimization (self)	Built	Ch. 9
RISC-V back end	Built	Ch. 9
6502 back end	Surveyed (contrast)	Ch. 9
Differential testing	Built	Ch. 8, 11
Hoare logic	Surveyed	Ch. 11
Type-safety proof (core)	Built	Ch. 11
Dependent-type proof checker	Built	Ch. 12
Typed-program generation (fuzzing)	Built	Ch. 13
Certifying register allocation	Built	Ch. 13
Graded (affine) mechanization	Built	Ch. 13

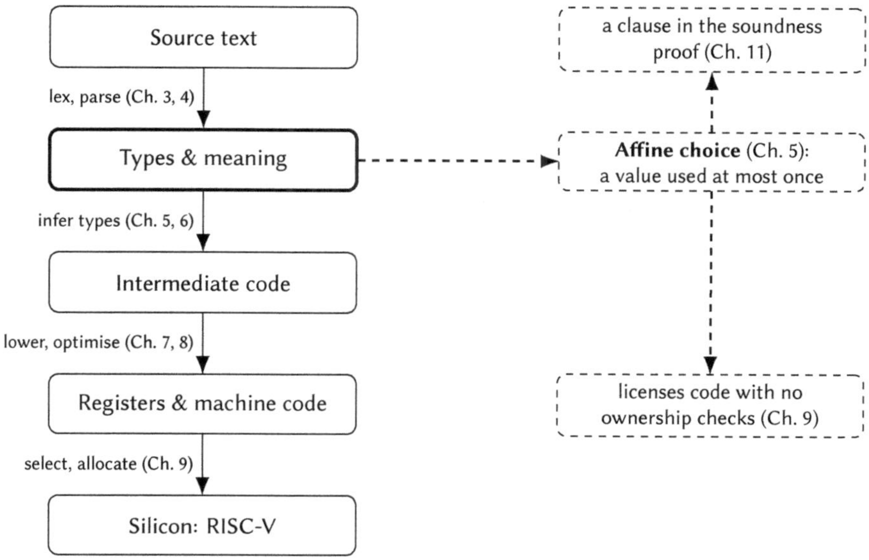

Figure 1: The book's spine, and one decision travelling it. Reading downward, each stage *lowers* the one above, trading abstraction for executability. Reading the other way, every stage is constrained from below. A single choice illustrates it: making affine types part of the language (Chapter 5) propagates *down* into code generation as a licence—values used once need no ownership checks (Chapter 9)—and *sideways* into the soundness proof as an obligation to discharge (Chapter 11). That propagation is the book's subject.

the next rung is dependent types, where the type checker and the proof checker become one program. Chapter 12 climbs that rung—reading the book's own machine-checked soundness proof as a program in such a language—and names the systems that inhabit it: Idris, Agda, Lean, and the `lcore` kernel this book builds to vouch for Lark. A reader who wants to continue has a precise place to go. The practical matters—the companion code, and how the book's two directory trees are organized—are laid out in the Foreword and in Appendix A. With the direction set, the construction can begin, at the silicon.

Part I

The Machine

Chapter 1

Instruction Sets and Memory

A programming language is a bridge. On one side: human intentions, expressed in abstract terms—types, functions, modules, patterns. On the other side: a processor that understands only three things. Fetch a sequence of bytes from memory. Decode those bytes as an instruction. Execute that instruction. The gap between these two sides is the subject of this book—but not the gap alone. What this book is really about is how a decision made at one end propagates to the other: how a constraint stated in the type system becomes a license taken by the code generator, how the shape of an instruction set reaches up to change what the language above it can afford to express. Closing the gap is the engineering; understanding what travels across it is the subject. Before we begin either, we need to understand what lies at the bottom.

This chapter is about the machine. Not in the abstract—not "a Turing machine" or "a von Neumann architecture"—but the actual, physical hardware that will eventually run the programs Lark compiles. Lark—Lambda Affine Resource Kernel—is the language we build throughout this book: a small, purely functional language with Hindley-Milner type inference, affine ownership, and RISC-V as its compilation target. Before we can build it, we need to understand what it runs on.

We look at two real instruction sets: the 6502, a minimal eight-bit processor from 1975, and RISC-V, a clean open standard from 2010. Between them they span most of what matters for a compiler writer. We also look at memory—not as a detail, but as a design force. The distinction between stack, heap, and static is not administrative. It shapes every language above it.

1.1 The Fetch-Decode-Execute Loop

Every processor, from the simplest microcontroller to a modern many-core chip, runs the same fundamental loop:

1. **Fetch**: read the bytes at the address stored in the *program counter* (PC).
2. **Decode**: interpret those bytes to determine which operation to perform and where the operands are.
3. **Execute**: carry out the operation. This may read or write registers, read or write memory, or update the PC to a new address.
4. Return to step 1.

The program counter is just a register that holds an address. After each instruction it advances automatically to the next one. A branch instruction overrides this by writing a new address into the PC. That is all that control flow is, at the bottom: an assignment to a register.

Memory, from the processor's point of view, is a flat array of bytes indexed by address. There is no structure to it. The processor does not know which bytes are code, which are data, and which are garbage from a previous program. That distinction is imposed by convention—by the compiler, the operating system, and the calling convention—not by hardware.

A small Python simulation makes this concrete. Below is a minimal stack machine with four instructions: `PUSH`, `ADD`, `HALT`, and nothing else.

Listing 1.1: A very minimal fetch-decode-execute loop

```
HALT = 0
PUSH = 1
ADD  = 2

memory = [
    PUSH, 3,    # push the literal 3
    PUSH, 4,    # push the literal 4
    ADD,        # pop two values, push their sum
    HALT,
]

pc    = 0
stack = []

while True:
    opcode = memory[pc]; pc += 1
```

```
    if opcode == HALT:
        break
    elif opcode == PUSH:
        stack.append(memory[pc]); pc += 1
    elif opcode == ADD:
        b = stack.pop()
        a = stack.pop()
        stack.append(a + b)

print(stack[-1])    # 7
```

This is not a toy simplification of how processors work. It *is* how processors work. The hardware version fetches from silicon instead of a Python list, runs at three billion iterations per second instead of one million, and keeps its working values in thirty-two registers instead of a Python list—but the loop is the same.

What this means for a compiler writer: a program is a sequence of bytes, and compilation is the art of producing the right sequence. Everything else in this book is in service of that goal.

1.2 Stack Machines and Register Machines

There are two main families of processor architecture, distinguished by where operands live between operations.

Stack machines keep operands on a stack. The ADD instruction pops two values from the top of the stack and pushes their sum. Instructions name no operands explicitly: they act on whatever is at the top of the stack. The JVM, the .NET CLR, WebAssembly, and CPython are all stack machines at the bytecode level.

Register machines maintain a fixed set of named registers. The ADD instruction names three registers explicitly: two sources and a destination. The x86-64, ARM, MIPS, and RISC-V are register machines.

Consider computing $3 + 4$ in each style. On a stack machine:

Listing 1.2: Adding on a stack machine

```
PUSH 3        ; stack: [3]
PUSH 4        ; stack: [3, 4]
ADD           ; stack: [7]
```

On a register machine (RISC-V style):

Listing 1.3: Adding on a register machine

```
li   t0, 3         ; t0 = 3
li   t1, 4         ; t1 = 4
add  t2, t0, t1    ; t2 = t0 + t1 = 7
```

The stack version is compact: instructions are short because there is nothing to name. The register version is explicit: every operand and destination is named, which costs bits in the encoding but saves memory traffic. Table 1.1 summarises the key differences.

Table 1.1: Stack machines vs. register machines

	Stack	**Register**
Instruction size	Small; no named operands	Wider; names registers
Memory traffic	Higher (push/pop)	Lower (registers first)
Code size	Smaller	Larger
Dispatch cost	Higher	Lower
Examples	JVM, Wasm, CPython	x86-64, ARM, RISC-V

Neither architecture is universally better. Stack machines produce denser bytecode, which matters for distribution over a network. Register machines are faster for native execution, which is why JIT compilers for the JVM translate stack bytecode to register operations before running it.[1]

Lark compiles to a custom virtual machine (Chapter 2) and ultimately to RISC-V (Chapter 9). Both are register machines. Understanding why that choice was made requires understanding what it costs.

1.3 The 6502: A Minimal ISA

In 1975 MOS Technology released a processor for $25 that could do most of what the competing $300 Motorola 6800 could do. The 6502 found its way into the Apple II, the Commodore 64, the BBC Micro, the Atari 2600, and the original Nintendo Entertainment System. It powered the early personal computer industry.

The 6502 has three *working* registers, each with a fixed role rather than a general one:

- `A` — the *accumulator*. Most arithmetic goes through here.
- `X`, `Y` — *index registers*. Used for counted loops and indexed memory access.

That is the full set. Three eight-bit registers, plus a sixteen-bit program counter (`PC`), an eight-bit stack pointer (`S`), and a status byte (`P`) that records flags like carry, zero, and overflow.

The stack is in memory page 1—addresses `0x0100` through `0x01FF`. It is exactly 256 bytes. There is no hardware support for a deeper stack. Nested subroutine calls consume this space directly; each `JSR` pushes a two-byte return address, so eight levels of nesting costs sixteen bytes.

Here is a loop that runs ten times—incrementing `X` from 0 until it reaches 10—in 6502 assembly:

Listing 1.4: A ten-iteration loop on the 6502

```
    LDX #0          ; X = 0
loop:
    INX             ; X += 1
    CPX #10         ; compare X with 10
    BNE loop        ; if X != 10, repeat
    BRK             ; done
```

Notice what is not here. There are no general-purpose temporaries: if you need to hold more than three values simultaneously, you must spill to memory explicitly. There are no compound addressing modes that let you say "the value at address `base + offset * 4`"—you must compute the address yourself, using the index registers and the processor's limited set of addressing modes.

Working with the 6502 teaches two things that are easy to forget on modern hardware. First, *registers are rare.* Three is a real constraint. A compiler targeting the 6502 must decide at every point which three values are worth keeping in registers and which must be stored to memory, a problem called *register allocation.* Chapter 9 treats this seriously. The 6502 makes its stakes visible.

Second, *every instruction is a choice that costs something.* The 6502 has 56 instructions; counting addressing-mode variants, these pack into 151 distinct single-byte opcodes. Each opcode encodes, in that one byte, both an operation and an addressing mode. The byte is not free: the processor must fetch it from memory, and memory is slow. A skilled 6502 programmer counted instruction bytes the way a poet counts syllables. The discipline carries over: a language implementer who has thought about instruction density thinks differently about what "compiling efficiently" means.

1.4 RISC-V: A Compiler-Friendly Design

RISC-V was designed at UC Berkeley starting in 2010 as a clean, open standard instruction set. Unlike x86-64—which grew from the 8086 through forty years of backward-compatible accretion—RISC-V started from a question: what does a compiler actually need from a processor?[2]

The answer is 32 general-purpose registers (named `x0` through `x31`), a load-store discipline, and fixed-width 32-bit instructions.

The registers have conventional roles assigned by the calling convention. A representative selection is shown in Table 1.2 (the full set runs to `x31`):

Table 1.2: Selected RISC-V registers and their ABI roles

Reg	**ABI**	**Role**
`x0`	`zero`	Always zero; writes discarded
`x1`	`ra`	Return address
`x2`	`sp`	Stack pointer
`x5--x7`	`t0--t2`	Temporaries (caller-saved)
`x10--x17`	`a0--a7`	Arguments / return values
`x18--x27`	`s2--s11`	Saved registers (callee-saved)

The *load-store discipline* means that arithmetic instructions operate only on registers, not on memory. To add the value at memory address 0x100 to a register, you first load it into a register, then add, then optionally store the result back. There are no "add-to-memory" instructions. This restriction sounds like a loss but is a gain for compilers: every arithmetic instruction has the same structure, and every memory access is explicit and separately schedulable.

Fixed-width instructions mean every instruction is exactly 32 bits. There is no need to figure out how long the current instruction is before fetching the next one. Instruction boundaries are always at addresses divisible by four. This makes the fetch stage of the pipeline trivial.

Here is the same ten-iteration loop in RISC-V assembly:

Listing 1.5: A ten-iteration loop on RISC-V

```
    li   t0, 0          ; t0 = 0
    li   t1, 10         ; t1 = 10 (loop bound, loaded once)
loop:
    addi t0, t0, 1      ; t0 += 1
    bne  t0, t1, loop ; if t0 != 10, repeat
```

The loop body is the same two instructions as on the 6502. The difference is in the setup. The 6502 can compare a register against a constant in a single instruction (`CPX #10`); RISC-V branches compare two *registers*, so the loop bound must first be materialised in `t1`. RISC-V spends an extra register and an extra setup instruction on that constant, and gets in return a uniform encoding a compiler can emit mechanically, with wider registers (64-bit in the RV64I base) and far more of them. The 6502 program is compact but demands hand-crafting; the RISC-V program is more regular and follows rules a compiler can apply reliably.

Calling conventions. The table above is not architecture—it is agreement. The RISC-V specification [Waterman and Asanović, 2019] says nothing about which register holds return addresses; the ABI convention does. A *calling convention* is a contract between the caller of a function and the callee: which registers the callee may destroy (*caller-saved*), which it must preserve (*callee-saved*), how arguments are passed, and how return values come back.

Without this contract, function calls would require full register saves on every call—expensive and unnecessary. With it, the compiler can reason locally about each function: "I need to use `t0` through `t2` here; these are caller-saved, so I do not need to save them around calls I make, but I do need to save them before making a call if I need them afterwards."

Chapter 9 implements Lark's code generator targeting RISC-V. The calling convention will be exactly this contract, made concrete in generated assembly. At the end of that chapter, Lark programs run as native machine code on a Raspberry Pi Pico 2/2W—an RP2350 microcontroller implementing RV32IMAC—verified on real hardware. The examples in this book use the RV64I base for exposition; the deployment target is a 32-bit RV32IMAC part. The instruction forms are nearly identical—chiefly the register width differs—so nothing in the reasoning above changes.

1.5 Memory Models

From the processor's perspective, memory is a flat array of bytes. A language implementation imposes structure on this flatness. The conventional division is into three regions, and the choice of which values go where has consequences that propagate all the way up to the language's type system.

The stack holds local variables and function call frames. It is managed automatically: calling a function allocates a frame on the stack; returning deallocates it. Allocation is as cheap as decrementing a register (the stack pointer). Lifetimes are strictly nested: a frame exists only as long as its function is active. The stack is bounded—typically one to eight megabytes on a modern system, far less on embedded hardware.

The heap holds values whose lifetimes cannot be determined statically. A value allocated with `malloc` may outlive the function that allocated it; it may be passed to a different subsystem; it may be freed anywhere. The heap is flexible and essentially unbounded. But flexibility costs: something must track which heap memory is in use and which is free.

There are three main strategies for managing the heap:

- *Manual management* (C, C++): the programmer calls `malloc` and `free` explicitly. Fast, but use-after-free and double-free bugs are endemic.
- *Garbage collection* (Java, Python, Go): the runtime tracks which heap objects are reachable and frees the rest automatically. Safe, but adds runtime overhead and non-deterministic pause times.
- *Static lifetime analysis* (Rust): the compiler proves at compile time that every heap allocation has exactly one owner, and that the owner frees the allocation when it goes out of scope. No runtime overhead, no GC pauses, no use-after-free—but the programmer must satisfy the type checker's proof obligations.

The static region holds global variables, string literals, and compiled code. It is allocated once, at program load time, and lives for the entire program's execution. There is no management question for static memory: it is always there.

The relationship between these regions and Lark is direct—but it is not the Rust relationship. Lark is purely functional: its values never share mutable heap cells, so the use-after-free and double-free bugs that ownership guards against in Rust cannot arise in the first place. What Lark takes from the ownership tradition is the static *guarantee*, not the reclamation machinery. Its affine type system proves at compile time, at no runtime cost, that a resource—a file handle, the `IO` token, any value not marked copyable—is used at most once, and so can never be silently duplicated or aliased.

That guarantee would *permit* a compiler to free each value the instant its single use ends. Lark's runtime does not bother: a whole-program batch with a bounded lifetime, it allocates from one bump-pointer arena and releases the arena when the program exits, keeping allocation a single pointer bump. The affine discipline buys *safety*, not storage reclamation—and that link, between a memory strategy at the hardware level and a type-theoretic constraint at the language level, is one of the book's central threads. Chapter 5 works it out in full.

1.6 The Embedded Constraint as a Clarity Instrument

Suppose you are writing a program for a system with 2 KB of RAM, no virtual memory, and no operating system. There is no `malloc`: the heap does not exist. There is no process isolation: a stack overflow does not produce a helpful error message; it silently corrupts whatever happened to be adjacent in memory.

Every local variable has a cost you can count in bytes. Every function call consumes stack space. Every global costs from a fixed budget of 2048 bytes. You cannot abstract any of this away, because there is nothing underneath to do the abstracting.

Here is what you must know at every moment:

- How deep is the current call stack? Each frame is at least two bytes (the return address on the 6502). Eight nested calls is sixteen bytes of stack. The 6502's stack is 256 bytes—at two bytes apiece, a hundred and twenty-eight calls exhausts it, and real frames carrying locals exhaust it sooner.

- What are all the global variables, and what do they total? On a 2 KB system, 200 bytes of globals is not trivial.

- Is any string literal large enough to matter? Every byte of literal is a byte of RAM.

These questions feel irrelevant on a modern system with 32 GB of RAM. A stack overflow on a Linux process sends a clean signal; the kernel enforces the boundary. `malloc` returns `NULL` gracefully. The programmer doesn't need to think about any of it.

But the questions are not irrelevant. They are hidden. The embedded constraint makes them visible again, and visible constraints are useful for understanding.

A language implementer who has thought seriously about what a local variable costs—not abstractly, but in bytes, on a specific processor, in a specific calling convention—reasons differently about register allocation, stack frame layout, and tail-call optimization. These are not micro-optimizations. They are the difference between a language that can run on constrained hardware and one that cannot, and they are the difference between a compiler that generates predictably efficient code and one that occasionally surprises its users.

Lark's eventual target is RISC-V, not the 6502. But the 6502 is where we sharpen the question: *what does this actually cost?* That question does not go away when the hardware has thirty-two registers instead of three. It just becomes easier to ignore—until it matters.

1.7 Exercises

1. Extend the toy fetch-decode-execute machine with two new instructions: `SUB` (pop two values, push their difference) and `JMP` (an unconditional jump). What extra byte does `JMP` read from memory, and how does its effect on pc differ from that of `PUSH`?

2. Rewrite the ten-iteration loop for a stack machine whose only instructions are `PUSH`, `ADD`, `SUB`, `DUP` (duplicate the top of stack), and `BNZ` (branch if the top of stack is non-zero). What is the greatest number of values on the stack at any one moment during your loop?

3. Consider the expression $(a \times b) + (c \times d)$. Count the minimum number of values that must be live at once to evaluate it. On the 6502, with its three registers, what does this force the compiler to do that it would not have to do on RISC-V?

4. RISC-V's load-store discipline forbids arithmetic directly on memory. Write the RISC-V sequence that increments the 32-bit value stored at the address held in `a0`. How many memory accesses does it take, and why can it not be fewer?

5. A function on the 2 KB embedded system declares a 300-byte local array. Explain, in terms of the three memory regions, why this is a different kind of risk than a 300-byte `malloc` on a desktop—and state what an affine type system would have to establish to place such a value safely.

Chapter 2 builds the first artifact: a virtual machine in software. Having seen what hardware actually does, we can understand why adding a layer of indirection is worth its cost—and what, precisely, we are buying.

Notes

[1]x86 is itself a register machine, yet its x87 floating-point unit is stack-based—operands live on an eight-deep register stack rather than in named registers. The pairing is a historical accident, and it makes floating-point code generation famously awkward.

[2]For an accessible tour of the architecture—the base integer instructions, the standard extensions, and the design rationale behind each—see Patterson and Waterman's *The RISC-V Reader: An Open Architecture Atlas* [Patterson and Waterman, 2017].

Chapter 2

A Virtual Machine in Software

Chapter 1 ended at hardware: the fetch-decode-execute loop, real instruction sets, real memory. This chapter adds a layer of software between that hardware and Lark. The question is why.

The answer has three parts. First, *portability*: compile once to bytecode and run the result on any machine that has a VM, regardless of whether it is x86-64, ARM, or RISC-V. Second, *isolation*: a VM can enforce boundaries that the hardware does not—no raw memory access, no undefined behaviour, bounds checking on every array access. Third, *productive indirection*: garbage collection, a step debugger, and a sampling profiler are all much easier to implement when all execution passes through a software layer you control.

The cost is performance. A software VM is an interpreter: every guest instruction requires several host instructions to decode and dispatch. On typical hardware, a naïve bytecode interpreter runs ten to one hundred times slower than equivalent native code. Whether this is acceptable depends on what the VM buys you. This chapter is partly about what it buys, and partly about how much of the overhead you can give back.

We build two VMs: a stack machine and a register machine. Both are real—they run the same programs and produce the same results. But they make different trade-offs, and understanding what changes between them is the main lesson of the chapter.

A word first on what this chapter is and is not, so nothing here is mistaken for a build step. It is a self-contained primer on how a software machine executes code—the frame model, the calling convention, the dispatch loop—and those ideas are load-bearing for the rest of the book. It is *not* a stage in Lark's pipeline. The production compiler emits no bytecode at all: it lowers the typed tree straight to three-address code and then to RISC-V (Chapters 7 and 9). What does carry forward is the *register machine* of Section 2.3. Its shape—a register file, an explicit call frame, one dispatch loop—is the shape of `tac_vm.py`, the interpreter that runs Lark's intermediate representation in Chapter 7 and serves as the correctness oracle in Chapters 8 and 11. Read the stack machine for contrast and the register machine as a first sketch of a tool we keep.

2.1 Why Virtual Machines?

The Java Virtual Machine, introduced in 1995, made a specific promise: write once, run anywhere. A Java compiler produces bytecode for a single hypothetical machine. The JVM interprets that bytecode—or, eventually, compiles it to native code at runtime—on whatever hardware is actually present. The hardware differences between a Sun workstation and a Windows PC were invisible to the programmer.

The promise was partly marketing and partly genuine, but the underlying mechanism is real and useful. A software VM decouples the compilation target from the execution platform. A compiler, once it can produce bytecode for a VM, runs everywhere that VM runs. Adding a new hardware target means porting the VM, not the compiler.

Isolation is a second benefit. A VM can be designed to make certain errors impossible at the bytecode level. If the instruction set has no way to express "read the byte at arbitrary address X," then bytecode cannot produce a buffer overrun regardless of what the compiler generates. WebAssembly takes this seriously: every memory access is bounds-checked, and the instruction set has no pointer arithmetic. The cost is some performance; the gain is a strong security boundary.

Productive indirection is harder to quantify but real. When a garbage collector runs inside a VM, it has access to the entire heap and can move objects safely because all references go through the VM. A step debugger can pause execution at any instruction boundary because instruction dispatch happens in one place. A sampling profiler can record the current instruction every millisecond and produce an accurate flame graph. None of these require changes to the language or the compiler.

Against these benefits sits the performance cost. An interpreter executes its dispatch loop on every single guest instruction. A guest ADD is not one host ADD; it is: load opcode, branch on opcode, pop two values, add, push result, increment program counter, repeat. On a modern out-of-order CPU, the indirect branch alone costs ten to twenty cycles if the branch predictor misses. A naïve Python interpreter running on CPython—itself a bytecode interpreter—runs roughly one thousand times slower than compiled C for typical numeric workloads.

Section 2.6 looks at this cost squarely. For now: the VM is a reasonable target for a language implementation, and we will build it.

A note of honesty, since the chapter spends real effort on these three motivations: Lark collects almost none of them directly. It ships no bytecode VM, no garbage collector, and no sandbox; it compiles ahead of time to native RISC-V over a bump-allocated arena. The motivations are why *most* of computing runs on virtual machines—the JVM, CPython, WebAssembly, the browser—and that is reason enough to understand them. The concrete thing this chapter leaves Lark is narrower, and was named in the opening: the register machine, kept on as the interpreter for the intermediate representation and as the oracle that checks the compiler.

2.2 A Stack Machine in Two Hundred Lines

We build from the toy of Chapter 1. That machine had three instructions and computed one thing. This one has fifteen instructions, a call stack, and local variable slots. It is sufficient to serve as a compilation target for a real language.

The instruction set. The opcodes are integer constants; the bytecode is a list of integers.[1]

Listing 2.1: Opcode definitions for the stack VM

```
HALT  = 0   # stop; top of stack is the return value
PUSH  = 1   # push the next byte as an integer literal
ADD   = 2   # pop b, pop a; push a + b
SUB   = 3   # pop b, pop a; push a - b
MUL   = 4   # pop b, pop a; push a * b
DIV   = 5   # pop b, pop a; push a // b
EQ    = 6   # pop b, pop a; push 1 if a == b, else 0
LT    = 7   # pop b, pop a; push 1 if a < b, else 0
NOT   = 8   # pop a; push 0 if a is nonzero, else 1
JMP   = 9   # next two bytes: target address; jump
JMPZ  = 10  # next two bytes: target; jump if stack top zero
LOAD  = 11  # next byte: slot index; push locals[slot]
STORE = 12  # next byte: slot index; pop into locals[slot]
CALL  = 13  # next two bytes: target; save frame, jump
RET   = 14  # pop return value, restore frame, push it
```

Fifteen instructions cover arithmetic, comparison, control flow, and function calls. That is enough to compile a real language. The JVM has about two hundred instructions; CPython's bytecode set grows over time. The number reflects a design choice: primitives kept primitive, complexity pushed into the compiler.

The dispatch loop. The VM is a class with three pieces of state: the bytecode array, the operand stack, and the call stack.

Listing 2.2: The stack VM: dispatch loop and frame model

```
class StackVM:
  def __init__(self, code):
    self.code   = code
    self.stack  = []          # operand stack
    self.frames = []          # (locals, return_pc)
    self.locals = [0] * 16    # current: 16 local slots
    self.pc     = 0

  def _u16(self):             # big-endian 16-bit operand
    hi = self.code[self.pc]
    lo = self.code[self.pc + 1]
    self.pc += 2
    return (hi << 8) | lo

  def run(self):
    code = self.code
    while True:
      op = code[self.pc]; self.pc += 1

      if op == HALT:
        return self.stack[-1] if self.stack else None
      elif op == PUSH:
        self.stack.append(code[self.pc])
        self.pc += 1
      elif op == ADD:
        b = self.stack.pop(); self.stack[-1] += b
      elif op == SUB:
        b = self.stack.pop(); self.stack[-1] -= b
      elif op == MUL:
        b = self.stack.pop(); self.stack[-1] *= b
      elif op == DIV:
        b = self.stack.pop(); self.stack[-1] //= b
      elif op == EQ:
        b = self.stack.pop()
        self.stack[-1] = int(self.stack[-1] == b)
      elif op == LT:
        b = self.stack.pop()
        self.stack[-1] = int(self.stack[-1] < b)
      elif op == NOT:
        self.stack[-1] = int(not self.stack[-1])
      elif op == JMP:
        self.pc = self._u16()
      elif op == JMPZ:
```

```
        target = self._u16()
        if not self.stack.pop():
          self.pc = target
      elif op == LOAD:
        s = code[self.pc]; self.pc += 1
        self.stack.append(self.locals[s])
      elif op == STORE:
        s = code[self.pc]; self.pc += 1
        self.locals[s] = self.stack.pop()
      elif op == CALL:
        target = self._u16()
        self.frames.append((self.locals[:], self.pc))
        self.locals = [0] * 16
        self.pc = target
      elif op == RET:
        val = self.stack.pop()
        self.locals, self.pc = self.frames.pop()
        self.stack.append(val)
```

The dispatch loop is an `if`/`elif` chain—the Python equivalent of a C `switch`. In Section 2.4 we look at how to make this faster.

One simplification to flag. Both VMs in this chapter implement `DIV` with Python's //, which rounds *toward negative infinity*: `(-7) // 2` is `-4`. RISC-V's `div` instruction truncates *toward zero*, giving -3—and real Lark follows the hardware, computing `int(a / b)` in its TAC interpreter and emitting `div` in its back end, so its integer division truncates. The two rules agree on non-negative operands and diverge only when the signs are mixed. The teaching // is kept here for readability, but the disagreement is exactly the kind of silent semantic gap that the differential oracle of Chapter 11 exists to catch—running the same program on two machines and demanding identical output—and Chapter 8 treats the analogous trap for floating-point identities with the same care.

The call model deserves attention. `CALL` saves the current locals array and return address, allocates a fresh set of 16 *zeroed* slots, and jumps to the target. `RET` reverses this: it pops the return value from the operand stack, restores the saved locals and program counter, then pushes the return value onto the caller's operand stack. Because `CALL` zeroes the new frame's locals, arguments are not passed there. They are passed on the *operand stack*, which `CALL` leaves untouched: the caller pushes each argument, and the callee's prologue moves it into a local slot. This is the simplest workable convention—arguments on the stack, one return value on the stack, no variable arity.

A worked example. Here is the program $3 \times (4 + 5)$ in bytecode, with addresses on the left:

Listing 2.3: Computing $3 \times (4 + 5)$ in bytecode

```
0   PUSH 3      ; stack: [3]
2   PUSH 4      ; stack: [3, 4]
4   PUSH 5      ; stack: [3, 4, 5]
6   ADD         ; stack: [3, 9]
7   MUL         ; stack: [27]
8   HALT
```

Each `PUSH` occupies two bytes (opcode + operand); `ADD`, `MUL`, and `HALT` occupy one. The program is nine bytes.

Function calls. To go further, here is a recursive factorial function. The convention follows from the call model: the argument arrives on the operand stack, the function's prologue stores it into local slot 0, and the return value is left on the operand stack at `RET`. A short bootstrap pushes the initial argument, calls `fact`, and halts with the result on top of the stack.

Listing 2.4: Recursive factorial in bytecode (addresses decimal)

```
; bootstrap: push the argument,
; call fact, halt with the result
0    PUSH   5       ; argument
2    CALL   [6]     ; call fact (entry at address 6)
5    HALT           ; result is on top of the stack
; fact: argument on the operand stack at entry;
; result on stack at RET
6    STORE 0        ; locals[0] = n   (pop the argument)
8    LOAD   0       ; push n
10   PUSH   1       ; push 1
12   LT             ; push 1 if n < 1, else 0
13   NOT            ; flip: 0 if n == 0 (base case), else 1
14   JMPZ   [29]    ; if n == 0, jump to base case
17   LOAD   0       ; push n     (kept for the multiply)
19   LOAD   0       ; push n again
21   PUSH   1       ; push 1
23   SUB            ; push n - 1   (arg for the recursive call)
24   CALL   [6]     ; fact(n-1); result left on the stack
27   MUL            ; n * fact(n-1)
28   RET
; base case
29   PUSH   1       ; fact(0) = 1
31   RET
```

The structure is visible: test the base case, branch to the base-case handler if true, otherwise recurse. One detail is worth dwelling on. Before the recursive `CALL`, the multiplicand n is sitting on the operand stack (pushed by the `LOAD 0` at address 17), beneath the argument $n-1$. The call consumes $n-1$ and leaves fact($n-1$) in its place, so n is still there for the `MUL`. The operand stack preserves it across the call for free—the same property that, in Section 2.3, the register machine has to work for. The pattern itself will appear again when we compile Lark's pattern-matching expressions in Chapter 6.

Running this VM is straightforward:[2]

Listing 2.5: Running a program on the stack VM

```
code = [
    # bootstrap: push the argument, call fact at 6, halt
    PUSH, 5, CALL, 0, 6, HALT,

    # fact: store the argument, test the base case (n == 0)
    STORE, 0, LOAD, 0, PUSH, 1, LT, NOT, JMPZ, 0, 29,

    # recursive case: keep n, compute n-1, call, multiply
    LOAD, 0, LOAD, 0, PUSH, 1, SUB, CALL, 0, 6, MUL, RET,

    # base case: return 1
    PUSH, 1, RET,
]
vm = StackVM(code)
print(vm.run())        # 120
```

2.3 The Register Machine Variant

The stack machine is clean and compact. The register machine is explicit and, on real hardware, faster. The distinction matters when we target RISC-V in Chapter 9. Here we build both and measure what changes.

The register machine replaces the operand stack with a fixed register file. Every instruction names its operands and destination explicitly. We use 16 registers, `r0` through `r15`; `r0` is hardwired to zero.

Listing 2.6: Opcode definitions for the register VM

```
RHALT  = 0    # stop; result is in r1
RMOVI  = 1    # rd, imm:          rd = imm
RMOV   = 2    # rd, rs:           rd = rs
```

```
RADD  = 3   # rd, rs1, rs2:  rd = rs1 + rs2
RSUB  = 4   # rd, rs1, rs2:  rd = rs1 - rs2
RMUL  = 5   # rd, rs1, rs2:  rd = rs1 * rs2
RDIV  = 6   # rd, rs1, rs2:  rd = rs1 // rs2
REQ   = 7   # rd, rs1, rs2:  rd = 1 if rs1 == rs2 else 0
RLT   = 8   # rd, rs1, rs2:  rd = 1 if rs1 < rs2 else 0
RNOT  = 9   # rd, rs:        rd = 0 if rs nonzero else 1
RJMP  = 10  # target:        jump unconditionally
RJMPZ = 11  # rs, target:    jump if rs == 0
RCALL = 12  # target:        save registers, jump
RRET  = 13  # rs:            return value in rs
```

Listing 2.7: The register VM

```
_THREE_REG = (RADD, RSUB, RMUL, RDIV, REQ, RLT)

class RegVM:
  def __init__(self, code):
    self.code   = code
    self.regs   = [0] * 16  # r0 always zero; r1 = result
    self.frames = []
    self.pc     = 0

  def _u16(self):
    hi = self.code[self.pc]
    lo = self.code[self.pc + 1]
    self.pc += 2
    return (hi << 8) | lo

  def run(self):
    code = self.code
    r    = self.regs
    while True:
      op = code[self.pc]; self.pc += 1
      r[0] = 0   # r0 hardwired to zero

      if op == RHALT:
        return r[1]
      elif op == RMOVI:
        rd = code[self.pc]; self.pc += 1
        r[rd] = code[self.pc]; self.pc += 1
      elif op == RMOV:
        rd = code[self.pc]; rs = code[self.pc+1]
        self.pc += 2
```

```
      r[rd] = r[rs]
    elif op in _THREE_REG:
      rd  = code[self.pc]
      rs1 = code[self.pc+1]; rs2 = code[self.pc+2]
      self.pc += 3
      if   op == RADD: r[rd] = r[rs1] + r[rs2]
      elif op == RSUB: r[rd] = r[rs1] - r[rs2]
      elif op == RMUL: r[rd] = r[rs1] * r[rs2]
      elif op == RDIV: r[rd] = r[rs1] // r[rs2]
      elif op == REQ:  r[rd] = int(r[rs1] == r[rs2])
      elif op == RLT:  r[rd] = int(r[rs1] < r[rs2])
    elif op == RNOT:
      rd = code[self.pc]; rs = code[self.pc+1]
      self.pc += 2
      r[rd] = int(not r[rs])
    elif op == RJMP:
      self.pc = self._u16()
    elif op == RJMPZ:
      rs = code[self.pc]; self.pc += 1
      target = self._u16()
      if not r[rs]: self.pc = target
    elif op == RCALL:
      target = self._u16()
      self.frames.append((r[:], self.pc))
      self.regs = [0] * 16; r = self.regs
      self.pc = target
    elif op == RRET:
      rs = code[self.pc]; self.pc += 1
      val = r[rs]
      r_saved, self.pc = self.frames.pop()
      self.regs = r_saved; r = self.regs
      r[1] = val
```

The same factorial program in register-machine bytecode, using r2 for the argument and r1 for the return value by convention:

Listing 2.8: Factorial on the register VM—**contains a deliberate bug, do not copy**; the fix is the calling-convention discussion that follows

```
; fact(n): n in r2 on entry; result in r1 at RET
0    RMOVI r3, 1          ; r3 = 1  (constant)
3    RLT   r4, r2, r3     ; r4 = (n < 1)
7    RNOT  r4, r4         ; r4 = not (n < 1)
10   RJMPZ r4, [base]     ; if n == 0, jump to base
14   RSUB  r5, r2, r3     ; r5 = n - 1
```

```
18  RMOV  r2, r5       ; argument for recursive call
21  RCALL [0]          ; fact(n-1); result in r1
24  RMUL  r1, r1, r2   ; BUG: r2 no longer holds n here
```

The listing reveals a real register-machine problem. The `MUL` at address 24 needs n, but by the time control returns, `r2` no longer holds it: `r2` was reused to pass the argument (address 18) and then zeroed by `RCALL` (address 21). Nothing preserved n across the call.[3] On the stack machine, the operand stack preserved values across calls for free; here, the compiler—or the programmer—must either spill the live value to a save slot before the call, or adopt a calling convention that designates which registers the callee must preserve.

This is not a defect in the register machine. It is the reason register allocation (Chapter 9) is a non-trivial problem.

Comparing the two machines. Table 2.1 sets the two styles side by side:

Table 2.1: Stack machine vs. register machine

	Stack VM	**Register VM**
Instruction encoding	1–3 bytes	2–4 bytes
Implicit operands	Yes (stack top)	No (named)
Operand traffic	Higher (push/pop)	Lower
Register save problem	Handled by stack	Explicit
Code size	Smaller	Larger
Native speed	Slower	Faster

Lark's VM, as implemented in this book, is a register machine.[4] The reasons mirror the RISC-V argument from Chapter 1: explicit operands make compiler code generation straightforward, and register-to-register operations are faster than stack traffic on modern hardware.

2.4 Dispatch Strategies

The performance of a bytecode interpreter depends heavily on how it dispatches each instruction. The dispatch loop runs once per guest instruction, so any overhead compounds immediately.

Switch dispatch is the most portable approach. The loop fetches an opcode byte, uses a `switch` (or Python `if/elif`) to branch to the handler, executes the handler, and loops. The `if/elif` chain we wrote above is exactly this.

In C, the equivalent is:

Listing 2.9: Switch dispatch in C

```
while (1) {
    uint8_t op = code[pc++];
    switch (op) {
        case PUSH:
            stack[sp++] = code[pc++];
            break;
        case ADD:
            stack[sp - 2] += stack[sp - 1]; sp--;
            break;
        /* ... */
        case HALT:
            return stack[sp - 1];
    }
}
```

Modern compilers often turn a dense `switch` into a jump table—an array of addresses indexed by opcode. Dispatch becomes a load followed by an indirect jump. This is already faster than a chain of comparisons.

Computed goto, a GCC extension, makes this explicit in the source:

Listing 2.10: Computed goto dispatch in C (GCC extension)

```
static void *table[] = {
    &&do_halt, &&do_push, &&do_add, /* ... */
};
#define NEXT() goto *table[code[pc++]]

NEXT();

do_push:
    stack[sp++] = code[pc++];
    NEXT();

do_add:
    stack[sp - 2] += stack[sp - 1]; sp--;
    NEXT();

do_halt:
    return stack[sp - 1];
```

The key difference from a `switch`: instead of one central branch instruction shared by all opcodes, each handler ends with its own indirect branch. This gives the branch predictor more information—it can learn that `ADD` is usually followed by `PUSH` in this particular trace—and reduces branch mispredictions.[5]

What profiling reveals. Profiling a simple numeric benchmark on a bytecode interpreter consistently finds the same result: the bottleneck is not the dispatch. It is the memory traffic. On the stack machine, every operation involves at least two reads from the stack array and one or two writes. The stack is in main memory (or L1 cache), and touching it repeatedly is not free. On the register machine, registers are in the VM's Python or C `locals`— still memory, but somewhat friendlier to the cache.

The lesson: optimising dispatch is worth doing once you have profiled and confirmed that dispatch is the bottleneck. It often is not. Start with clarity and measure before you optimise.

2.5 Bytecode as a Language

The instruction set of a VM is itself a language. It has a vocabulary (the opcodes), a syntax (the encoding of operands), and a semantics (what each instruction does). Designing it well is language design.

What should be primitive? The minimal approach: only operations the compiler cannot synthesise from smaller ones. Arithmetic operators are primitive because the hardware provides them. Conditional branches are primitive because the hardware provides them. String concatenation is not primitive if it can be implemented as a sequence of loads, stores, and a loop.

A smaller primitive set makes the VM simpler. A larger set can make the compiler simpler by offloading work. The right balance depends on who is writing the compiler and what the compiler's job is. The VM described here has arithmetic, comparison, control flow, and function calls as primitives. Everything else is built from these.

Operand encoding. Embedding literal values directly in the instruction stream works for small integers—a one-byte PUSH operand covers 0 to 255. For larger values, there are two approaches.

The first is to use multi-byte operands: a `PUSH32` instruction followed by four bytes of value. This keeps the bytecode self-contained but complicates the decoder (instructions are no longer fixed-width).

The second is a *constant pool*: a separate array of values, referenced by index.

Listing 2.11: A constant pool and LOADK instruction

```
LOADK = 15   # next byte: index into constant pool

class StackVMWithPool:
```

```
def __init__(self, code, constants):
  self.code      = code
  self.constants = constants  # list of int, float, or str
  # ... rest of __init__ as before

def run(self):
  # ... same dispatch loop; add this branch:
  elif op == LOADK:
    idx = self.code[self.pc]; self.pc += 1
    self.stack.append(self.constants[idx])
```

The constant pool has two advantages: it deduplicates constants (the string "hello" appears once in the pool even if it is used many times), and it keeps the instruction stream narrow (an index fits in one byte, even when the constant value does not).

The JVM, CPython, and the Lua VM all use constant pools. Chapter 7 will introduce a similar structure in Lark's intermediate representation.

A minimal assembler. Hand-encoding bytecode as a list of integers is error-prone. A tiny assembler—even twenty lines—makes the bytecode readable and maintainable. The key capability is *label resolution*: forward references to addresses that are not yet known when the instruction is emitted.

Listing 2.12: A two-pass assembler for the stack VM

```
def assemble(program):
  """program: list of label strings or (op, *args) tuples"""
  OPCODE = {
    'HALT': 0,   'PUSH': 1,    'ADD': 2,  'SUB': 3,
     'MUL': 4,    'DIV': 5,     'EQ': 6,   'LT': 7,
     'NOT': 8,    'JMP': 9,   'JMPZ': 10,
    'LOAD': 11, 'STORE': 12, 'CALL': 13, 'RET': 14,
  }
  WIDTHS = {                  # opcode -> instruction byte width
     0: 1,  1: 2,  2: 1,  3: 1,   4: 1,  5: 1,
     6: 1,  7: 1,  8: 1,  9: 3,  10: 3,
    11: 2, 12: 2, 13: 3, 14: 1,
  }
  # First pass: compute label positions
  labels = {}
  pos = 0
  for item in program:
    if isinstance(item, str):
      labels[item.rstrip(':')] = pos
    else:
```

```
    pos += WIDTHS[OPCODE[item[0]]]

# Second pass: emit bytes
code = []
for item in program:
  if isinstance(item, str):
    continue
  op, *args = item
  code.append(OPCODE[op])
  for arg in args:
    if isinstance(arg, str):     # label reference
      addr = labels[arg]
      code += [addr >> 8, addr & 0xFF]
    else:
      code.append(arg)
return code
```

With the assembler, the factorial program becomes readable. The bootstrap and the `STORE 0` prologue carry the same argument convention as before; the assembler resolves `fact` and `base` to their byte addresses:

Listing 2.13: Factorial expressed with the assembler

```
factorial_src = [
  ('PUSH',  5),      # bootstrap: push the argument
  ('CALL', 'fact'),
  ('HALT',),         # result is left on the operand stack
  'fact:',           # entry point
  ('STORE', 0),      # pop the argument into local slot 0
  ('LOAD',  0),
  ('PUSH',  1),
  ('LT',),
  ('NOT',),
  ('JMPZ', 'base'),
  ('LOAD',  0),
  ('LOAD',  0),
  ('PUSH',  1),
  ('SUB',),
  ('CALL', 'fact'),
  ('MUL',),
  ('RET',),
  'base:',
  ('PUSH',  1),
  ('RET',),
```

```
]
# assemble(factorial_src) ->
# bytecode; StackVM(...).run() == 120
```

Two-pass assembly is the canonical approach: the first pass computes label addresses, the second emits bytes with resolved references. Chapter 9 uses exactly the same strategy for RISC-V assembly.

2.6 Counting the Cost

A Python implementation of a VM like this is slow. How slow depends on what we compare it to, but we should not evade the question.

A rough measurement: a tight loop computing the sum of integers from 0 to one million takes about 0.001 seconds in compiled C. The same loop on our Python stack VM takes about 2–3 seconds. That is a factor of roughly two thousand. This is not a defect in the VM design—it is the overhead of Python (itself a VM) interpreting our VM's dispatch loop.

A production VM written in C narrows the gap considerably. CPython, which is itself a bytecode interpreter written in C, runs the same loop about ten to twenty times slower than equivalent compiled C. LuaJIT's baseline interpreter runs about five times slower than C. JIT compilation can close the remaining gap to two or three times slower for numeric workloads—though the JIT itself has startup overhead that hurts short-running programs. Table 2.2 puts approximate numbers on these tiers.

Table 2.2: Approximate performance ratios for different interpreter implementations

Implementation	Slowdown vs. native C
Our Python stack VM	$\sim$1000–2000$\times$
C switch-dispatch VM	$\sim$10–50$\times$
C computed-goto VM	$\sim$5–20$\times$
Production JIT (LuaJIT, V8)	$\sim$2–5$\times$
Ahead-of-time compiled (Lark Ch. 9)	$\sim$1$\times$

When a VM is the right answer. The ratios above look discouraging, but they measure the wrong thing for many use cases.

For a scripting language embedded in a game or application, a ten-times overhead is often irrelevant: the language is used for configuration and event handling, not inner loops. For a sandboxed execution environment (WebAssembly in a browser, bytecode in a plugin system), the isolation properties are worth significant overhead. For development and debugging, the ability to pause, inspect, and resume execution at arbitrary bytecode boundaries is worth more than the performance of a release build.

When it is not. For numerical computing, scientific simulation, or any application where the inner loop is the bottleneck, interpreter overhead is unacceptable. This is why Python is rarely used for the critical inner loops of machine-learning frameworks: those loops are compiled C++ or CUDA, called from Python for convenience.

These two targets suit different parts of the development cycle. A bytecode VM serves well as an early development target: fast to iterate on, easy to debug, portable across platforms. Chapter 9 compiles to RISC-V for deployment, where native performance matters.

2.7 Exercises

1. Add a `MOD` instruction (pop `b`, pop `a`, push `a % b`) to the stack VM. Give its opcode number, the dispatch branch that implements it, and the entry it needs in the assembler's `WIDTHS` table.

2. The factorial passes its argument on the operand stack. Trace, value by value, what sits on the operand stack at the moment of the deepest recursive `CALL` when computing fact(3). Explain why each multiplicand is still present when its `MUL` finally executes.

3. Rewrite the stack-VM factorial iteratively, with a loop and no recursion. Does your version use the call stack (`frames`) at all? What is the maximum operand-stack depth it reaches, and how does that compare with the recursive version?

4. The register VM's `RCALL` zeroes every register. Modify `RCALL` and `RRET` to implement a caller-saved/callee-saved split: `r2`–`r7` may be clobbered by the callee, while `r8`–`r15` must be preserved across the call. Which registers does each instruction now copy, and where does the saved copy live?

5. Implement two dispatch strategies for the stack VM—the `if`/`elif` chain shown here and a dictionary mapping each opcode to a handler function—and time both on the sum-to-one-million loop. Which is faster under CPython? Does the ordering match the C intuition from Section 2.4, and if not, why might the host interpreter change the answer?

The VM model developed in this chapter is complete: a register machine with sixteen registers, a frame-based call model, and an instruction set covering arithmetic, comparison, control flow, and function calls. Chapters 3 and 4 build the front end: a lexer and a parser that turn Lark source text into an abstract syntax tree. Chapter 6 will interpret that tree directly. Chapters 7 through 9 will compile it through a three-address intermediate representation and emit native instructions for RISC-V—and the register machine returns there too, as `tac_vm.py`, the interpreter that runs that representation.[6]

Notes

[1]A production VM uses a bytearray or a C array of `uint8_t`—not a Python list. The Python list makes the exposition clear; the performance implications are addressed in Section 2.6.

[2]In practice, the bytecode would come from the compiler, not from a hand-assembled list. Chapter 7 generates code from Lark's intermediate representation.

[3]The companion `ch02/reg_vm.py` omits this register-zeroing line. Zeroing the callee's registers has a second consequence this listing glosses over: it would also wipe the argument in `r2` *before* the callee could read it, so arguments could not be passed in registers at all. The repository's `RegVM` therefore has the callee inherit the caller's register file, and it ships both the buggy factorial—where the bug instead surfaces as `r2` being *restored* to $n - 1$ on return—and a fixed version that saves n in a register preserved across the call. The two tell the same lesson; the runnable code is the cleaner vehicle for it.

[4]The `StackVM` and `RegVM` in this chapter are teaching models; neither appears as a file in the repository. The production Lark pipeline (`lark/05/src/`, Phase 5 onward—see the companion map in the foreword) does not use a bytecode interpreter of this kind: source text is lexed, parsed, type-checked, lowered to three-address code (`tac.py`), and assembled directly to RV32I machine code (`riscv_asm.py`). Two VMs do exist in the production source: `tac_vm.py` interprets the three-address IR for correctness testing, and `riscv_vm.py` is a full RV32I+M emulator used for integration tests before deployment to the RP2350. Their *encoding* differs from the byte-array machine here—they interpret structured instructions, not packed opcodes in a list—but their *model* is the register machine of Section 2.3: a register file, explicit call frames, and a single dispatch loop. The frame model and calling-convention reasoning of this chapter carry over directly to both, and Chapter 7 shows `tac_vm.py` running.

[5]CPython 3.11 introduced a "specialising adaptive interpreter" (PEP 659), which goes further: it rewrites bytecode in place when it detects repeated patterns, replacing a generic `BINARY_OP` with a specialised `BINARY_OP_ADD_INT`. The gain is similar in spirit to computed goto, and works without C extensions.

[6]An earlier plan had Chapters 7–9 emitting bytecode for the register VM described here before targeting RISC-V. In the actual implementation (`lark/05/src/`) that intermediate bytecode stage was dropped: the compiler lowers directly from typed AST to three-address code (`tac.py`) and then to RV32I assembly (`riscv_asm.py`). The register-machine concepts from this chapter still inform the TAC design and the register allocator.

Part II

From Text to Structure

Chapter 3

Lexical Analysis

Raw source text is a poor thing to parse. It is a flat sequence of bytes in which a keyword, a comment, and the middle of an identifier all look alike until you have read enough context to tell them apart. The parser built in Chapter 4 does not want to work at that level, and it does not have to. Its input is a list of *tokens*: atomic units of meaning—a keyword, a name, a literal, an operator—each already classified and located. Producing that list is the scanner's job. It reads a stream of characters and emits a stream of tokens, discarding whitespace and comments on the way.

The split into two stages is not mere tidiness. A scanner recognises a *regular language*: a class of patterns that a finite-state machine can accept in one left-to-right pass, with no memory beyond its current state. A parser recognises a *context-free grammar*, a strictly larger class. Each stage is simpler for being handed only the work its formalism can do, and the boundary between them turns out to be forced rather than chosen—a point Section 3.3 makes precise.

This chapter builds Lark's scanner from the contract it must satisfy down to the last operator. Along the way it develops the model that justifies the design (finite automata), the limits of that model, and the concrete decisions a real lexer faces: token classes, literal decoding, keyword resolution, multi-character operators, and a comment syntax that nests.

3.1 The Scanner's Contract

A scanner turns a source string into a sequence of tokens. Each token carries four things: a *kind* (which category it belongs to), the *raw text* copied from the source, a *processed value* (the integer 42, not the string `"42"`), and a *location* (line and column, for diagnostics).

Listing 3.1: The Token type

```
from dataclasses import dataclass
from enum import Enum, auto

@dataclass(frozen=True)
class Token:
    kind:  TK      # enumerated token kind
    text:  str     # raw source text
    value: object  # decoded: int, float, str, bool, or None
    line:  int
    col:   int
```

The output is a flat list, terminated by a sentinel `EOF` token so the parser never has to test for the end of the list separately. Once the list exists, the parser treats it as the whole of the program and never touches the source text again. That is why location has to travel inside the token: a message like `foo.lark:4:12: unexpected token` is only possible if the scanner recorded where each token began.

The `kind` field is an enumeration. A representative slice:

Listing 3.2: Selected token kinds

```
class TK(Enum):
    INT       = auto()  # integer literal
    FLOAT     = auto()  # floating-point literal
    STRING    = auto()  # string literal
    NAME      = auto()  # lowercase id: variables, functions
    UPPER     = auto()  # uppercase id: types, constructors
    WILDCARD  = auto()  # standalone _ in a pattern
    FN        = auto()  # keyword: fn
    LET       = auto()  # keyword: let
    IF        = auto()  # keyword: if
    # ... and so on ...
    EOF       = auto()
```

The full enumeration is modest, and its shape is typical of a small language: six literal kinds (`INT`, `FLOAT`, `STRING`, `TRUE`, `FALSE`, and `UNIT`), two identifier classes, twenty-three reserved words, ten operators, and thirteen punctuation marks. Two of the reserved words, `true` and `false`, double as literals: they are spelled like keywords but carry boolean values.

Why two identifier classes? Lark distinguishes `NAME`, which starts with a lowercase letter, from `UPPER`, which starts with an uppercase one. The parser leans on the distinction: a type annotation expects an `UPPER`, a variable binding expects a `NAME`. Deciding it in the scanner—where the very first character settles the question—keeps that information out of the grammar, where it would otherwise need extra rules.

A worked example. The fragment

Listing 3.3: A Lark function definition

```
fn max(a: Int, b: Int) : Int = if a >= b then a else b
```

scans to the following token stream (kind, text, value, location):

Listing 3.4: Token stream for the fragment above

```
FN        "fn"      fn      1:1
NAME      "max"     max     1:4
LPAREN    "("       (       1:7
NAME      "a"       a       1:8
COLON     ":"       :       1:9
UPPER     "Int"     Int     1:11
COMMA     ","       ,       1:14
NAME      "b"       b       1:16
COLON     ":"       :       1:17
UPPER     "Int"     Int     1:19
RPAREN    ")"       )       1:22
COLON     ":"       :       1:24
UPPER     "Int"     Int     1:26
ASSIGN    "="       =       1:30
IF        "if"      if      1:32
NAME      "a"       a       1:35
GE        ">="      >=      1:37
NAME      "b"       b       1:40
THEN      "then"    then    1:42
NAME      "a"       a       1:47
ELSE      "else"    else    1:49
NAME      "b"       b       1:54
EOF
```

Several small acts of classification have already happened. The scanner resolved the keywords `fn`, `if`, `then`, and `else` while leaving the lookalikes `max`, `a`, and `b` as plain `NAME`s; it kept `Int` apart from those names on the strength of one capital letter; and it fused the adjacent characters > and = into a single `GE`. Note too the two roles of the colon: the parameter annotations at columns 9 and 17, and the return-type annotation at column 24—one token kind, `COLON`, that the parser will later read in two different grammatical positions. Fifty-four characters of source became twenty-two tokens. Everything downstream reasons about those twenty-two, never the fifty-four.

3.2 A Model for Tokens: Finite Automata

Behind every scanner is a finite-state machine, whether the code names it or not. A *deterministic finite automaton* (DFA) has a finite set of states, a designated start state, a set of accepting states, and a transition function that, given the current state and the current input character, names the next state. It reads one character at a time, left to right, with no memory but the state it is in. If it lands in an accepting state when the input runs out, the string is accepted.

An identifier DFA. Figure 3.1 shows the automaton that accepts Lark names: a lowercase letter, then zero or more letters, digits, or underscores.

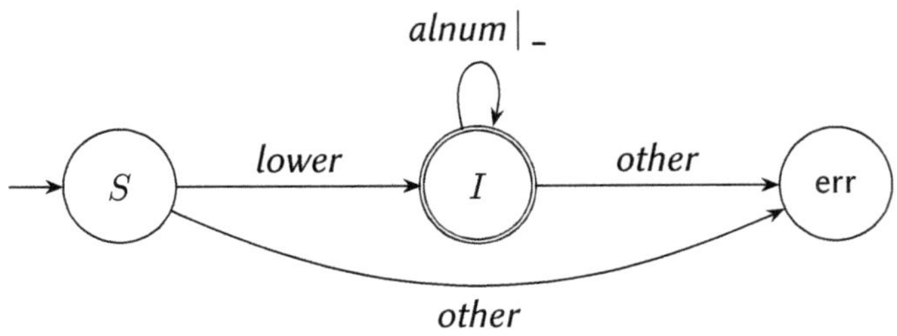

Figure 3.1: A DFA for Lark identifiers. State I (double border) accepts. In a real scanner the "other" edge out of I is not an error—it signals that the current token is finished and the character belongs to the next one.

The figure's one subtlety is the edge labelled *other* leaving the accepting state. In the abstract machine it goes to an error sink. In a scanner it means the opposite of failure: the name is complete, and the character that ended it has not been consumed. Translated to code, that "do not consume the terminator" rule is the whole trick.

Listing 3.5: A finite-state tokenizer for names and integers

```
def tokenize_simple(source):
    tokens = []
    state  = "START"
    buf    = ""
    i      = 0
    while i < len(source):
        ch = source[i]
```

```
        if state == "START":
            if ch.islower():
                state = "IDENT"
                buf = ch
            elif ch.isdigit():
                state = "INT"
                buf = ch
            elif ch.isspace():
                pass
            else:
                raise ValueError(f"unexpected: {ch!r}")
        elif state == "IDENT":
            if ch.isalnum() or ch == "_":
                buf += ch
            else:
                tokens.append(("IDENT", buf))
                buf = ""
                state = "START"
                continue           # reprocess ch from START
        elif state == "INT":
            if ch.isdigit():
                buf += ch
            else:
                tokens.append(("INT", int(buf)))
                buf = ""
                state = "START"
                continue           # reprocess ch from START
        i += 1
    if buf:
        tokens.append((state, buf))
    return tokens
```

The two `continue` statements are the terminator rule in disguise. When a token ends, the character that ended it is left unconsumed and re-examined from the start state. Lark's real scanner makes the same move with a `_peek` method that looks ahead without advancing; the effect is identical, and the bookkeeping is cleaner.

Non-deterministic automata. A *non-deterministic finite automaton* (NFA) relaxes the DFA in two ways: a state may offer several transitions on the same character, and it may take ε-transitions that consume no input at all. An NFA accepts a string if *any* path of transitions reaches an accepting state. That freedom makes NFAs easy to build from pattern descriptions—they compose cleanly under alternation, concatenation, and repetition—but it makes them awkward to run, since the machine must keep track of every state it might currently be in.

The bridge is the *subset construction*: an NFA becomes an equivalent DFA whose states are *sets* of NFA states. The DFA can be exponentially larger in the worst case, but for scanner patterns it stays small. Lexer generators such as Flex and re2c perform this construction for you and emit a table-driven DFA. Lark's scanner is written by hand, so the construction never appears as code—yet the machine the code implements is a DFA in every sense that matters.

3.3 What Regular Languages Cannot Do

Finite automata and regular expressions describe exactly the same class of languages. Kleene's theorem makes the equivalence official: every regular expression has an equivalent DFA, and every DFA an equivalent regular expression.[1] This is why regular expressions are the standard notation for specifying tokens—each one is a DFA you can read. Table 3.1 shows a selection for Lark.

Table 3.1: Selected Lark tokens as regular expressions

<table>
<tr><th>Token</th><th>Regular expression</th></tr>
<tr><td>Integer literal</td><td><code>[0-9]+</code></td></tr>
<tr><td>Float literal</td><td><code>[0-9]+\.[0-9]+</code></td></tr>
<tr><td>Name</td><td><code>[a-z][a-zA-Z0-9_]*</code></td></tr>
<tr><td>Upper identifier</td><td><code>[A-Z][a-zA-Z0-9_]*</code></td></tr>
<tr><td>Arrow</td><td><code>-></code></td></tr>
<tr><td>String literal</td><td><code>"([^"\]|\.)*"</code></td></tr>
</table>

Where the model stops. Every token in any practical programming language fits a regular pattern. The thing a finite automaton cannot do is *count*. The language $\{a^n b^n \mid n \geq 0\}$—some number of `a`s followed by an equal number of `b`s—is not regular, because a machine with finitely many states cannot remember an arbitrary n.

The *pumping lemma* turns that intuition into a proof. Every regular language has a length p such that any member at least p long contains, *within its first p characters*, a non-empty segment that can be repeated any number of times with the result still in the language. Apply this to $a^p b^p$: its first p characters are all `a`s, so the guaranteed segment lies wholly inside the run of `a`s, and repeating it produces more `a`s than `b`s—a string outside the language, and a contradiction.

Balanced parentheses are the same problem wearing programming-language clothes, and they explain the division of labour between the two stages directly. The scanner does not try to balance anything. It emits a `LPAREN` here and a `RPAREN` there and moves on; matching them is the parser's job, because matching them requires the counting a finite automaton provably lacks. The boundary between scanner and parser is not a matter of taste. It is the line between what a finite automaton can recognise and what it cannot.

Nested block comments. Lark's block comments open with `(*`, close with `*)`, and may nest:

Listing 3.6: A nested block comment

```
(* outer (* inner *) still outer *)
```

Recognising matched nesting means counting depth, which is precisely the counting that puts $\{a^n b^n\}$ out of reach of regular languages.[2] The scanner therefore steps briefly outside the regular world to handle them, with a depth counter rather than a state machine. The departure is harmless: a comment is consumed in full and produces no token, so nothing downstream ever learns that the scanner did something a DFA could not.

3.4 Building Lark's Scanner

The scanner is a class with four pieces of state—the source string, the current offset into it, and the current line and column—and a single public method, `tokenize`, that returns the token list.

Listing 3.7: The Lexer class: state and entry point

```
class Lexer:
    def __init__(
      self, source: str, filename: str = "<stdin>"
    ) -> None:
        self.source   = source
        self.filename = filename
        self.pos      = 0
        self.line     = 1
        self.col      = 1

    def tokenize(self) -> list[Token]:
        tokens: list[Token] = []
        while True:
            tok = self._next()
```

```
            tokens.append(tok)
            if tok.kind == TK.EOF:
                break
        return tokens
```

Peek and advance. Every other method is built on two primitives. `_peek` reads a character relative to the cursor without moving it; `_advance` consumes one character and keeps the line and column in step.

Listing 3.8: The two fundamental operations

```
def _peek(self, offset: int = 0) -> str:
    i = self.pos + offset
    return self.source[i] if i < len(self.source) else ""

def _advance(self) -> str:
    ch = self.source[self.pos]
    self.pos += 1
    if ch == "\n":
        self.line += 1
        self.col = 1
    else:
        self.col += 1
    return ch
```

Returning the empty string past the end of input is a small but load-bearing choice. Because `_peek` never raises at end of file, every caller can compare its result against a character without first checking bounds, and the end of input simply matches none of the patterns.[3]

Skipping whitespace and comments. Before each token, `_skip` runs down whitespace and block comments. The comment handler is where the depth counter from Section 3.3 earns its place.

Listing 3.9: Whitespace and nested-comment skipping

```
def _skip(self) -> None:
    while self.pos < len(self.source):
        ch = self._peek()
        if ch in " \t\r\n":
            self._advance()
        elif ch == "(" and self._peek(1) == "*":
            self._skip_comment()
        else:
            break
```

```
def _skip_comment(self) -> None:
    # remember where it opened
    line, col = self.line, self.col
    self._advance()       # consume (
    self._advance()       # consume *
    depth = 1
    while self.pos < len(self.source):
        if self._peek() == "(" and self._peek(1) == "*":
            self._advance()
            self._advance()
            depth += 1
        elif self._peek() == "*" and self._peek(1) == ")":
            self._advance()
            self._advance()
            depth -= 1
            if depth == 0:
                return
        else:
            self._advance()
    raise self._error("unterminated comment", line, col)
```

The location is captured before the comment is consumed, so that if the comment never closes the error points at the (* that opened it rather than at the far end of the file where the scanner finally noticed.

The main dispatch. After skipping, the first character decides the token's class outright.

Listing 3.10: First-character dispatch

```
def _next(self) -> Token:
    self._skip()
    if self.pos >= len(self.source):
        return Token(
            TK.EOF, "", None, self.line, self.col
        )
    line, col = self.line, self.col
    ch = self._peek()
    if ch.isdigit():
        return self._read_number(line, col)
    if ch == '"':
        return self._read_string(line, col)
    if ch.islower():
        return self._read_name(line, col)
```

```
    if ch.isupper():
        return self._read_upper(line, col)
    if ch == "_":
        return self._read_wildcard(line, col)
    return self._read_symbol(line, col)
```

The dispatch is a single chain of tests because the token classes are *prefix-disjoint*: no character can legally begin two of them. A digit opens a number, a quote opens a string, lowercase opens a name, uppercase an upper, an underscore the wildcard, and anything else falls through to a symbol. There is no ambiguity to resolve at this level, and so no lookahead is needed to choose the right reader—only, sometimes, inside it.

Numbers. Integers and floats share a leading run of digits. What separates them is a decimal point followed by at least one more digit.

Listing 3.11: Integer and float scanning

```
def _read_number(self, line: int, col: int) -> Token:
    start = self.pos
    while self._peek().isdigit():
        self._advance()
    if self._peek() == "." and self._peek(1).isdigit():
        self._advance()                  # consume the dot
        while self._peek().isdigit():
            self._advance()
        text = self.source[start:self.pos]
        return self._tok(
            TK.FLOAT, text, float(text), line, col
        )
    text = self.source[start:self.pos]
    return self._tok(TK.INT, text, int(text), line, col)
```

The two-character lookahead matters. Testing `_peek(1).isdigit()` before committing to a float is what keeps the dot in a field access like `point.x` out of the number: there the dot is punctuation, not a decimal separator, and the scanner stops at `point` with the dot unconsumed.

Strings. String literals are delimited by double quotes, with escape sequences resolved as they are read.

Listing 3.12: String scanning with escape handling

```
_ESCAPES: dict[str, str] = {
    '"': '"', "\\": "\\", "n": "\n", "t": "\t", "r": "\r",
```

```
}

def _read_string(self, line: int, col: int) -> Token:
    start = self.pos
    self._advance()                           # opening quote
    chars: list[str] = []
    while True:
        if self.pos >= len(self.source):
            raise self._error(
                "unterminated string", line, col
            )
        ch = self._advance()
        if ch == '"':
            break
        if ch == "\\":
            esc = self._advance()
            chars.append(self._ESCAPES.get(esc, esc))
        else:
            chars.append(ch)
    text  = self.source[start:self.pos]  # with quotes
    value = "".join(chars)               # decoded content
    return self._tok(TK.STRING, text, value, line, col)
```

Here the difference between `text` and `value` stops being incidental and starts doing work. For the literal `"hello\n"`, `text` is the six source characters between and including the quotes, while `value` is the five-character string `hello` followed by an actual newline. The parser uses `value`; an error message that wants to echo what the programmer wrote uses `text`. Keeping both means neither use has to reconstruct the other.

One small policy is worth making explicit: the `.get(esc, esc)` on the escape table means an *unrecognised* escape passes through as the bare character—\q becomes a literal q, not an error. That is a deliberate choice, not an oversight; a stricter lexer would reject unknown escapes instead, and either policy is defensible so long as it is the one the language definition actually promises.

Names and keyword resolution. A name is read in one pass and then looked up in a table. There is no separate machinery for keywords: a keyword is just a name that happens to be in the table.

Listing 3.13: Name scanning with keyword resolution

```
_KEYWORDS: dict[str, TK] = {
    "and": TK.AND,  "else": TK.ELSE,   "end": TK.END,
     "fn": TK.FN,     "if": TK.IF,      "in": TK.IN,
```

```
    "let": TK.LET, "match": TK.MATCH, "type": TK.TYPE,
    # ... twenty-three reserved words in all ...
}

def _read_name(self, line: int, col: int) -> Token:
    start = self.pos
    while self._peek().isalnum() or self._peek() == "_":
        self._advance()
    text = self.source[start:self.pos]
    kind = _KEYWORDS.get(text, TK.NAME)
    value = (True  if kind == TK.TRUE  else
             False if kind == TK.FALSE else
             text)
    return self._tok(kind, text, value, line, col)
```

The lookup folds keyword recognition into name scanning at no extra cost: read the identifier, ask the table what it is, and default to `NAME` when the table has nothing. The value column is uniform except for the two boolean keywords, where `true` and `false` carry Python booleans rather than their own spelling.

Uppercase identifiers are simpler still—there are no uppercase keywords, so there is no table to consult:

Listing 3.14: Upper identifier scanning

```
def _read_upper(self, line: int, col: int) -> Token:
    start = self.pos
    while self._peek().isalnum() or self._peek() == "_":
        self._advance()
    text = self.source[start:self.pos]
    return self._tok(TK.UPPER, text, text, line, col)
```

Symbols. Operators and punctuation are dispatched through a table for the unambiguous single characters, with one-character lookahead for the cases where a character can begin more than one token.

Listing 3.15: Symbol and operator scanning

```
def _read_symbol(self, line: int, col: int) -> Token:
    ch = self._advance()

    # single-character tokens with no ambiguity
    single: dict[str, TK] = {
        "+": TK.PLUS, "*": TK.STAR, "/": TK.SLASH,
        "|": TK.PIPE, ":": TK.COLON, ",": TK.COMMA,
```

```
        "[": TK.LBRACKET, "]": TK.RBRACKET,
        "{": TK.LBRACE,   "}": TK.RBRACE,
        ")": TK.RPAREN,
}
if ch in single:
    return self._tok(single[ch], ch, ch, line, col)

# ( or ()
if ch == "(":
    if self._peek() == ")":
        self._advance()
        return self._tok(TK.UNIT, "()", None, line, col)
    return self._tok(TK.LPAREN, "(", "(", line, col)

# - or ->
if ch == "-":
    if self._peek() == ">":
        self._advance()
        return self._tok(
            TK.ARROW, "->", "->", line, col
        )
    return self._tok(TK.MINUS, "-", "-", line, col)

# = or == or =>
if ch == "=":
    if self._peek() == "=":
        self._advance()
        return self._tok(TK.EQEQ, "==", "==", line, col)
    if self._peek() == ">":
        self._advance()
        return self._tok(
            TK.FAT_ARROW, "=>", "=>", line, col
        )
    return self._tok(TK.ASSIGN, "=", "=", line, col)

# ! must be the start of !=
if ch == "!":
    if self._peek() == "=":
        self._advance()
        return self._tok(TK.NEQ, "!=", "!=", line, col)
    raise self._error(
        "expected '=' after '!'", line, col
    )

# < or <=
```

```
    if ch == "<":
        if self._peek() == "=":
            self._advance()
            return self._tok(TK.LE, "<=", "<=", line, col)
        return self._tok(TK.LT, "<", "<", line, col)

    # > or >=
    if ch == ">":
        if self._peek() == "=":
            self._advance()
            return self._tok(TK.GE, ">=", ">=", line, col)
        return self._tok(TK.GT, ">", ">", line, col)

    raise self._error(
        f"unexpected character {ch!r}", line, col
    )
```

The `UNIT` token earns a note. In Lark `()` is the unit literal—the sole value of the unit type, the cousin of `()` in Haskell and of `void` in C. Recognising it here, as a two-character sequence at the symbol level, means the parser never sees a bare `LPAREN` followed by an immediate `RPAREN` and never has to ask whether that pair is an empty argument list or a unit value. It sees `UNIT`, and the grammar stays shorter for it.

The wildcard. Lark reserves a lone `_` as the wildcard pattern, and forbids identifiers from beginning with an underscore so that the two can never be confused.

Listing 3.16: Wildcard scanning

```
def _read_wildcard(self, line: int, col: int) -> Token:
    self._advance()                    # consume _
    if self._peek().isalnum() or self._peek() == "_":
        raise self._error(
            "identifiers may not start with '_'",
            line, col
        )
    return self._tok(TK.WILDCARD, "_", None, line, col)
```

All the dispatch cases are now in place. The scanner handles every token class that Lark's grammar requires.[4]

3.5 Reporting Lexical Errors

When a scanner meets input it cannot tokenize it has two choices: stop at the first error, or skip the offending character and carry on. Lark stops. Lexical errors almost always come from a typo or a wrong encoding—the kind of mistake that would poison everything downstream if it were waved through—so failing at once, with an exact location and an exact message, serves the programmer better than struggling on over corrupted input.

The error type carries everything a diagnostic needs, and formats the familiar `file:line:col: message` string in its constructor:

Listing 3.17: The LexError type

```
class LexError(Exception):
    def __init__(self, msg: str, filename: str,
                 line: int, col: int) -> None:
        self.msg      = msg
        self.filename = filename
        self.line     = line
        self.col      = col
        super().__init__(f"{filename}:{line}:{col}: {msg}")
```

Only three lexical errors can arise in Lark source, and the scanner has raised each of them already in the sections above:

1. An *unexpected character* at the start of a token—raised at the end of `_read_symbol` when no case matches, as in `unexpected character '$'`.
2. An *unterminated string*—the input ends while the scanner is still inside a string literal.
3. An *unterminated comment*—the input ends while the comment depth counter is still positive.

All three obey one rule: the location is the *start* of the offending construct, not the point where the scanner ran out of input. The unterminated string points at its opening quote; the unterminated comment points at its opening `(*`. The programmer is looking for the place the mistake was made, not the place the scanner happened to give up, and those are rarely the same.

The road not taken. The other strategy—emit a diagnostic, skip the bad character, and keep scanning—has its place. An editor or an incremental build tool has to produce useful results from half-written, momentarily invalid source, and cannot afford to halt on the first stray character. Supporting it means adding an error-token kind (or an out-of-band channel for diagnostics) and a recovery policy that decides how much to discard: one character, or everything up to the next whitespace. Lark needs none of this at the lexical level. The more interesting version of the same question—how a *parser* recovers and resynchronises after an error—returns in Chapter 4, where the trade-offs genuinely bite.

3.6 Exercises

1. Extend `_read_number` to accept an exponent suffix, so that `1.5e10` and `3e8` scan as floats. State precisely the new lookahead your change requires, and give an input on which a naive version would misclassify the dot.
2. Lark forbids identifiers that begin with an underscore. Suppose instead they were allowed. Which method in Section 3.4 would change, which case in the main dispatch would become ambiguous, and how would you resolve the ambiguity?
3. Draw a DFA that accepts the comparison operators <, <=, >, >=, ==, and `!=`, and no other strings. How many accepting states does it need, and why can it not be merged into fewer?
4. Add single-line comments (-- to end of line) to `_skip`. Unlike block comments, these are a regular pattern. Explain why, and confirm that your addition needs no depth counter.
5. Using the pumping lemma, prove that the set of correctly nested Lark block comments is not regular. Identify, in the proof, exactly where the finite-memory limitation bites—and relate that point to the depth counter the scanner already uses (Section 3.3): the body *counts* nesting depth; this exercise shows the counter is a necessity, not a convenience, because no finite automaton could replace it.

The Lark scanner is now complete: a hand-written lexer that turns source text into a flat token list in a single left-to-right pass. Chapter 4 takes that list and builds an abstract syntax tree from it, working through recursive descent, the theory of context-free grammars, and the shift-reduce techniques that handle the cases recursive descent cannot.

Notes

[1]Both directions are constructive. Thompson's construction [Thompson, 1968] turns a regular expression into an NFA in linear time;

the subset construction turns that NFA into a DFA; state elimination turns a DFA back into a regular expression.

[2]Line comments—say `--` to end of line—are regular and could live inside the DFA. Lark uses nesting block comments instead, and the hand-written scanner tracks depth with a counter.

[3]The source file (`lark/01/src/lexer.py`) defines two further helpers alongside `_peek` and `_advance` that are called throughout the listings in this chapter but omitted here: `_error(msg, line, col)` constructs a `LexError`, substituting `self.line`/`self.col` when `line` or `col` are `None`; and `_tok(kind, text, value, line, col)` is a one-line wrapper for the `Token` constructor. Readers assembling the chapter's code into a runnable file should add both from the source.

[4]The scanner as built in this chapter lives in `lark/01/src/lexer.py` (Phase 0 of the Lark build; see the companion map in the foreword). Later phases extended the token set as the language grew—trait and module keywords were added in Phase 2 (`lark/02/`) onward—but the architecture is unchanged: the same `Token` dataclass, the same `Lexer` class, the same single-pass state machine. The final version of the scanner is `lark/07/src/lexer.py`. Readers following the build step by step should start from `lark/01/`.

Chapter 4

Parsing

The scanner delivered twenty-two tokens for `fn max(a: Int, b: Int) : Int = if a >= b then a else b`. The parser's job is to recover something the token list does not explicitly contain: the *relationships* between those tokens. Which name is being defined, which are its parameters, what is the return type, what expression forms its body—these are structural facts buried in the order and kind of the tokens, not in the tokens themselves.

The obstacle is that programming language structure is recursive. A function body contains expressions. An expression may contain a function call. A function call has arguments that are themselves expressions. This recursive nesting cannot be described by a regular language—the class the scanner worked in—because a finite automaton cannot remember how many levels deep it has entered. Something more powerful is needed.

The right formalism is the *context-free grammar*, and the machine that recognises context-free languages is the *pushdown automaton*—a finite automaton extended with an unbounded stack. This chapter works through two parsing strategies—top-down recursive descent, which Lark uses, and bottom-up shift-reduce, which it does not—to show why the first is the right choice here and when the second is the better tool. The chapter ends with the abstract syntax tree that Lark's parser produces, which every subsequent chapter receives.

A word on what to read closely and what to skim. The *load-bearing* part of this chapter—the part Lark is actually built from—is the line from context-free grammars through recursive descent and the LL(1) property to the abstract syntax tree and its error handling. The treatment of *bottom-up* parsing (shift-reduce and the LR family) is a survey: Lark uses none of it, and it is here so that you can read the many compilers and parser generators that do. A first reading can take the bottom-up section lightly and lose nothing that the rest of the book depends on.

4.1 Context-Free Grammars

A *context-free grammar* (CFG) has four parts: a finite set of *terminals* (the tokens the scanner produces), a finite set of *nonterminals* (named syntactic categories to be defined), a distinguished *start symbol* (a nonterminal from which all strings are derived), and a set of *productions*. Each production maps a single nonterminal to a sequence of terminals and nonterminals:

$$N \rightarrow X_1 X_2 \cdots X_k$$

A production with an empty right-hand side is written $N \rightarrow \varepsilon$. A string of terminals belongs to the language of the grammar if it can be derived from the start symbol by repeatedly replacing any nonterminal with the right-hand side of one of its productions, until only terminals remain.

An arithmetic grammar. Operator precedence can be encoded directly in the grammar's nesting structure. The grammar G_0 below makes multiplication bind more tightly than addition, with both left-associative:

Listing 4.1: Grammar G_0: arithmetic with operator precedence

```
E  ->  E '+' T  |  T          (* addition, left-assoc  *)
T  ->  T '*' F  |  F          (* mult, left-assoc *)
F  ->  num  |  '(' E ')'      (* atoms and grouping *)
```

Uppercase letters are nonterminals; quoted symbols are terminals; `num` stands for any numeric token. The hierarchy enforces precedence: a sum (E) can only reach a product (T) through the nonterminal, so a product always binds more tightly. A string belongs to the language of G_0 exactly when it can be derived from E.

Derivation. A step-by-step derivation of `1 + 2 * 3` shows both the grammar at work and the structure it assigns to the string. Each step replaces one nonterminal with the right-hand side of one of its productions:

$$\begin{aligned} E &\Rightarrow E+T \\ &\Rightarrow T+T \\ &\Rightarrow F+T \\ &\Rightarrow 1+T \\ &\Rightarrow 1+T*F \\ &\Rightarrow 1+F*F \\ &\Rightarrow 1+2*F \\ &\Rightarrow 1+2*3 \end{aligned}$$

The sequence of production choices is simultaneously a proof that `1 + 2 * 3` is in the language and a record of its structure: the $*$ was reached through T

before the E production resolved the +, which is precisely the higher-precedence binding.

Why context-free? In a context-free grammar any occurrence of a nonterminal may be rewritten regardless of what surrounds it—that is the context-free property. A *regular* grammar, by contrast, may only expand a nonterminal into a terminal followed by at most one nonterminal, which prevents the arbitrary nesting that programming languages require. Every regular language is context-free, but not the converse.[1]

Lark's grammar. Lark's surface grammar is specified in EBNF in `lark/01/docs/grammar.ebnf`. EBNF shorthands—$\{x\}$ for zero or more repetitions, $[x]$ for optional—keep the rules concise. The expression fragment:

Listing 4.2: Lark expression grammar (from `grammar.ebnf`, simplified)

```
expr        = let_expr | if_expr | match_expr
              | lambda_expr | infix_expr ;
let_expr    = "let" name [ ":" type ] "=" expr "in" expr ;
if_expr     = "if" expr "then" expr "else" expr ;
match_expr  = "match" expr "with"
              { "|" pattern "=>" expr } "end" ;
lambda_expr= "fn" "(" [ params ] ")" "=>" expr ;
infix_expr  = unary_expr { op unary_expr } ;
apply_expr  = atom { "(" [ args ] ")" } ;
```

The `infix_expr` rule, as written, does not specify operator precedence. That information lives in the parser, not the grammar. Section 4.2 shows how the function chain encodes it.

4.2 Recursive Descent

The most direct route from a grammar to a parser is a mechanical translation: one function per nonterminal, one conditional branch per alternative, one matched token per terminal. The resulting parser is called *recursive descent* because productions that refer to their own nonterminal become recursive function calls.

A toy parser. Grammar G_0 is left-recursive, which breaks naive recursive descent (the problem is addressed below). For a first illustration, take a simpler grammar $E \to T(+T)^*$, $T \to \texttt{num} \mid (E)$, which generates sums of numbers and grouped expressions with no further precedence levels:

Listing 4.3: Recursive descent for simple sums

```
def parse_expr(tokens, pos):
```

```
    left, pos = parse_term(tokens, pos)
    while pos < len(tokens) and tokens[pos][0] == '+':
        pos += 1                            # consume '+'
        right, pos = parse_term(tokens, pos)
        left = ('add', left, right)
    return left, pos

def parse_term(tokens, pos):
    kind, value = tokens[pos]
    if kind == 'num':
        return ('num', value), pos + 1
    if kind == '(':
        pos += 1
        node, pos = parse_expr(tokens, pos)
        assert tokens[pos][0] == ')'
        return node, pos + 1
    raise SyntaxError(f"unexpected: {tokens[pos]!r}")
```

The while loop in parse_expr mirrors the EBNF repetition $(+T)^*$: read one term, then keep reading more terms as long as a + follows. When no + is next, the loop exits and the accumulated left-associative tree is returned. The mutual recursion between parse_expr and parse_term—the latter calls the former inside parentheses—handles nested grouping to any depth, something no finite automaton can do.

The left-recursion problem. For the rule $E \to E + T \mid T$, a literal translation would call parse_E from inside parse_E before consuming any token—immediate infinite recursion. This is left recursion, and it is fatal for top-down parsers. The fix is *left-recursion elimination*: rewrite each left-recursive rule to introduce a new nonterminal that handles the tail.

$$E \to E + T \mid T \quad \longrightarrow \quad E \to T\,E', \quad E' \to +T\,E' \mid \varepsilon$$
$$T \to T * F \mid F \quad \longrightarrow \quad T \to F\,T', \quad T' \to *F\,T' \mid \varepsilon$$

The primed nonterminals E' and T' handle the repetition; their right-hand sides are right-recursive, which translates to ordinary recursive calls. In practice, recursive descent parsers express this pattern as a `while` loop rather than introducing the primed nonterminals explicitly.

Lark's parser. Lark's expression grammar encodes precedence through a chain of functions, one per level. Each function handles the operators at its own precedence level and calls the next-higher level for its operands:

Listing 4.4: Precedence chain in Lark's parser (from `lark/02/src/parser.py`)

```
def _parse_add(self) -> Expr:
    left = self._parse_mul()
    while self._at(TK.PLUS, TK.MINUS):
        op   = self._advance().text
        left = BinOp(op, left, self._parse_mul())
    return left

def _parse_mul(self) -> Expr:
    left = self._parse_unary()
    while self._at(TK.STAR, TK.SLASH):
        op   = self._advance().text
        left = BinOp(op, left, self._parse_unary())
    return left

def _parse_unary(self) -> Expr:
    if self._at(TK.MINUS, TK.NOT):
        op = self._advance().text
        # right-recursive
        return UnaryOp(op, self._parse_unary())
    return self._parse_apply()
```

The full precedence chain, from lowest to highest, is: `or` → `and` → comparisons → `_parse_add` → `_parse_mul` → `_parse_unary` → `_parse_apply` → `_parse_atom`. Binary operators use the while loop for left associativity; unary negation recurses on itself, giving it right associativity so that `--x` parses as `-(-(x))`.

Beyond expressions. The same pattern scales to declarations. The top-level loop reads declarations until EOF; each declaration begins with a keyword that uniquely determines its kind:

Listing 4.5: Declaration dispatch (from `lark/02/src/parser.py`)

```
def _parse_top_decl(self) -> Decl:
    exported = bool(self._match(TK.EXPORT))
    tok = self._peek()
    if tok.kind == TK.FN:
        return self._parse_fn_decl(exported)
    if tok.kind == TK.LET:
        return self._parse_let_decl(exported)
    if tok.kind == TK.TYPE:
        return self._parse_type_decl(exported)
    if tok.kind == TK.TRAIT:
        return self._parse_trait_decl(exported)
    if tok.kind == TK.IMPL:
```

```
        return self._parse_impl_decl()
    raise self._error(
        f"expected declaration (fn/let/type/trait/impl), "
        f"got {tok.kind.name} ({tok.text!r})")
```

No lookahead beyond the first token is ever needed to choose a branch. The grammar is *prefix-disjoint* at this level: each keyword opens exactly one kind of declaration. That is the property which LL(1) parsers formalise.

4.3 LL(1): Making Recursive Descent Formal

Recursive descent works because the parser can always determine, from a single token of lookahead, which production to apply. Formalising this leads to *LL(1)* parsing: **L**eft-to-right input, **L**eftmost derivation, **1** token of lookahead.

First sets. For a grammar symbol or string α, the set $\mathrm{FIRST}(\alpha)$ contains every terminal that can begin a string derived from α, plus ε if α can derive the empty string. For the left-recursion-eliminated arithmetic grammar, the values are (Table 4.1):

Table 4.1: FIRST sets for the arithmetic grammar

Symbol	FIRST
F	$\{\mathtt{num},\ (\}$
T'	$\{*,\ \varepsilon\}$
T	$\{\mathtt{num},\ (\}$
E'	$\{+,\ \varepsilon\}$
E	$\{\mathtt{num},\ (\}$

Follow sets. $\mathrm{FOLLOW}(N)$ is the set of terminals that can appear *immediately after* nonterminal N in any sentential form derived from the start symbol, plus $\$$ for the start symbol itself (Table 4.2):

The parse table. The LL(1) parse table $M[N, t]$ specifies which production to apply when nonterminal N is to be expanded and the lookahead token is t. The construction rule: for each production $N \to \alpha$, add it to $M[N, t]$ for every $t \in \mathrm{FIRST}(\alpha) \setminus \{\varepsilon\}$; if $\varepsilon \in \mathrm{FIRST}(\alpha)$, also add it to $M[N, t]$ for every $t \in \mathrm{FOLLOW}(N)$.

Every cell is either empty (a syntax error if reached) or holds exactly one production. That is the LL(1) condition: the lookahead uniquely determines the action. A grammar is LL(1) if and only if its parse table has no cell with two or more entries.

Table 4.2: FOLLOW sets

Nonterminal	FOLLOW
E	$\{), \$\}$
E'	$\{), \$\}$
T	$\{+,), \$\}$
T'	$\{+,), \$\}$
F	$\{*, +,), \$\}$

Table 4.3: LL(1) parse table for the arithmetic grammar

	num	(	)	+	*
E	$T\,E'$	$T\,E'$			
E'			ε	$+T\,E'$	
T	$F\,T'$	$F\,T'$			
T'			ε	ε	$*F\,T'$
F	num	(E)			

Table-driven parsing. The parse table can be used directly by a generic driver that maintains a stack of expected grammar symbols:

Listing 4.6: A table-driven LL(1) parser

```
def ll1_parse(table, tokens, start):
    stack = ['$', start]
    pos   = 0
    while stack:
        top   = stack.pop()
        token = tokens[pos]
        if top == '$' == token:
            # accept: both stack and input empty
            return
        # terminal: must match current token
        if top == token:
            pos += 1
        # nonterminal: look up and push
        elif top in table:
            production = table[top].get(token)
            if production is None:
```

```
                raise SyntaxError(
                  f"unexpected {token!r} "
                  f"when expanding {top!r}"
                )
            stack.extend(reversed(production))
        else:
            raise SyntaxError(
              f"expected {top!r}, got {token!r}"
            )
```

What LL(1) cannot handle. Three conditions cause a grammar to fail the LL(1) test. *Left recursion* ($A \to A\,\alpha$) must be eliminated before table construction, as it causes infinite loops in top-down parsers. *First-first conflicts* arise when two alternatives for the same nonterminal can begin with the same terminal. *First-follow conflicts* arise when a nullable alternative (ε in its FIRST set) overlaps with the nonterminal's FOLLOW set.

Lark's grammar avoids all three. Every declaration begins with a unique keyword; every expression alternative begins with a token not shared with any other alternative at the same level. The `if--then--else` construct avoids the classic dangling-else conflict by requiring both `then` and `else`.[2]

Seen through this lens, the table-driven LL(1) parser is a *pushdown automaton*: a finite control plus an explicit stack holding the grammar symbols still to be matched. That stack is exactly the call stack recursive descent keeps *implicitly*, one pending function call per expected symbol. The pushdown automaton is the abstract machine behind every top-down parser; the recursive functions are simply a more readable way to run it.[3]

4.4 Bottom-Up Parsing

Top-down parsing builds the parse tree from the root, choosing a production before seeing the terminals it covers. Bottom-up parsing works the other way: it consumes terminals first, assembles them into larger structures, and names the production afterward. The canonical bottom-up strategy is *shift-reduce* parsing.

Shift and reduce. The parser maintains a stack and reads the token stream from left to right. At each step it either *shifts*—moves the next token onto the stack—or *reduces*—recognises that the top of the stack matches the right-hand side of some production, and replaces it with that production's left-hand side nonterminal. Parsing succeeds when the start symbol sits alone on the stack with the input exhausted.

Table 4.4 shows the parse of `1 + 2 * 3` under G_0. Note that G_0's left recursion poses no obstacle: the bottom-up strategy handles it directly.

Table 4.4: Shift-reduce trace for `1 + 2 * 3` under G_0

Stack	Remaining input	Action
$\$$	`1 + 2 * 3 $`	shift
$\$\,1$	`+ 2 * 3 $`	reduce $F \to \mathtt{num}$
$\$\,F$	`+ 2 * 3 $`	reduce $T \to F$
$\$\,T$	`+ 2 * 3 $`	reduce $E \to T$
$\$\,E$	`+ 2 * 3 $`	shift
$\$\,E+$	`2 * 3 $`	shift
$\$\,E+2$	`* 3 $`	reduce $F \to \mathtt{num}$
$\$\,E+F$	`* 3 $`	reduce $T \to F$
$\$\,E+T$	`* 3 $`	**shift** (not reduce: $*$ binds tighter)
$\$\,E+T*$	`3 $`	shift
$\$\,E+T*3$	`$`	reduce $F \to \mathtt{num}$
$\$\,E+T*F$	`$`	reduce $T \to T*F$
$\$\,E+T$	`$`	reduce $E \to E+T$
$\$\,E$	`$`	accept

Row 9 is the critical moment. The stack holds $E + T$ and the next token is `*`. One option is to reduce $E \to E+T$, placing E on the stack with `* 3` still ahead—but $*$ cannot follow E (it is not in FOLLOW(E)), and reducing now would leave the multiplication unresolvable. The parser shifts instead, deferring the E-reduction until the multiplication is complete. The lookahead token determines the choice.

The LR family, in brief. The shift-versus-reduce decision is driven by a finite automaton over *items*—productions with a dot marking how far the parse has reached, such as $[E \to E + \bullet T]$ (“`E +` seen, T expected”)—whose states the stack tracks so that the choice needs no backtracking.[4] The payoff is reach: LR parsers accept left-recursive grammars directly and cover a strictly larger class than LL(1) (every LL(1) grammar is LR(1), not the converse), which makes LR the natural target for a *generated* parser. The cost is opacity—the automaton states are not human-readable, and good error messages take extra engineering on top of the generated tables—and it is that cost the next section weighs against recursive descent for Lark.

4.5 Choosing a Strategy

Lark's parser is recursive descent. The choice holds on three dimensions.

Power. Lark's grammar is LL(1), verified during design. Every declaration begins with a unique keyword; every expression alternative begins with a token not shared at the same level. An LR generator would accept the grammar without difficulty, but it would offer nothing that the grammar does not already require.

Readability. A function named `_parse_fn_decl` is immediately legible as the parser for function declarations. Its body lists exactly the tokens it consumes; its call sites name the structure they expect. The precedence chain—`_parse_add` calling `_parse_mul` calling `_parse_unary`—documents the grammar in the code. A table of LR automaton states does not.

Error quality. When the parse fails, the call stack reveals the parser's current intent. The function `_parse_fn_decl` knows it is parsing a function declaration; if the next token is wrong it says so precisely. A table-driven parser trades this context for generality. For a language meant to be used, error messages that name the construct being parsed are worth the cost.

Two alternatives deserve mention. *Parser combinators*—libraries that represent grammar rules as first-class values composed with higher-order functions—produce code that reads almost like a grammar specification.[5] *Earley parsers* handle all context-free grammars—including ambiguous ones—in $O(n^3)$ worst-case time. They are the right tool for natural language processing, where ambiguity is inherent, not a design error.

4.6 Abstract Syntax Trees

Every derivation produces a *parse tree* (or *concrete syntax tree*): a tree whose shape mirrors exactly the grammar productions used. Each internal node is a nonterminal; each leaf is a terminal. The parse tree for `1 + 2 * 3` under G_0 has fourteen nodes (Figure 4.1).

The intermediate nodes E, T, F are structurally load-bearing during the parse—they are what gives the precedence hierarchy its meaning—but semantically empty once the tree is built. Every subsequent pass cares only about the operators and their operands. An *abstract syntax tree* (AST) discards the scaffolding and keeps only the nodes that carry semantic information (Figure 4.2).

The AST for `1 + 2 * 3` has three nodes. The parse tree has fourteen. Both represent the same structure; the AST is what the compiler actually uses.

Lark's AST. The tree is defined in `lark/02/src/tree.py` as a collection of frozen dataclasses. `frozen=True` makes every node immutable: once built by the parser, no code can alter it. A representative selection of the expression hierarchy:

Listing 4.7: Selected expression nodes (from `lark/02/src/tree.py`)

```
@dataclass(frozen=True)
```

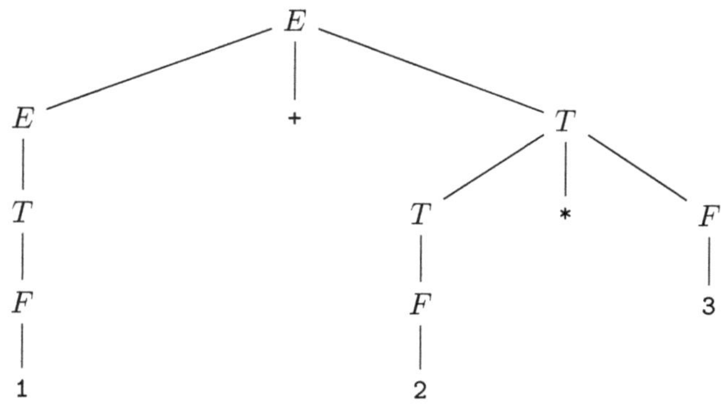

Figure 4.1: Parse tree for `1 + 2 * 3` under G_0. The chains $E \to T \to F$ enforce precedence but carry no semantic content once the parse is complete.

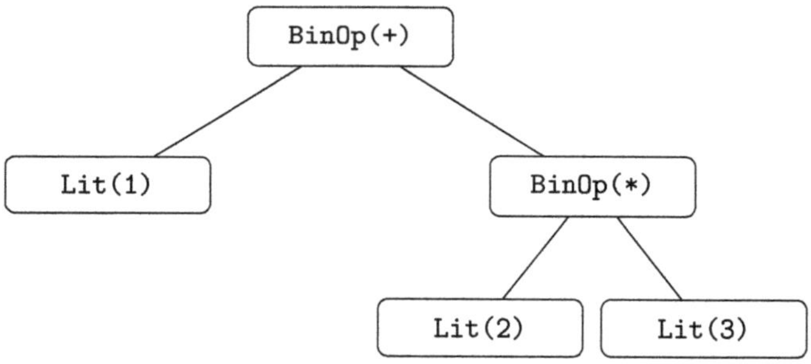

Figure 4.2: AST for `1 + 2 * 3`: three nodes. The precedence that required eleven nonterminal nodes in the parse tree is now captured by nesting alone.

```
class Lit:
    value: object    # int | float | str | bool | None

@dataclass(frozen=True)
class Var:
    name: str

@dataclass(frozen=True)
class BinOp:
    op:    str
    left:  Expr
    right: Expr

@dataclass(frozen=True)
```

```
class LetExpr:
    name:  str
    ann:   Type | None  # optional type annotation
    value: Expr
    body:  Expr

@dataclass(frozen=True)
class MatchExpr:
    scrutinee: Expr
    arms:      tuple[tuple[Pat, Expr], ...]

Expr = Union[Lit, Var, Con, TupleExpr, Apply,
             BinOp, UnaryOp, LetExpr, IfExpr,
             MatchExpr, Lambda]
```

The type alias `Expr` is the union of all eleven expression node types. Every subsequent pass in the compiler dispatches on the concrete type of each node; the type checker in Chapter 5 is written almost entirely as a recursive walk over this union.

From grammar to nodes. Each grammar production maps to one of three fates in the AST. *Transparent* productions—parentheses, operator-level helper rules such as E' and T'—leave no trace; the parser absorbs them silently. *Operator* productions produce a `BinOp` or `UnaryOp` node carrying the operator string. *Structural* productions produce a dedicated node: `LetExpr`, `IfExpr`, `MatchExpr`, `Lambda`, or a declaration type.

The parser builds each node at the point where its production is complete. For `let x = 1 + 2 in x`:

Listing 4.8: Building a `LetExpr` node (from `_parse_let_expr`)

```
def _parse_let_expr(self) -> LetExpr:
    self._expect(TK.LET)
    name = self._expect(TK.NAME).text
    ann  = None
    if self._match(TK.COLON):
        ann = self._parse_type()
    self._expect(TK.ASSIGN)
    value = self._parse_expr()     # builds BinOp(+, 1, 2)
    self._expect(TK.IN)
    body  = self._parse_expr()     # builds Var('x')
    return LetExpr(name, ann, value, body)
```

The result is:

Listing 4.9: AST for `let x = 1 + 2 in x`

```
LetExpr(
    name  = 'x',
    ann   = None,
    value = BinOp('+', Lit(1), Lit(2)),
    body  = Var('x')
)
```

This tree is what every subsequent pass receives. The type checker assigns types to it; the interpreter evaluates it; the lowerer emits three-address code from it. Location information is not stored in AST nodes: the parser has consumed the tokens, and any later error messages use the locations recorded during scanning.[6]

Parsing `match`. One expression form deserves to be followed all the way through, because the rest of the book leans on it: the `match` expression, the characteristic construct of an ML-family language. Its grammar was given above (`match e with | pat => expr ...end`); parsing it is a direct transcription of that production, no harder than `let`.

Listing 4.10: Parsing a `match` expression (from `lark/02/src/parser.py`)

```
def _parse_match_expr(self) -> MatchExpr:
    self._expect(TK.MATCH)
    scrutinee = self._parse_expr()
    self._expect(TK.WITH)
    arms: list[tuple[Pat, Expr]] = []
    while self._match(TK.PIPE):  # each arm begins with '|'
        pat  = self._parse_pattern()
        self._expect(TK.FAT_ARROW)  # '=>'
        expr = self._parse_expr()
        arms.append((pat, expr))
    self._expect(TK.END)               # 'end' closes the match
    return MatchExpr(scrutinee, tuple(arms))
```

The arms loop is the same `while self._match(...)` shape that drove operator precedence: keep consuming while the leading token (here `|`) says another arm follows. The only new piece is the *pattern* on the left of each `=>`, which has its own small recursive parser—wildcards, variables, literals, and constructor patterns that may nest:

Listing 4.11: Parsing a pattern, abbreviated (from `lark/02/src/parser.py`)

```
def _parse_pattern(self) -> Pat:
    tok = self._peek()
```

```
if tok.kind == TK.WILDCARD:
    self._advance(); return PWild()
if tok.kind == TK.NAME:
    self._advance(); return PVar(tok.text)
if tok.kind in _LIT_KINDS:
    self._advance(); return PLit(tok.value)
if tok.kind == TK.UPPER:  # a constructor pattern
    self._advance()
    args: tuple[Pat, ...] = ()
    if self._match(TK.LPAREN):      # e.g. Rect(w, h)
        pats = [self._parse_pattern()]
        while self._match(TK.COMMA):
            pats.append(self._parse_pattern())
        self._expect(TK.RPAREN)
        args = tuple(pats)
    return PCon(tok.text, args)
# tuple patterns and negative-number literals omitted
raise self._error("unexpected token in pattern")
```

Constructor patterns recurse through `_parse_pattern` for their arguments, so `Rect(w, h)` and a nested `Cons(x, Cons(y, rest))` parse by the same rule. That is the whole of the *syntax* of matching. What a `match` *means*—how its arms are type-checked against the scrutinee's constructors and checked for exhaustiveness (Chapter 5), how it is evaluated (Chapter 6), and how it is lowered to a chain of tag tests (Chapter 7)—is the thread this one production opens and the next several chapters follow to the ground.

4.7 Error Handling

When a parse fails the parser must decide how much to report and whether to continue. The scanner's fail-fast approach—stop at the first bad character—is the simplest choice and the one Lark currently uses. It suits a batch compiler that processes a complete file expecting well-formed input. An IDE or incremental build tool cannot stop at the first error; it needs to recover and continue so that the programmer sees all the mistakes in one pass.

ParseError. The error type mirrors `LexError` from Chapter 3: filename, line, column, and message, formatted in the standard `file:line:col: message` style.

Listing 4.12: ParseError (from `lark/02/src/parser.py`)

```
class ParseError(Exception):
    def __init__(self, msg: str, filename: str,
                 line: int, col: int) -> None:
```

```
        self.msg      = msg
        self.filename = filename
        self.line     = line
        self.col      = col
        super().__init__(f"{filename}:{line}:{col}: {msg}")
```

_expect and _error. The two error-producing primitives are `_expect` and `_error`. `_expect` consumes a mandatory token and raises immediately if it is absent; the location is taken from the offending token, not from wherever the exception is eventually caught.

Listing 4.13: The `_expect` and `_error` primitives

```
def _expect(self, kind: TK) -> Token:
    tok = self._peek()
    if tok.kind != kind:
        raise self._error(
          f"expected {kind.name}, got "
          f"{tok.kind.name} ({tok.text!r})"
        )
    return self._advance()

def _error(
    self, msg: str, tok: Token | None = None
) -> ParseError:
    t = tok or self._peek()
    return ParseError(msg, self.filename, t.line, t.col)
```

The message `foo.lark:7:12: expected IN, got NAME ("then")` is precise because the parser was working through a `let` expression, expected the closing `in` keyword, and found a name instead. The programmer sees the expected and actual tokens in their source file; they do not need to know what "parse" means to act on the message.

Panic mode. The simplest recovery strategy is *panic mode*: after an error, discard tokens until a reliable *synchronisation token* is found, then continue from that point. Synchronisation tokens delimit clearly-bounded units—in a statement-level language, semicolons or closing braces; in Lark, the declaration-opening keywords.

Listing 4.14: Panic-mode recovery at the declaration level (illustrative)

```
SYNC = {TK.FN, TK.LET, TK.TYPE, TK.TRAIT, TK.IMPL, TK.EOF}
```

```
def _parse_decls_with_recovery(self) -> list[Decl]:
    decls = []
    while not self._at(TK.EOF):
        try:
            decls.append(self._parse_top_decl())
        except ParseError as e:
            print(f"error: {e}", file=sys.stderr)
            while not self._at(*SYNC):
                self._advance()  # discard until sync
    return decls
```

Lark does not implement recovery at present: it stops at the first error, matching the scanner's behaviour. For a file-level batch compiler this is the right default—a single syntax error typically corrupts the parse state in ways that produce misleading secondary errors. The recovery sketch above is the pattern for any reader building a language server or IDE plugin that must tolerate partial programs.

Error quality. Location accuracy is necessary but not sufficient. The most useful error messages name the *construct* being parsed, not just the mismatched token. A function `_parse_fn_decl` that has consumed `fn` and a name and then finds the wrong next token can say "in function declaration: expected parameter list, got ="—a message pointing directly at the missing parentheses. A table-driven parser dispenses with this context in exchange for generality. For a hand-written parser the context is free: it is already present in the function names and the call stack.

4.8 Exercises

1. Write a recursive descent parser for Boolean expressions built from variables (`a`, `b`, ...), `not`, `and`, and `or` (standard precedence: `not` highest, `or` lowest). State the grammar in EBNF first, verify it is LL(1) by computing FIRST for each nonterminal, then implement one function per nonterminal.

2. Compute the LL(1) parse table for the right-recursive variant of G_0: $E \to T\,(+T)^*$, $T \to F\,(*F)^*$, $F \to \mathtt{num} \mid (E)$. First rewrite the grammar using standard production notation (no EBNF shorthands), then compute FIRST and FOLLOW sets and fill in the table. Compare the result with Table 4.3: are there any differences?

3. The grammar $S \to a\,S\,b \mid \varepsilon$ generates $\{a^n b^n \mid n \geq 0\}$. Show it is LL(1) by computing FIRST(S) and FOLLOW(S), constructing the parse table, and verifying each cell has at most one entry. Implement a recursive descent

parser for it. Then explain, using the pumping lemma from Chapter 3, why no finite automaton can accept $\{a^n b^n\}$.

4. Lark's `match` expression currently requires one pattern per arm. Extend `_parse_match_expr` to allow multiple patterns separated by |: for example, `| A | B => expr`. (a) Write the revised EBNF rule for an arm. (b) Show the code change to `_parse_match_expr`. (c) Modify the `MatchExpr` node in `tree.py` to store a tuple of patterns per arm rather than a single pattern.

5. Trace the shift-reduce parse of `(1 + 2) * 3` under G_0, using the same table format as Table 4.4. At the step where the stack is $\$ \ (\ E$ and the remaining input begins with), what action does the parser take? Explain why the closing parenthesis does not trigger a reduce at this point, and identify the production that eventually consumes it.

Lark's parser is complete: a hand-written recursive descent machine that turns a token list into an abstract syntax tree in a single left-to-right pass. Chapter 5 takes that tree and assigns types to it, building the symbol table, Hindley-Milner type inference, and the affine ownership rules that give Lark its resource discipline.

Notes

[1]The Chomsky hierarchy places these classes in a strict inclusion: regular $\subset$ context-free $\subset$ context-sensitive $\subset$ recursively enumerable. Programming language syntax sits firmly at the context-free level. The context-sensitive checks—name resolution, type checking—are deferred to later passes.

[2]The *dangling-else* ambiguity—`if` c `then` `if` c' `then` a `else` b—creates a first-follow conflict: the `else` may attach to either `if`. Most languages resolve it by convention (else attaches to the nearest open if), then patch the grammar or the parser to enforce the convention. Lark's mandatory `then` and `else` keywords leave nothing dangling.

[3]The pushdown automaton is to context-free grammars what the finite automaton of Chapter 3 was to regular expressions: the machine model that recognises exactly that class of languages. A *nondeterministic* pushdown automaton recognises all context-free languages; the *deterministic* one recognises a smaller class that still includes every practical programming-language grammar—which is why a single token of lookahead suffices for parsers like Lark's.

[4]LR(0) items use no lookahead; conflicts are addressed by adding Follow information (SLR), merging item sets with identical cores (LALR), or full one-token

lookahead per item (LR(1)). Practical generators (yacc, bison, ANTLR in LALR mode) produce LALR(1) parsers, which handle every grammar a real programming language requires.

[5]Representative combinator libraries include Haskell's Parsec, Rust's `nom`, and Python's `lark-parser`. A combinator encoding of the addition level might read `chainl1(parse_mul, lit("+") $> BinOp("+"))`. They suit projects where compactness matters more than custom error messages.

[6]The parser and AST as built in this chapter live in `lark/02/src/parser.py` and `lark/02/src/tree.py` (Phase 2 of the Lark build; see the companion map in the foreword). Later phases extended the implementation with trait declarations, module imports, and a REPL—visible in `lark/07/src/` (Phase 7)—but the structural grammar introduced in Phase 2 is unchanged. Readers who want a compact, standalone version of the parsing stage should start from `lark/02/`.

Part III

Meaning

Chapter 5

Names, Scope, and Types

The abstract syntax tree from Chapter 4 is structurally complete but semantically empty. It contains names—`x`, `add`, `Int`—but says nothing about what they refer to. A variable `x` in a function body must reach back to the binding that introduced it. The annotation `Int` in a signature must agree with the type of the expression it annotates. The call `eq(a, b)` must confirm that `a` and `b` belong to a type for which equality is defined. None of this can be checked by reading a single node in isolation; it requires a pass that threads state through the whole tree.

That pass is the type checker. It does three things simultaneously: it resolves names by tracking which bindings are in scope; it assigns a type to every expression node; and it enforces a resource discipline—affine ownership—that the value-level language cannot state on its own. The chapter builds each of these in turn, from the symbol table up through Hindley-Milner inference to the ownership rules and the trait system that gives Lark its ad-hoc polymorphism. All three parts land at the same implementation: a single inference pass (Algorithm W) that traverses the AST once and either produces a fully annotated tree or names the first inconsistency precisely.

5.1 Names and the Symbol Table

A *symbol table* is a map from names to everything the compiler currently knows about them. For a variable `x` the minimum is a type; for a function `add` it includes parameter types and return type; for a type name `Pair` it includes the structure of the type and its constructors. When the emphasis is on the mathematical object, compilers call this the *environment*; when the emphasis is on the textual region over which a name is visible, they call it the *scope*.

Lark's type checker represents the environment as a persistent linked chain of dictionaries. Each time a new name is introduced—by a `let` binding, a function parameter, or a declaration—a fresh dictionary is constructed that extends the current one without modifying it.

Listing 5.1: The type environment (simplified; `lark/03/src/infer.py` uses `Env = dict[str, Scheme]`)

```
@dataclass
class Env:
    bindings: dict[str, Scheme]
    parent:   Env | None = None

    def lookup(self, name: str) -> Scheme:
        if name in self.bindings:
            return self.bindings[name]
        if self.parent is not None:
            return self.parent.lookup(name)
        raise TypeError(f"unbound name: {name!r}")

    def extend(self, name: str, scheme: Scheme) -> Env:
        return Env({name: scheme}, parent=self)

    def extend_many(self, pairs: dict[str, Scheme]) -> Env:
        return Env(dict(pairs), parent=self)
```

The `extend` method returns a *new* environment. This is a design requirement, not a performance choice. When the checker descends into the body of `let x =` e_1 `in` e_2, it creates an environment that includes `x`; when it returns to the surrounding expression, `x` must no longer be in scope. Immutable extension makes this free: the extended environment is simply not passed back up.

What the table stores. Each binding maps a name to a *type scheme*: either a plain type with no quantified variables (a *monotype*), or a universally quantified type that can be freshly instantiated at each use (a *polytype*). The distinction—developed in Section 5.5—is what allows a single definition of `id` to be applied to integers, strings, and records without duplication.

Listing 5.2: Type representation (simplified; `lark/03/src/ty.py` uses integer type variables `TVar(id)`, names the function and applied types `TFn` and `TApp(head, args)`, and adds a tuple type `TTup`)

```
@dataclass(frozen=True)
class TVar:
    name: str                    # type var: 'a', 'b', ...

@dataclass(frozen=True)
```

```
class TCon:
    name: str                          # base type: Int, Bool, ...

@dataclass(frozen=True)
class TApp:
    func: Type
    arg:  Type                         # List Int = TApp(...)

@dataclass(frozen=True)
class TFun:
    param: Type
    ret:   Type                        # Int -> Bool

@dataclass(frozen=True)
class Scheme:
    params: tuple[str, ...]            # quantified variables
    ty:     Type

Type = TVar | TCon | TApp | TFun
```

The prelude. The checker begins with a non-empty environment containing the built-in operations. Every Lark program can use these without declaring them.

Listing 5.3: Built-in operators as schemes (the implementation generates these in _binop_type)

```
INT  = TCon("Int");  BOOL = TCon("Bool")
STR  = TCon("String")

a = TVar("a")

PRELUDE: dict[str, Scheme] = {
    "+":  Scheme(("a",), TFun(a,     TFun(a,     a))),
    "-":  Scheme(("a",), TFun(a,     TFun(a,     a))),
    "*":  Scheme(("a",), TFun(a,     TFun(a,     a))),
    "/":  Scheme(("a",), TFun(a,     TFun(a,     a))),
    "==": Scheme(("a",), TFun(a,     TFun(a,     BOOL))),
    "not":Scheme((),     TFun(BOOL, BOOL)),
}
```

The arithmetic and equality operators are polymorphic: each carries an unconstrained scheme ($\forall a.\ a \to a \to a$ for the arithmetic operators, $\forall a.\ a \to a \to$ Bool for equality) that is instantiated fresh at each call site. One consequence is that the same + applies to both `Int` and `Float`; a genuinely ill-typed mix such as `1 + true` is still rejected, because unifying the two operand types fails.

This scheme is looser than arithmetic warrants, and the chapter should not pretend otherwise. Because it constrains only that both operands and the result share *one* type, it accepts not just `Int` and `Float` but also `true + false`, `() + ()`, and `"a" + "b"`. The last is deliberate—Lark spells string concatenation +, and the trait examples of Section 5.8 rely on it—but the first two are nonsense the checker waves through. The principled fix is a *bounded* scheme, $\forall a\ [\mathrm{Num}\ a].\ a \to a \to a$, restricting `a` to the types that actually implement addition; and that is exactly the trait machinery of Section 5.8. The reason + is left fully polymorphic here is the same reason those bounds are not enforced—trait constraints are recorded but not checked (Chapter 11)—so arithmetic is intentionally over-permissive, and a reader should not mistake "it type-checks" for "it means something." One corner of this looseness turns out to be worse than permissive: an operator whose operand type is *still a type variable* when its declaration is generalised leaves every back end to guess, and the guesses need not agree. Chapter 13 tells that story—a real miscompilation, found by fuzzing—and ends it by making the ambiguity a type error.

The prelude also contains `show` as a polymorphic builtin ($\forall a.\ a \to \mathrm{String}$); it is a function, not a trait. For types that need user-supplied behaviour, the trait mechanism in Section 5.8 provides the right tool.

5.2 Scope

A language has *lexical scope* when the meaning of a free name is determined by the textual region where the expression is written—the definition site. It has *dynamic scope* when the meaning is determined at runtime by the chain of active calls—the call site. The two regimes give different answers, and for a language with first-class functions the difference is not a matter of taste.

A concrete case.

Listing 5.4: A scope experiment in Lark

```
let x = 1 in
let f = fn(n : Int) => x + n in
let x = 2 in
f(0)
```

Under lexical scope `f` captures the `x` from its definition environment, so `f(0)` returns `1`. Under dynamic scope `f` looks up `x` in the current call stack at the moment it is called, finding the more recent `x = 2`, and returns 2.

Why lexical scope. A function definition under lexical scope creates a *closure*: the function's code paired with the environment active at the point of definition. That closure is self-contained—it carries the bindings it needs, and those bindings cannot be altered by any code that later calls the function. Reasoning about a lexically scoped function requires only its text and its definition environment. Under dynamic scope the closure carries only the code; the bindings it depends on are resolved at runtime against the current call stack, which means any caller can accidentally shadow a name the function expects. Every language that takes first-class functions seriously—Haskell, ML, Scheme from R5RS onward, Rust, Python—uses lexical scope.[1]

Environments as nested maps. The `Env.extend` method models lexical scope directly. Each call creates a child environment linked to its parent; lookup walks the chain, finding the innermost binding that matches. Shadowing—an inner `x` hiding an outer `x`—is the natural behaviour.

Listing 5.5: Scope as nested environments

```
e0 = Env({"x": Scheme((), INT)})              # outer: x : Int
e1 = e0.extend("x", Scheme((), BOOL))         # inner: x : Bool
assert e1.lookup("x").ty == BOOL
assert e0.lookup("x").ty == INT
```

The type checker threads an environment through every recursive call. For `let x =` e_1 `in` e_2: check e_1 in the current environment, then check e_2 in the current environment extended with `x`. When the call returns, the extended environment is not passed upward; no cleanup is needed. The stack of recursive calls mirrors the nesting of scopes, and the two coincide by construction.

5.3 Types as Ontology

A type system answers a question that looks technical but is in fact philosophical: *what kinds of things can exist in this universe?*

Gottlob Frege distinguished *sense*—how something is presented—from *reference*—what it picks out. The expression `2 + 2` and the literal `4` have the same reference (both denote the same mathematical object) but different senses. A type assigns expressions to *kinds*, not to particular values: the type `Int` says nothing about which integer an expression denotes, only that it denotes some integer. Type checking is the discipline of confirming that every operation receives arguments of the kinds it expects.[2]

Types as predicates. The simplest account says a type is a predicate on values: `Int` is the predicate "is an integer," `Int -> Bool` is the predicate "is a function from integers to booleans." A well-typed expression is one whose runtime value satisfies the assigned predicate. This account is useful but not quite right. Type checking is a *syntactic* operation—it reads the program text, not the execution. A more precise formulation says that a type is a static *approximation* of the set of values an expression can produce. The approximation is coarser than the runtime truth (`Int` rather than "the integer 42"), but coarser-and-static beats precise-but-unavailable.

What Lark's types say. Lark's type system partitions its value universe into classes: integers, booleans, strings, the unit value, function types, product types, and sum types. The type checker's task is to assign a class to every expression node and confirm the assignments are consistent: a + node receives two integers; an `if` node has a boolean condition and branches of the same type; a function application supplies an argument of the type the function expects.

Types also serve a communication function. When the checker rejects `1 + true`, it is not finding a runtime bug—the program would fail at that point regardless. It is naming the conceptual error: the programmer applied an integer operation to a boolean. That naming is independent of execution. It is the type system's statement about what the program *means*.

Lark's type system is a descendant of Church's simply typed lambda calculus (1940), extended by Hindley's (1969) and Milner's (1978) inference algorithm and by Damas's (1982) completeness proof. These are not historical curiosities. They are the formal foundation that specifies precisely what Lark's checker does and what it guarantees.

5.4 The Simply Typed Lambda Calculus

The smallest type system worth calling one is the *simply typed lambda calculus* (STLC). Its term grammar has three forms:

$$e \ ::= \ x \mid \lambda x{:}T.\, e \mid e_1\, e_2$$

A variable x; an abstraction $\lambda x{:}T.\, e$ (a function taking x of type T returning e); and an application $e_1\, e_2$. Types are base types ι (standing for `Int`, `Bool`, and so on) or function types:

$$T \ ::= \ \iota \mid T_1 \rightarrow T_2$$

Typing judgements. A *typing judgement* $\Gamma \vdash e : T$ reads: under the type environment Γ, the expression e has type T. The rules that define which judgements are valid are the *typing rules.* The STLC has three. This is the first of the book's formal notations, and a reader meeting inference rules for the first time may want Appendix C open beside this section: it decodes the notation, piece by piece, into the Python it describes.

Variable (Var). A variable has whatever type the environment assigns:

$$\frac{(x : T) \in \Gamma}{\Gamma \vdash x : T}$$

Abstraction (Abs). A function $\lambda x{:}T_1.\, e$ has type $T_1 \to T_2$ if the body e has type T_2 when $x : T_1$ is in scope:

$$\frac{\Gamma,\ x : T_1\ \vdash\ e : T_2}{\Gamma\ \vdash\ \lambda x{:}T_1.\, e\ :\ T_1 \to T_2}$$

Application (App). An application $e_1\ e_2$ has type T_2 if e_1 has function type $T_1 \to T_2$ and e_2 supplies the argument type T_1:

$$\frac{\Gamma \vdash e_1 : T_1 \to T_2 \qquad \Gamma \vdash e_2 : T_1}{\Gamma \vdash e_1\ e_2 : T_2}$$

A proof of $\Gamma \vdash e : T$ is a tree of rule applications with a leaf for every variable occurrence and a branching node for every abstraction or application. Constructing that tree is precisely what the type checker does.

What STLC cannot do. The simply typed lambda calculus requires every type annotation to be written by the programmer. The identity function must be declared as λx:Int. x or λx:Bool. x; there is no way to write a single identity that works for all types. This is *monomorphism*: every expression has exactly one type. It is sound and decidable, but too restrictive for practical use.

Adding base types and products. The full STLC adds rules for constants (integers, booleans) and product types $T_1 \times T_2$ with projection and introduction rules. Lark further adds sum types—user-defined algebraic data declared with `type`—and recursive types. The typing machinery is the same; only the rule set grows.

5.5 Hindley-Milner Type Inference

Lark does not require type annotations. The types are inferred from the structure of the program by *Hindley-Milner* (HM) inference, independently discovered by Roger Hindley (1969) [Hindley, 1969] and Robin Milner (1978) and proved complete by Luis Damas (1982).

The key idea: unification. HM inference generates constraints— equations between types—and solves them by *unification*. When the checker sees an application `f x` and knows `f : ?a -> ?b` and `x : Int`, it generates the constraint `?a` = Int, records the solution `?a` ↦ Int, and propagates it. When `f : Int -> Bool` and `x : Bool`, the constraint Int = Bool has no solution: a type error.

Type variables (?a, ?b, ...) are placeholders for unknown types. A *substitution* maps type variables to types; applying it replaces each variable with its bound value.

Listing 5.6: Unification (simplified from `lark/03/src/ty.py`)

```
def unify(t1: Type, t2: Type, subst: dict) -> dict:
    t1 = apply_subst(t1, subst)
    t2 = apply_subst(t2, subst)
    if t1 == t2:
        return subst
    if isinstance(t1, TVar):
        return bind(t1.name, t2, subst)
    if isinstance(t2, TVar):
        return bind(t2.name, t1, subst)
    if isinstance(t1, TFun) and isinstance(t2, TFun):
        subst = unify(t1.param, t2.param, subst)
        return  unify(t1.ret,   t2.ret,   subst)
    if isinstance(t1, TApp) and isinstance(t2, TApp):
        subst = unify(t1.func, t2.func, subst)
        return  unify(t1.arg,  t2.arg,  subst)
    raise TypeError(f"cannot unify {t1} with {t2}")

def bind(name: str, ty: Type, subst: dict) -> dict:
    if occurs(name, ty, subst):
        raise TypeError(f"infinite type: {name} in {ty}")
    return {**subst, name: ty}
```

The `occurs` check prevents binding a variable to a type that contains the variable itself. Without it, unifying `?a` with `?a -> Bool` would produce the infinite expansion `(?a -> Bool) -> Bool -> ...`, which is not a type. The check catches this immediately.[3]

Algorithm W. The inference algorithm—Algorithm W—combines constraint generation and unification into one recursive traversal. It returns a type and an updated substitution.

Listing 5.7: Algorithm W: core cases (simplified from `lark/03/src/infer.py`)

```
_fresh_n = 0
def fresh() -> TVar:
    global _fresh_n  # production: use a Counter/closure
    _fresh_n += 1
    return TVar(f"?{_fresh_n}")
```

```
def infer(
    expr: Expr, env: Env, subst: dict
) -> tuple[Type, dict]:

    if isinstance(expr, Lit):
        return lit_type(expr.value), subst

    if isinstance(expr, Var):
        return instantiate(env.lookup(expr.name)), subst

    if isinstance(expr, BinOp):
        op_scheme = env.lookup(expr.op)
        t_op  = instantiate(op_scheme)
        t1, subst = infer(expr.left,  env, subst)
        t2, subst = infer(expr.right, env, subst)
        t_ret = fresh()
        subst = unify(
            t_op, TFun(t1, TFun(t2, t_ret)), subst
        )
        return apply_subst(t_ret, subst), subst

    if isinstance(expr, Lambda):
        t_p  = fresh()
        env2 = env.extend(expr.param, Scheme((), t_p))
        t_b, subst = infer(expr.body, env2, subst)
        return TFun(apply_subst(t_p, subst), t_b), subst

    if isinstance(expr, Apply):
        t_f, subst = infer(expr.func, env, subst)
        t_a, subst = infer(expr.arg,  env, subst)
        t_r = fresh()
        subst = unify(t_f, TFun(t_a, t_r), subst)
        return apply_subst(t_r, subst), subst

    if isinstance(expr, LetExpr):
        t_v, subst = infer(expr.value, env, subst)
        scheme     = generalise(t_v, env, subst)
        env2       = env.extend(expr.name, scheme)
        return infer(expr.body, env2, subst)

    raise NotImplementedError(type(expr).__name__)
```

Instantiation and generalisation. Two operations make polymorphism work.

Instantiation replaces a scheme's quantified variables with fresh type variables, so that each use of `id` gets its own independent `?a`:

Listing 5.8: Instantiation and generalisation

```
def instantiate(scheme: Scheme) -> Type:
    renaming = {p: fresh() for p in scheme.params}
    return substitute(scheme.ty, renaming)

def generalise(ty: Type, env: Env, subst: dict) -> Scheme:
    ty   = apply_subst(ty, subst)
    free = free_vars(ty) - env_free_vars(env, subst)
    return Scheme(tuple(free), ty)
```

Generalisation wraps a monotype in a scheme, quantifying over every type variable that is free in the type but not in the surrounding environment. Variables free in the environment are the ones the caller can still constrain; they must not be generalised.

Let-polymorphism. The `LetExpr` case generalises before extending the environment. This is *let-polymorphism*: the expression `let id = fn(x) => x in (id(1), id(true))` type-checks because `id` is generalised to $\forall a.\ a \rightarrow a$ and freshly instantiated at each use. Lambda-bound variables are *not* generalised: in `fn(x) => (x(1), x(true))` the parameter `x` cannot simultaneously be an integer function and a boolean function. The asymmetry between `let` and `fn` is a theorem, not an accident—it is precisely the condition that keeps HM inference decidable and complete.[4]

A worked example. To infer the type of `let f = fn(x) => x + 1 in f(3)`:

1. Infer the lambda body. `x` is assigned a fresh variable `?1`. In the body `x + 1` the operator `+` is instantiated to $\text{Int} \rightarrow \text{Int} \rightarrow \text{Int}$ against the literal `1 : Int`; unifying forces `?1` $= \text{Int}$. The lambda has type $\text{Int} \rightarrow \text{Int}$.

2. Generalise. No free type variables remain; the scheme is $\forall.\ \text{Int} \rightarrow \text{Int}$ (no quantified variables). `f` is a monomorphic integer function.

3. Infer the body `f(3)`. Instantiate `f`: $\text{Int} \rightarrow \text{Int}$. The argument `3` has type Int; the application has type Int.

The whole expression has type `Int`.

Typing a recursive function. The `infer` cases above cannot, on their own, type the book's running example. To check the body of `sum_to`, the checker must already know that the name `sum_to` is in scope and what type it has—but that is the very type it is in the middle of inferring. A top-level `fn` is therefore checked not by `infer` but by a small routine that does one extra thing first: it binds the function's own name to a fresh type variable *before* descending into the body, so a recursive call type-checks against that variable, and afterwards unifies the variable with the signature the body actually produced.

Listing 5.9: Typing a (possibly recursive) function declaration (simplified from `lark/03/src/infer.py`)

```
def check_fn_decl(decl, env, fresh, copy_types):
    rec_var = fresh.var()  # the fn's own type: unknown

    # ...but in scope already:
    local_env = {**env, decl.name: Scheme((), rec_var)}
    param_types, tracked = bind_params(
        decl.params, local_env, fresh, copy_types
    )
    tbody, bt, s = infer(
        local_env, tracked, decl.body, fresh, copy_types
    )
    fn_t = curry(param_types, bt)  # params -> body type

    # recursion meets the signature:
    s = compose(unify(apply(s, rec_var), fn_t), s)
    return (
        TFnDecl(decl.name, ...),
        generalise(env, apply(s, fn_t)),  # general OUTSIDE
    )
```

Two points are worth drawing out. The name is bound with `Scheme((), rec_var)`—a *monomorphic* scheme, no quantifiers—so within its own body `sum_to` has a single fixed type; only `generalise`, applied to the *outer* environment after the body is checked, makes it polymorphic for callers. This is standard *monomorphic recursion*: a recursive function may not call itself at two different types, which is the price HM pays to keep inference decidable.[5] And the `rec_var` binding is precisely the static counterpart of the `rec_name` field the interpreter will use in Chapter 6: where the type checker binds the name to a type before checking the body, the evaluator binds the name to the closure before running it. The same knot—a definition that must refer to itself—tied once in the types and once in the values.

5.6 Algebraic Data Types and Pattern Matching

Hindley-Milner gives Lark functions, tuples, and the base types. A real language needs to let a programmer name new types with several shapes—a value that is *either* this *or* that. These are *algebraic data types* (ADTs), and they are introduced with `type`:

Listing 5.10: Two algebraic data types

```
type Color = | Red | Green | Blue

type Shape = | Rect of Float, Float | Circle of Float
```

`Color` is a *sum* of three constructors that carry no data; `Shape` is a sum of two that do—a `Rect` carries a width and a height, a `Circle` a radius. A value of type `Shape` is exactly one of these alternatives, tagged so the program can later tell which.

A constructor is a function into its type. The type checker does not treat constructors as a special form. When it registers a `type` declaration, it adds one ordinary entry to the environment for each constructor—a function from its fields to the type being declared. The fields are *curried* into the result exactly as a multi-argument function would be.

Listing 5.11: Registering an ADT's constructors (simplified from `lark/03/src/infer.py`)

```
def _register_type_decl(decl, env, fresh, copy_types):
    # one fresh type variable per declared parameter,
    # shared across constructors
    param_vars = {p: fresh.var() for p in decl.params}
    result_t = (TApp(decl.name, tuple(param_vars.values()))
                if decl.params else TCon(decl.name))
    for v in decl.body:                              # each variant
        con_t = result_t
        fields = field_monos(v, param_vars, fresh)
        for fm in reversed(fields):
            # curry the fields into the result
            con_t = TFn(fm, con_t)
        env[v.name] = Scheme(
            tuple(sorted(free_vars(con_t))), con_t
        )
```

For the two declarations above this records exactly these schemes:

$$\texttt{Red, Green, Blue} : \text{Color}$$

$$\texttt{Rect} : \text{Float} \to \text{Float} \to \text{Shape} \qquad \texttt{Circle} : \text{Float} \to \text{Shape}.$$

Because a constructor is just a function, building a value needs no new typing rule. The bare name `Rect` is looked up like any other variable, and the application `Rect(2.0, 3.0)` type-checks through the ordinary `Apply` rule against the scheme above—the only thing the checker adds is a clear error when a name is used as a constructor but was never declared.

Listing 5.12: A constructor use is an ordinary lookup (from `lark/03/src/infer.py`)

```
case Con(name=n):
    if n not in env:
        raise TypeError(f"unbound constructor: {n!r}")
    t = instantiate(fresh, env[n])
    return XCon(n, t), t, {}
```

Taking a value apart: patterns. Construction has a dual. To *use* a `Shape` you must discover which constructor built it and recover its fields, and that is what a `match` expression does. Each arm pairs a *pattern*—a constructor name with sub-patterns for its fields—with an expression to evaluate when the pattern fits.

Listing 5.13: A function defined by pattern matching

```
fn area(s : Shape) : Float =
    match s with
    | Rect(w, h) => w * h
    | Circle(r)  => 3.14159 * r * r
    end
```

A pattern is checked by its own small judgement. Given a pattern, the checker returns the *type* the pattern can match and the *bindings* it introduces—a wildcard matches anything and binds nothing, a variable matches anything and binds itself, a literal matches its own type, and a constructor pattern matches the constructor's type and binds whatever its sub-patterns bind.

Listing 5.14: Typing a pattern: the type it matches and the names it binds (simplified from `lark/03/src/infer.py`)

```
def infer_pat(pat, fresh):
    match pat:
        case PWild():
            return TPWild(t := fresh.var()), t, {}
        case PVar(name=n):
            t = fresh.var()
            return TPVar(n, t), t, {n: Scheme((), t)}
```

```
        case PLit(value=v):
            t = _lit_type(v)
            return TPLit(v, t), t, {}
        case PCon(name=n, args=args):
            # recurse into each field sub-pattern,
            # collecting their bindings (no repeats)
            ...
```

The match rule ties these together. It infers the scrutinee's type, then for each arm unifies the pattern's type *with the scrutinee* (so an arm that cannot apply is a type error), checks the arm body in an environment extended with the pattern's bindings, and unifies every arm body against a single result type (so all arms agree on what the match produces).

Listing 5.15: The match typing rule (simplified from lark/03/src/infer.py)

```
case MatchExpr(scrutinee=scrut, arms=arms):
    ts, st, s = infer(
        env, tracked, scrut, fresh, copy_types
    )
    result_v  = fresh.var()
    for (pat, body) in arms:
        tp, pt, pat_env = infer_pat(pat, fresh)
        # pattern fits scrutinee
        s = compose(unify(apply(s, st), apply(s, pt)), s)
        arm_env = {**env, **pat_env}
        ta, at, s = infer(
            arm_env, tracked, body, fresh, copy_types
        )
        # arms agree on the result type
        s = compose(
            unify(apply(s, at), apply(s, result_v)), s
        )
    return (
        TMatchExpr(ts, ..., apply(s, result_v)),
        apply(s, result_v),
        s,
    )
```

For area, the scrutinee s is Shape; the pattern Rect(w, h) unifies with Shape and binds w and h; both arm bodies produce Float, so the match—and the function—has type Float.[6]

Exhaustiveness: the check Lark does not make. There is one more thing a type checker can do for match, and it is the characteristic one for an ML-family language: verify that the arms are *exhaustive*—that together they cover every constructor of the scrutinee's type. The check is a small set computation. From the type, take the full set of constructors; {`Rect`, `Circle`} for `Shape`. Walk the arms, removing each constructor a pattern covers (a variable or wildcard arm covers all that remain). If the set is empty at the end, the `match` is exhaustive; if not, the uncovered constructors are exactly the cases the programmer forgot.

Lark does *not* perform this check. A `match` that omits a case is accepted by the type checker; the omission becomes a *runtime* failure instead, because the compiler lowers a non-matching fall-through to a trap (Chapter 7 shows the `__lark_match_fail` call it emits). So a well-typed Lark program can still get stuck on a `Shape` it has no arm for. This is the same character as the dynamic trait dispatch of Section 5.8: a guarantee that *could* be static is deferred to a runtime check, and Chapter 11 scopes the soundness theorem accordingly. Exhaustiveness checking is squarely a type-checker's job, and the set computation above is the heart of the algorithm. It is left unbuilt *here*—but not forever: when Chapter 13 needs a language with no undefined corners, this is one of the corners it closes, and the missing pattern itself becomes the error message.

5.7 Affine Types and Ownership

HM inference answers the question "what kind of thing is this?" Lark's type system asks a second, independent question: "who is responsible for this value?" The answer is expressed through *affine types*, and the motivation begins with a problem that exists even in a purely functional language.

The resource problem. If there is no mutable state, what problem does ownership solve? Some values are not freely copyable. A file handle is a contract with the operating system: opening it allocates a kernel descriptor, and that descriptor must be closed exactly once. A network connection, a lock, a cryptographic context—all carry obligations the type system can enforce by restricting how the values that represent them flow through the program. The classical response is garbage collection: track references, reclaim when the count falls to zero. Lark's response is *ownership*: the type system statically guarantees that every resource is consumed by exactly one user, so no runtime tracking is needed.

Linear and affine types. A *linear* type marks a value that must be used *exactly once*—neither dropped nor duplicated. An *affine* type marks a value that must be used *at most once*—it may be dropped but not duplicated. The formal distinction lies in the *structural rules* of the type theory (Table 5.1):
Ordinary (intuitionistic) logic permits all three. Linear logic forbids weakening and contraction; affine logic forbids only contraction. Lark uses affine types: a resource may be dropped (the programmer decided it was unnecessary) but may never be duplicated.[7]

Table 5.1: Structural rules: intuitionistic, linear, and affine

Rule	Meaning	Linear	Affine
Weakening	a binding may be ignored	forbidden	allowed
Contraction	a binding may be used twice	forbidden	forbidden
Exchange	order of bindings may change	allowed	allowed

The `Copy` trait as the gating mechanism. Lark does not mark individual types as affine with a special keyword. Instead, the *absence of a `Copy` implementation* makes a type affine. The primitive types—`Int`, `Float`, `Bool`, `String`, `()`—are freely copyable by definition. Any user-defined type that does not declare `impl Copy for T = {}` is affine by default.

Listing 5.16: Opting in and out of free copyability

```
(* affine by default *)
type Color = | Red | Green | Blue

(* now Color is freely copyable *)
impl Copy for Color = {}

(* no Copy impl → still affine *)
type Handle = | Handle of Int
```

Ownership in Lark: the `IO` type. The canonical example of an affine resource in Lark is `IO`. Every program that performs output receives an `IO` token and must thread it through each operation in sequence—the token is consumed by the first call and a fresh one is returned, which is then consumed by the next call. Attempting to reuse the original token is an affine violation.

Listing 5.17: IO threading in Lark

```
fn main(io : IO) : IO =
    let io = print(io, "first")  in
    let io = print(io, "second") in
    let io = print(io, "third")  in
    print(io, "fourth")
```

Each `let io = ...` rebinds the name `io` to the fresh token returned by the previous call. The old token is consumed and the name is no longer accessible. The program can produce output in a defined order without mutable state, because the type system enforces that each `IO` value flows through exactly one operation.

How the checker enforces this. The type checker maintains a *use-count map*, `Tracked`, alongside the type environment. When a variable is bound whose type is non-`Copy`, it is entered into `Tracked` with a count of zero. Each use of the variable increments the count; a count greater than one raises an `AffineError` immediately.[8]

Listing 5.18: Affine tracking (from `lark/03/src/infer.py`)

```
# name -> use count; only non-Copy bindings
Tracked = dict[str, int]

class AffineError(Exception):
    def __init__(self, name: str) -> None:
        super().__init__(
            f"affine variable '{name}' used more than once")

# Inside the Var case of infer():
if n in tracked:
    tracked[n] += 1
    if tracked[n] > 1:
        raise AffineError(n)

# When binding a lambda parameter whose type is non-Copy:
if not is_copy(param_type, copy_types):
    tracked[param_name] = 0
```

The limit of a syntactic count: closures. This mechanism counts the *textual* uses of an affine name in a single pass over the AST, and that is exactly where it stops being airtight. A closure captures the bindings in scope where it is written; if it captures an affine value and is then *invoked more than once*, it consumes that value once per call at run time—but the static pass sees the lambda body only once and has no way to count how often the closure is later applied. Lark does not forbid the capture: a lambda is checked with a *copy* of the enclosing use-counts (`tracked2 = dict(tracked)` in the `Lambda` case), so a captured affine variable can be used inside the body without that use being charged to the outer binding's budget. The single-use discipline is therefore guaranteed for straight-line code and not for values that escape into closures—one of the concrete reasons the mechanised soundness proof of Chapter 11 is scoped to the functional core and excludes the affine fragment. Closing this gap is what the substructural type systems behind Rust and Clean spend most of their complexity on; Lark stops, for now, at the version a reader can hold in their head. Mark this paragraph: the gap it describes is a genuine soundness hole, and Chapter 13 returns to it with a concrete counterexample, a repaired rule, and a machine-checked model of the whole affine discipline—capture included—that retires the exclusion above.

What Lark takes from Rust—and what it leaves out. Rust's ownership system handles mutable memory: values live on the heap, borrows track references, lifetimes prevent dangling pointers. Lark takes the *idea*— ownership enforced statically by the type system—and applies it to a purely functional setting. There is no mutable heap, so there are no mutable borrows and no lifetime parameters. The "use at most once" discipline governs *resources* (external state, I/O handles) not allocations. The simplification is principled: the parts of Rust's system that are irrelevant in a purely functional language are removed; the part that matters is kept.

The research precedent is Clean's *uniqueness types* (Barendsen and Smetsers, 1993): in a purely functional setting, a value marked with `*T` ("unique T") may not be aliased, enabling in-place array update without sacrificing referential transparency. Cogent (Rizkallah et al., 2016) carries this further into a systems fragment with proof-carrying guarantees. Lark's ownership is the same family of ideas at a scale a single reader can build and understand completely.

5.8 Traits

Parametric polymorphism—the $\forall a$ of HM—applies uniformly: the same code works for every type without knowing anything specific about it. *Ad-hoc polymorphism* is the opposite: the same name (`eq`, `show`, `compare`) denotes different operations on different types, with the correct implementation selected at the call site. Lark provides ad-hoc polymorphism through *traits*: named collections of operations that a type may implement.

Haskell calls them *type classes*; Rust calls them *traits*. The idea is the same. A trait declaration says what operations the trait requires; an `impl` block says how a particular type provides them.

Declaring a trait. A trait declaration introduces a name, a type parameter (a lowercase variable), and a block of method signatures. Each signature gives only the type—the implementation comes later, separately, in an `impl` block.

Listing 5.19: Trait declarations in Lark (from `lark/03/tests/08_traits.lark`)

```
trait Describe a = {
    fn describe : a -> String
}

trait Area a = {
    fn area : a -> Float
```

```
}
```

The type parameter a stands for the implementing type. The signature `fn describe : a -> String` says: any type implementing `Describe` must provide a function from itself to a string.

Implementing a trait. An `impl` block provides the method bodies for a specific type. The keyword `for` separates the trait name from the implementing type; the body uses `= { ...}`.

Listing 5.20: Implementing traits for a sum type

```
type Color = | Red | Green | Blue

type Shape = | Rect of Float, Float | Circle of Float

impl Describe for Color = {
    fn describe(c) =
        match c with
        | Red   => "red"
        | Green => "green"
        | Blue  => "blue"
        end
}

impl Area for Shape = {
    fn area(s) =
        match s with
        | Rect(w, h)   => w * h
        | Circle(r)    => 3.14159 * r * r
        end
}
```

Trait bounds. A function that requires its argument to satisfy a trait declares a *bound* in square brackets before the parameter list. The bound is written as the trait name followed by the constrained type variable. Multiple bounds on different variables are separated by commas.

Listing 5.21: Trait-bounded functions

```
fn label[Describe a](x : a) : String =
    "the color is " + describe(x)

fn compare_areas[Area a, Area b](x : a, y : b) : String =
    "areas: " + show(area(x)) + " and " + show(area(y))
```

The bound `[Describe a]` is parsed and recorded on the declaration, but the current checker does *not* enforce it. Trait methods are registered in the environment as ordinary polymorphic functions—`describe`, for instance, simply gets the scheme $\forall a.\ a \rightarrow \text{String}$—so a call to `describe(x)` type-checks against that scheme without the checker selecting any `impl`. Choosing the right implementation is deferred to run time.

This deferral has a consequence worth naming now, because the book's soundness claim depends on it. A well-typed program can call a trait method on a type that provides no `impl`; the checker accepts it, and the program then gets stuck at run time. That is a real exception to "well-typed programs do not go wrong," and it is a deliberate one—trait dispatch is dynamic. Chapter 11 states the exact scope of Lark's soundness guarantee: it covers the functional core and deliberately excludes trait dispatch (and the affine discipline).

Trait resolution at run time. Because the checker does not pick an `impl`, resolution happens during evaluation. The type checker's job is only to register the method bodies: a checked `impl` block becomes a `TImplDecl` in the typed tree. The evaluator (Chapter 6) walks those declarations and fills a dispatch table keyed by *(method name, concrete type name)*, and each trait method becomes a `VDispatch` value that selects from it using the runtime type of its argument:

Listing 5.22: Trait dispatch (from `lark/04/src/cek.py`)

```
# m.dispatch: dict[(method_name, type_name) -> closure]
# Populated while evaluating each TImplDecl.

case VDispatch(method=meth):
    type_name = runtime_type(arg, m)
    impl = m.dispatch.get((meth, type_name))
    if impl is None:
        raise RuntimeError(
            f"no impl of {meth!r} for type {type_name!r}"
        )
    return apply(impl, arg, kont, m)
```

Coherence. Lark assumes *coherence*: at most one implementation of any trait for any type, so the dispatch key *(method, type)* names a unique closure. The assumption is currently a convention rather than a checked invariant—two `impl` blocks for the same pair are not flagged; the second simply overwrites the first in the dispatch table. Haskell enforces coherence globally. Rust enforces it through the *orphan rule*: either the trait or the implementing type must be defined in the current crate. Lark relies on global coherence—the whole program is one namespace—which keeps dispatch simple and unambiguous.[9]

Traits and the `Copy` discipline. The `Copy` trait itself is the clearest example of how traits and ownership interact. Any type with `impl Copy for T = {}` is removed from affine tracking. The trait carries no methods—its body is empty—because its only effect is to tell the checker "this type is freely copyable." A user-defined resource type like `Handle` must never receive a `Copy` impl; the type system relies on its absence to enforce the single-use discipline.

5.9 Type Errors as Design

The type checker has two outputs: a fully annotated AST (every expression node labelled with its inferred type, including the type-checked `impl` blocks the evaluator later dispatches on) and, on failure, a precisely located error message. Both are products of a single recursive pass—an implementation of *Algorithm W*.

One mode: synthesis. The checker works in a single direction. Every expression node is handled by `infer`, which *synthesises* a type from the node's structure and returns it alongside an updated substitution. There is no separate "check" judgement for expressions; where an expected type is already known—a function's declared return type, a `let` annotation—the checker simply *unifies* the synthesised type against it.

Listing 5.23: The inference interface (simplified from `lark/03/src/infer.py`)

```
def infer(
    env: Env, tracked: Tracked, expr: Expr,
    fresh: Fresh, copy_types,
) -> tuple[TExpr, Mono, Subst]:
    """Synthesise the type of expr.
    Returns (typed_node, type, substitution)."""
    ...
```

Expected types flow into the traversal only through unification. The branches of an `if` expression are the clearest case: the condition is unified with `Bool`, both branches are inferred, and the two branch types are unified with each other so that the arms are forced to agree.

Listing 5.24: `IfExpr` by synthesis and unification (simplified from `lark/03/src/infer.py`)

```
case IfExpr(cond=cond, then_=then_, else_=else_):
    _, ct, s = infer(env, tracked, cond, fresh, copy_types)
```

```
    s = compose(unify(apply(s, ct), T_BOOL), s)
    _, tt, s = infer(env, tracked, then_, fresh, copy_types)
    _, et, s = infer(env, tracked, else_, fresh, copy_types)
    s = compose(unify(apply(s, tt), apply(s, et)), s)
    return apply(s, tt), s
```

A possible refinement: bidirectionality. A natural next step would split `infer` into two judgements—a *synthesis* mode that produces a type and a *checking* mode that consumes an expected one—the design introduced by Pierce and Turner (2000) to extend inference without annotations everywhere. It would pay off in two ways. Fewer fresh variables and unifications, because a known expected type is pushed inward rather than generated as a constraint; and sharper error messages, because a failing check holds both the expected type (from context) and the synthesised type (from the expression). Lark's checker does not yet make this split—it is pure synthesis—but nothing in its structure prevents it.[10]

Error quality. The same discipline that produces good parse errors produces good type errors. Each error carries a source location—taken from the AST node where the inconsistency was detected—a description of what was expected, and a description of what was found.

Listing 5.25: Error types (from `lark/03/src/infer.py`)

```
class TypeError(Exception):
    def __init__(self, msg: str) -> None:
        super().__init__(msg)

class AffineError(Exception):
    def __init__(self, name: str) -> None:
        super().__init__(
            f"affine variable '{name}' used more than once")
```

Source location is attached when the error propagates to the top-level runner, which has access to the original source file and the parser's position map. The checker itself carries only the message; the runner wraps it in `filename:line:col: message` before reporting to the user.

The two error kinds name different violations. A *type error* names a kind mismatch: `expected Int, got Bool`. An *affine error* names a use-count violation: `affine variable 'io' used more than once`. Both are raised by the same traversal. A third kind of failure—calling a trait method on a type that has no `impl`—is *not* caught here: trait dispatch is resolved at run time by the evaluator (Chapter 6), which raises `no impl of 'describe' for type 'Handle'` if the lookup misses. Like the parser, the checker is currently fail-fast: it stops at the first violation. Error recovery—continuing past a type mismatch by substituting a sentinel type—follows the same panic-mode pattern as the parser, and can be added without restructuring the traversal.

What the type system forecloses. A type system is not merely a diagnostic tool. It is a design decision about what the language can say. By including affine types, Lark forecloses the possibility of accidentally duplicating a resource. By assigning every expression a single consistent type, it forecloses the possibility of applying an integer operation to a boolean. The things the type system rejects are not arbitrary—they are the expressions the language designer judged to be either meaningless or dangerous. That judgment is encoded in the typing rules. Every type error is the rules speaking.

5.10 Exercises

1. Write out the full typing derivation—the tree of rule applications—for the expression $(\lambda f{:}(\text{Int} \to \text{Int}).\ f\ 1)\ (\lambda x{:}\text{Int}.\ x + 1)$ in the STLC. Identify the rule applied at each node and the environment in use at each leaf. What is the type of the whole expression?

2. Trace the execution of Algorithm W on `let f = fn x => x in (f 1, f true)`. Show: (a) the fresh variables generated, (b) the substitution after inferring the lambda, (c) the scheme assigned to `f` after generalisation, (d) the fresh instantiation of `f`'s scheme at each call site, and (e) the types of the pair's two components. Identify the step where let-polymorphism becomes visible—where a lambda-bound parameter would fail but a `let`-bound name succeeds.

3. The occurs check prevents infinite types. Construct a term—in Lark or directly using the Python `infer` function—that would trigger an infinite type if the occurs check were removed. Show the sequence of unification steps, name the variable and the type it would be bound to, and explain why the resulting infinite type is not a valid member of the `Type` datatype.

4. A programmer writes the following Lark code:

Listing 5.26: Double-consume of an affine IO token

```
fn two_prints(io : IO) : IO =
    (* old io consumed; new io bound *)
    let io = print(io, "hello") in
    (* new io used once: count = 1 *)
    let _  = print(io, "world") in
    (* new io used again: count = 2, error *)
```

```
    io
```

The checker raises `AffineError` on the final bare `io`. (a) Trace through the `Tracked` map at each line: what is the count for `io` after line 2, after line 3, and at the point the error fires? (b) Rewrite the function so that it prints both strings without violating the affine constraint. (c) The rewritten version shadows `io` at each step. Explain why shadowing a non-`Copy` binding does *not* count as a second use, and trace what the checker does with `Tracked` when the `let io = ...` rebinding is introduced (see the `LetExpr` case: `tracked.pop(n, None)`).

5. Lark's `Copy` trait carries no methods—`impl Copy for T = {}` is always an empty body. (a) What does the checker actually do when it encounters this declaration? Trace through the `is_copy` function and `copy_types` set. (b) Define a user type `type Point = | Point of Int, Int` and implement `Copy` for it. Write a function that uses a `Point` value twice and verify that no `AffineError` is raised. (c) Now define `type Handle = | Handle of Int` *without* implementing `Copy`. Write the same two-use function for `Handle` and explain at which step the error fires. (d) State the precise rule: which trait declaration, and which absence, determines whether a binding enters `Tracked`.

Lark's type checker is complete: a Hindley-Milner inference engine that assigns types and enforces affine ownership in a single pass over the AST, registering the trait implementations the evaluator later dispatches on at run time. The affine decision in particular does not stay here. Because it is enforced statically, the code generator of Chapter 9 may assume every resource is consumed exactly once and emit no runtime ownership checks; and the soundness of that assumption is what the machine-checked proof of Chapter 11 establishes. A choice made in the type system has become a license taken in the back end and an obligation discharged in the formal model—the propagation this book is about. Chapter 6 takes the typed tree and evaluates it—building closures, threading environments, handling tail calls—and confronts the ceiling that tree-walking evaluation places on a serious functional language.

Notes

[1]Dynamic scope did not disappear. Common Lisp retains it through `defvar`; Emacs Lisp uses it by default; Clojure exposes it explicitly via `binding`. It is the

right tool for propagating contextual information—a current output stream, an exception handler—through a call tree without threading a parameter through every intermediate function. The point is not that dynamic scope is always wrong, but that it is the wrong *default* for a language with first-class closures.

[2]The connection to philosophy runs deeper than the vocabulary. Bertrand Russell introduced type theory in 1908 precisely to block the paradoxes—including the paradox bearing his name—that arise when sets are allowed to contain themselves. The type-theoretic resolution is the same move a programming language type system makes when it prevents a function from being applied to itself without qualification. The Curry-Howard correspondence, made exact in Chapter 12, makes the connection precise: types are propositions, well-typed terms are proofs, and checking a program for type correctness is checking a claimed proof for validity.

[3]Some languages skip the occurs check to gain speed—Prolog among them. The price is infinite types that hang the printer. For a statically typed programming language the check is non-negotiable.

[4]Milner's 1978 paper [Milner, 1978] proves soundness (only correct programs accepted) and Damas's 1982 paper [Damas and Milner, 1982] proves completeness: Algorithm W infers the *most general* type, the *principal type*, of which every other valid type is an instance. An extension to `let` that generalises lambda bindings as well—called *rank-2* polymorphism—is undecidable in general.

[5]*Polymorphic recursion*—a function that calls itself at a type more general than the one it is being checked at—makes type inference undecidable (Henglein 1993). Languages that allow it, such as Haskell, require an explicit type signature on the recursive function, which turns inference back into the easier problem of *checking* a given type. Lark sidesteps the issue by not offering it.

[6]Phase 3's `infer_pat` records a constructor pattern's shape but leaves the field types to be pinned by unification at the surrounding `match`, and it does not itself check that the constructor belongs to the scrutinee's type. The hardened checker (`lark/07/src/infer.py`) strengthens the `PCon` case: it looks the constructor up in the environment, recovers its declared field types from the curried scheme, and unifies each field sub-pattern against the matching field type—so in `Rect(w, h)` the variables `w` and `h` are known to be `Float` independently of how the arm body uses them.

[7]The choice of affine over linear is deliberate. Linear types force every resource to be consumed, which eliminates leaks but burdens the programmer with mandatory consumption even for provisional values. Affine types preserve the "no duplication" guarantee while tolerating discard. Rust makes the same

choice: values are moved, not copied, unless the type implements `Copy`—which corresponds to lifting the affine constraint.

[8]The choice of a use-count rather than a Boolean flag is deliberate: the count allows the error message to report the *second* use, where the violation is detected, while the first use (count 1) passes silently. A Boolean would require more book-keeping to recover the offending location.

[9]Global coherence is the right default while Lark has no module system. Once modules are introduced, the orphan rule becomes necessary: without it, two modules could each define `impl Describe for Color` with different behaviour, and the choice of implementation would depend on import order. The orphan rule prevents this by requiring that either the trait or the type being implemented belongs to the defining module.

[10]Bidirectional checking is the architecture used in dependently typed proof assistants such as Agda, Lean, and Idris, where synthesis and checking become the two judgements of bidirectional dependent type theory. The Conclusion describes the step from Lark's level to dependent types.

Chapter 6

A Working Interpreter

The typed tree from Chapter 5 is meaning-ready but inert. Every node carries a type; names resolve; the affine discipline has been checked. Nothing, however, *runs.* An interpreter is the first artefact in this book that takes a Lark program and produces an answer—the first point at which the language stops being a description and becomes a thing that computes.

This chapter builds that interpreter. It begins with the design anyone would write first: a recursive function that walks the tree and returns a value for each node. That design is correct, short, and—for a purely functional language—fatally incomplete. A single requirement, proper tail calls, breaks it, and the break is not a bug to be patched but a structural fact that forces a different organisation. The fix is to make the interpreter's control state explicit: to stop relying on the host language's call stack and carry the "what to do next" as data. The result is an *abstract machine*—the CEK machine—which is Lark's actual interpreter.[1] The reference implementation discussed throughout is `lark/04/src/cek.py`: the front-end of Chapters 3–5 plus this one evaluator, with none of the compiler machinery the later chapters add.

6.1 Tree-Walking Evaluation

Evaluation needs two universes that the earlier chapters kept apart. *Expressions* are the nodes of the typed tree—syntax that has been given a type but not yet a meaning. *Values* are what expressions evaluate *to*: the integers, closures, and constructors that exist only at run time. The type checker reasoned about types; the interpreter manufactures values. The first design decision is the value domain.

Listing 6.1: The value domain (`lark/04/src/cek.py`; abbreviated)

```
@dataclass
class VInt:    n: int
@dataclass
class VFloat: f: float
@dataclass
class VBool:   b: bool
@dataclass
class VStr:    s: str
@dataclass
class VUnit:   pass
@dataclass
class VTuple: elems: tuple[Value, ...]

@dataclass
class VCon:                           # fully-applied ADT constructor
    tag: str
    payload: tuple[Value, ...]

@dataclass
class VClosure:   # function value: code + captured env
    param: str
    body:  TExpr
    env:   dict
    rec_name: str | None = None

Value = Union[
    VInt, VFloat, VBool, VStr, VUnit, VTuple,
    VCon, VClosure, VBuiltin, VPrintIO, VDispatch, VIO,
]
```

Two things are worth noting before any evaluation rule is written. First, `VClosure` carries a `body` that is still a `TExpr`: a function value is unevaluated code paired with the environment it was created in. Second, there is a value for everything the language can produce, including the I/O token `VIO` and the trait-dispatch placeholder `VDispatch` that Chapter 5 left to "the evaluator" to resolve. The value domain is the interpreter's ontology, just as the type domain was the checker's.

The obvious evaluator is one recursive function. It takes an expression and an environment—a map from names to values—and returns the value the expression denotes. Each case mirrors one node of the typed tree, and the recursion mirrors the tree's structure exactly.

Listing 6.2: The direct recursive evaluator (illustrative—*not* Lark's actual interpreter; see Section 6.4)

```
def eval(e: TExpr, env: dict) -> Value:
    match e:
        case TLit(value=v):
            return _lit_val(v)
        case TVar(name=n):
            return env[n]
        case TBinOp(op=op, left=l, right=r):
            return binop(op, eval(l, env), eval(r, env))
        case TIfExpr(cond=c, then_=t, else_=f):
            return (
                eval(t, env) if eval(c, env).b
                else eval(f, env)
            )
        case TLetExpr(name=n, value=v, body=b):
            return eval(b, {**env, n: eval(v, env)})
        case TLambda(params=((p, _),), body=b):
            return VClosure(p, b, dict(env))
        case TApply(fn=fn, args=(arg,)):
            f = eval(fn, env)
            a = eval(arg, env)
            # fatal
            return eval(f.body, {**f.env, f.param: a})
```

This is honest about what it is: a transliteration of the typing rules into value rules. Where Chapter 5's `infer` returned a type for each node, `eval` returns a value. The structure is identical; only the codomain has changed. For straight-line and branching code it works, and it is the right thing to understand first.

It has two gaps, not one, and only the deeper is marked. The shallow one is visible immediately: the `TLambda` case builds `VClosure(p, b, dict(env))` with no self-reference, and the application case never rebinds the function's own name. A top-level function that calls itself—`sum_to`, the running example—therefore cannot resolve that call: it fails with an unbound name *before* it ever runs deep enough to matter. Recursion is not free here. It is the `rec_name` mechanism introduced with closures in the next section. The deeper gap is the line marked *fatal*: even once recursion works, each recursive call nests a host-level `eval`, and Section 6.4 is about what that costs. First, the part that every interpreter must get right regardless of its control structure: closures.

6.2 Environments and Closures

A closure is the value of a function expression. The word names a precise idea that is easy to state and easy to get wrong: a function value is its code *together with* the environment in which it was created. The environment is not optional baggage. It is what makes a free variable in the function body refer to the right thing.

Consider a function that builds adders:

Listing 6.3: A closure capturing its environment

```
fn adder(n : Int) : Int -> Int = fn(x : Int) => n + x
```

When `adder(5)` is evaluated, the inner `fn(x) => n + x` becomes a value. That value must remember that `n` is `5`, because by the time anyone calls the returned function, the call to `adder` has long since finished and `n` would otherwise be gone. Lexical scope is the rule that `n` refers to the binding visible *where the function was written*, not where it is eventually called. A closure enforces that rule by capturing the environment at creation time:

Listing 6.4: Closure creation captures the defining environment (`lark/04/src/cek.py`)

```
case TLambda(params=params, body=body):
    name0, _ = params[0]
    if len(params) == 1:
        return Return(
            VClosure(name0, body, dict(env)), kont
        )
    # more than one parameter: curry by nesting a lambda
    inner = TLambda(params[1:], body, ty.T_UNIT)
    return Return(
        VClosure(name0, body=inner, env=dict(env)), kont
    )
```

The `dict(env)` is the capture. It copies the current bindings into the closure so that later mutation of the surrounding environment cannot leak in, and so that the captured environment outlives the scope that produced it. This is why Chapter 5's environments were built by immutable extension: a closure can safely hold a reference to an environment that the rest of the program has moved on from.

One parameter at a time. Every Lark function takes exactly one argument. A two-parameter function is sugar for a function that returns a function—this is *currying*, and the listing above performs it mechanically by wrapping the remaining parameters in a nested `TLambda`. The payoff is uniformity: the application rule has a single case to handle, and partial application falls out for free. `adder` above is genuinely a one-parameter function whose body happens to be another one-parameter function.

This is worth squaring with the running example, which is written and called as `sum_to(acc, n)`—plainly two arguments. The two views agree: a multi-argument call is surface syntax that the parser collects into a single node, and the interpreter discharges it one argument at a time, applying `sum_to` to `acc` and the resulting one-parameter function to `n`. Currying is the *semantics*; the two-argument form is how it is written. The compiler of Chapter 7 will take advantage of the fact that `sum_to` is a top-level function of *known arity* and emit a single direct call that passes both arguments at once, skipping the currying—but that is an optimisation the type checker's knowledge licenses, not a change to what the program means.

Recursion. A closure created for a top-level `fn` declaration needs to be able to call itself. The `rec_name` field is how: when the closure is entered, the machine rebinds that name to the closure itself before evaluating the body.

Listing 6.5: Applying a closure rebinds parameter and (if recursive) self (`lark/04/src/cek.py`)

```
case VClosure(param=p, body=body, env=cenv, rec_name=rn):
    new_env = dict(cenv)
    new_env[p] = arg
    if rn:
        new_env[rn] = fn        # self-reference for recursion
    return Eval(body, new_env, kont)
```

The new environment starts from the *captured* `cenv`, not from the caller's environment—lexical scope again—and extends it with the argument and, for a recursive definition, the function itself.[2]

6.3 Attribute Grammars

The recursive evaluator computes one thing per node: a value. The type checker, in Chapter 5, computed a different thing per node: a type. Both are instances of a single, older idea—the *attribute grammar*, introduced by Knuth in 1968—and naming it makes the shared structure visible.

An attribute grammar augments a context-free grammar by associating *attributes* with grammar symbols and *semantic rules* with productions. Each rule says how to compute the attributes of one node from the attributes of its neighbours in the parse tree. Attributes come in two directions. A *synthesised* attribute flows *up*: a node's value is computed from its children's values. An *inherited* attribute flows *down*: a node receives context from its parent.

Evaluation is exactly an attribute-grammar computation, and the two directions have concrete names in the interpreter:

- The **value** of an expression is a *synthesised* attribute. `TBinOp` computes its value from the values of its left and right children; a leaf such as `TLit` synthesises its value directly. This is why `eval` is structurally recursive—synthesis is a bottom-up fold.
- The **environment** is an *inherited* attribute. A node does not compute its own environment; it receives one from its parent and passes a possibly-extended copy down to its children. `TLetExpr` inherits an environment, extends it with the new binding, and passes the extension down to its body.

Chapter 5's typed tree is, in this vocabulary, an *attributed tree*: the checker decorated every node with a synthesised `typ` attribute and left the result in the tree for this chapter to consume. The interpreter performs a second attribution over the same tree, synthesising values instead of types, with the environment threaded as the inherited attribute. Seeing both passes as attribute evaluations is more than tidy bookkeeping: it explains why a single recursive traversal suffices for each, and it draws the clean line between the two flows—what a node *is told* (inherited context) and what a node *reports* (synthesised result)—that the next section must make explicit to do anything more.

6.4 Tail Calls and the CEK Machine

Return to the fatal line. In the recursive evaluator, applying a function evaluates its body with a *recursive Python call*:

```
return eval(f.body, {**f.env, f.param: a})
```

Every Lark function call becomes one Python function call. The host language's call stack grows by one frame for each Lark call and shrinks only when the call returns a value. For a language with loops this would be tolerable, because loops do not nest the stack. Lark has no loops. It is purely functional: iteration *is* recursion. A program that counts to a million is written as a tail-recursive function, and under the recursive evaluator that program nests a million Python frames and crashes with a stack overflow long before it finishes.

Listing 6.6: A loop in Lark is a tail-recursive function

```
fn sum_to(acc : Int, n : Int) : Int =
    if n == 0 then acc
    (* tail call: the last thing done *)
    else sum_to(acc + n, n - 1)
```

The recursive call to `sum_to` is in *tail position*: it is the last action of the function, and its result is the function's result. There is nothing left to do after it returns. A correct implementation must therefore *reuse* the current frame rather than push a new one—this is *proper tail call* elimination, and for a functional language it is not an optimisation but a correctness requirement. Without it, the language cannot express a loop.

The recursive evaluator cannot provide it, because it has delegated control to Python, and Python does not eliminate tail calls. The fix is to take control back: stop using the host call stack, and represent "what to do next" explicitly as a data structure that the interpreter manages itself. That data structure is a *continuation*, and an interpreter built around an explicit continuation is an *abstract machine*.

States, frames, and the loop

The CEK machine—Control, Environment, Kontinuation—has exactly two kinds of state. It is either reducing an expression, or delivering a finished value to the pending work.

Listing 6.7: The two machine states (`lark/04/src/cek.py`)

```
@dataclass
class Eval:     # reduce expr in env, then run kont
    expr: TExpr
    env:  dict
    kont: list[Frame]

@dataclass
class Return:   # deliver val to the first frame of kont
    val:  Value
    kont: list[Frame]
```

The continuation `kont` is a list of *frames*, used as a stack.[3] Each frame is one deferred obligation—a piece of context that was set aside while some subexpression is evaluated, to be resumed when its value comes back. They are precisely the inherited-context fragments that the recursive evaluator kept implicitly on the Python stack, now made into first-class data.[4]

Listing 6.8: Continuation frames, one per deferred obligation (`lark/04/src/cek.py`; abbreviated)

```
# evaluating left; right pending
@dataclass
```

```
class BinOpLF:   op: str; right: TExpr; env: dict
# left done; combine with right
@dataclass
class BinOpRF:   op: str; left_val: Value
@dataclass
class IfF:       then_: TExpr; else_: TExpr; env: dict
@dataclass
class LetF:      name: str; body: TExpr; env: dict
# evaluating the function
@dataclass
class ApplyFnF: args: list[TExpr]; env: dict
@dataclass
class ApplyArgF:
    fn_val: Value; remaining: list[TExpr]; env: dict
```

The interpreter is now a single loop. It repeatedly takes one step, and a step is a total function from a state to its successor state. Reducing an expression either produces a value directly (a literal, a variable lookup) or sets up the first sub-expression and pushes a frame to remember the rest.

Listing 6.9: Reducing an expression: each compound form defers its context as a frame (`lark/04/src/cek.py`; abbreviated)

```
def step_eval(expr, env, kont, m):
    match expr:
        case TLit(value=v):
            return Return(_lit_val(v), kont)
        case TVar(name=n):
            return Return(env[n], kont)
        case TBinOp(op=op, left=l, right=r):
            return Eval(
                l, env, [BinOpLF(op, r, env)] + kont
            )
        case TIfExpr(cond=c, then_=t, else_=e):
            return Eval(c, env, [IfF(t, e, env)] + kont)
        case TLetExpr(name=n, value=v, body=body):
            return Eval(v, env, [LetF(n, body, env)] + kont)
        case TApply(fn=fn, args=args):
            return Eval(
                fn, env, [ApplyFnF(list(args), env)] + kont
            )
```

Delivering a value pops the first frame and resumes its obligation. Evaluating the left operand of a + leaves a `BinOpLF` on the stack; when the left value arrives, the machine starts the right operand, leaving a `BinOpRF` that remembers the left value; when the right value arrives, the two are combined.

Listing 6.10: Delivering a value: each frame says how to resume (`lark/04/src/cek.py`; abbreviated)

```
def step_ret(val, frame, rest, m):
    match frame:
        case BinOpLF(op=op, right=r, env=env):
            return Eval(r, env, [BinOpRF(op, val)] + rest)
        case BinOpRF(op=op, left_val=lv):
            return Return(binop(op, lv, val), rest)
        case IfF(then_=t, else_=e, env=env):
            return Eval(t if val.b else e, env, rest)
        case LetF(name=n, body=body, env=env):
            return Eval(body, {**env, n: val}, rest)
```

The driver loop runs steps until the continuation is empty and a value is in hand—that value is the program's result.

Listing 6.11: The entire control structure: one loop (`lark/04/src/cek.py`)

```
def run(init: State, m: Machine) -> Value:
    state = init
    while True:
        match state:
            case Return(val=v, kont=[]):
                return v  # nothing pending: done
            case _:
                state = step(state, m)
```

There is exactly one `while` in the interpreter and no per-call Python recursion in the program's evaluation. The Lark call stack lives in `kont`, a Python list on the heap, which can grow to millions of entries without troubling the host. The two states and the steps between them form a single cycle (Figure 6.1).

Why tail calls are now free

The point of the rebuild appears in the application rule. When the last argument of a call has been evaluated, the machine applies the function and hands it the *current* continuation unchanged:

Listing 6.12: The tail position: no frame is pushed (`lark/04/src/cek.py`)

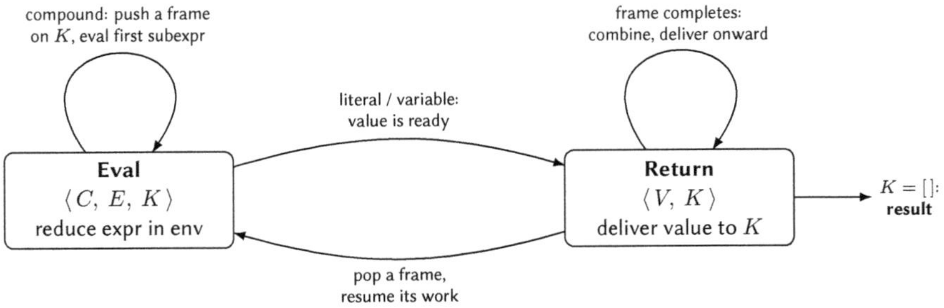

Figure 6.1: The CEK machine is a loop over two states. `step_eval` drives the arrows out of **Eval**: a literal or variable yields a value (top edge), while a compound form pushes a frame onto the continuation K and recurses into its first sub-expression (self-loop). `step_ret` drives the arrows out of **Return**: it pops the first frame and either resumes evaluation (bottom edge) or finishes the frame and delivers the value to the next one (self-loop). When K is empty the value in hand is the program's result. A tail call is the case where **Eval** re-enters **Eval** with K *unchanged*—no frame added—which is why the continuation does not grow.

```
case ApplyArgF(fn_val=fn, remaining=[], env=_):
    # last argument done: apply and pass the
    # SAME continuation onward
    return apply(fn, val, rest, m)
```

Apply, for a closure, returns `Eval(body, new_env, kont)`—reducing the body under the *same* `kont` it was given. No frame was added for the call. So when `sum_to` calls itself in tail position, the continuation does not grow: the machine simply begins evaluating the body again with a new environment and the identical pending work. A million iterations run in bounded continuation space. That is proper tail call elimination, and it is not a special case bolted on—it is the default behaviour of a machine whose control is explicit. A *non*-tail call, by contrast, is one that left a frame on the stack before the call (an `ApplyArgF` with arguments still `remaining`, or a `BinOpRF` waiting to combine the result); that frame is exactly the record of work that must happen after the call returns, and it is exactly what grows the stack. The machine distinguishes the two for free, by whether a frame is present.

Pattern matching as a frame

The ADTs of Chapter 5 arrive at the interpreter as a single runtime shape: a *tagged value*, `VCon(tag, payload)`, where the tag is the constructor name and the payload is the list of field values. Evaluating `Rect(2.0, 3.0)` produces `VCon("Rect", [2.0, 3.0])`. A `match` is then nothing more exotic than the `if` above: it has a scrutinee to evaluate first and a decision to make once its value is in hand, so it reduces by pushing a frame.

Listing 6.13: A match defers its arms as a frame (`lark/04/src/cek.py`)

```
case TMatchExpr(scrutinee=s, arms=arms):
    return Eval(s, env, [MatchF(arms, env)] + kont)
```

When the scrutinee's value comes back, the `MatchF` frame tries each arm in order, asking a small recursive matcher whether the pattern fits the value. The matcher returns either an environment extended with the pattern's bindings—success—or `None`—this arm does not apply, try the next.

Listing 6.14: Matching a pattern against a value (`lark/04/src/cek.py`; abbreviated)

```
def match_pat(pat, val, env):
    match pat:
        case TPWild():
            return env
        case TPVar(name=n):
            return {**env, n: val}  # binds the value
        case TPLit(value=v):
            if _val_eq(val, _lit_val(v)):
                return env
            return None
        case TPCon(name=n, args=sub_pats):
            # wrong constructor
            if not isinstance(val, VCon) or val.tag != n:
                return None
            e = env
            # match each field
            for sp, sv in zip(sub_pats, val.payload):
                e = match_pat(sp, sv, e)
                if e is None:
                    return None
            return e
        # TPTuple is analogous: match each element
```

```
        # against its sub-pattern.
```

Listing 6.15: Resuming a match: first fitting arm wins (lark/04/src/cek.py)

```
case MatchF(arms=arms, env=env):
    for (pat, body) in arms:
        new_env = match_pat(pat, val, env)
        if new_env is not None:
            return Eval(body, new_env, rest)
    raise RuntimeError(f"non-exhaustive match on {val!r}")
```

Two things connect this to earlier chapters. First, `MatchF` is a reified evaluation context of the same kind as `IfF`—the match's pending work, set aside while the scrutinee runs—which is why the attribute-grammar lens of Section 6.3 fits it so cleanly: the bindings a pattern produces are an *inherited* attribute, flowing *down* into the chosen arm exactly as a `let` binding flows into its body. Second, the final `raise`: when no arm fits, the machine fails at run time. Nothing earlier ruled this out, because the type checker of Chapter 5 does not check exhaustiveness (Section 5.6); a well-typed program can reach this line. The compiler of Chapter 7 emits the same failure as an explicit trap, and Chapter 11 states where this leaves the soundness guarantee. (The story has an ending: Chapter 13 adds the static check, after which no program that reaches this line exists to be run.)

Effects without mutation

Lark is pure, yet a program must be able to print. The interpreter reconciles these by threading the I/O capability as a value. The `print` built-in is curried: applied to the I/O token it yields an intermediate that remembers the token; applied then to a string, it performs the write and returns the token, ready to be threaded onward.

Listing 6.16: I/O as a threaded value, not a side effect on the language level (lark/04/src/cek.py)

```
case VPrintIO(io=io):
    if not isinstance(arg, VStr):
        raise RuntimeError(
            f"print expected String, got {arg!r}"
        )
    print(arg.s)
    return Return(io, kont)
```

The whole program is launched by applying `main` to a fresh I/O token, `VIO()`, and running the machine to a final value. Because the token is affine—the type checker of Chapter 5 guaranteed it is used at most once per step—the threading is forced to be linear: each `print` consumes the token and produces a new one, and there is no way to write to a stale handle. The purely functional surface and the imperative reality of a terminal are bridged by one value passed hand to hand.

6.5 The Ceiling of the Interpreter

The CEK machine is correct, complete, and—for what it is—efficient: it runs every Lark program the type checker accepts, with proper tail calls and bounded host-stack use. It is also, irreducibly, slow, and understanding *why* slow is what motivates the rest of the book.

The interpreter walks the source program's tree, repeatedly. Every step matches on the syntactic form of a node and dispatches accordingly; every arithmetic operation unwraps boxed Python objects (`VInt`, `VFloat`) and re-wraps the result; every variable reference is a dictionary lookup; every function entry copies an environment dictionary; every trait method call is a runtime lookup in the dispatch table. None of this work is about the *computation* the program expresses—it is overhead intrinsic to interpreting a tree shaped for human reading rather than for a machine to execute. The structure being walked is the program's syntax, and syntax is the wrong shape for fast execution.

There is no way to remove this cost from *within* the interpreter paradigm. One can tune the dispatch, intern the environments, cache lookups— and each buys a constant factor while leaving the fundamental arrangement intact: a node is examined, its meaning is looked up, its operands are fetched from a heap of boxes. To go genuinely faster the representation itself must change. The tree must be lowered to a linear sequence of simple operations over explicit locations—an *intermediate representation*—which can then be analysed, simplified, and finally turned into the real machine instructions of Chapter 1.

That is the ceiling, and it is a precise one. The interpreter establishes *what* Lark programs mean—it is the executable specification of the language's dynamic semantics, and the compiler chapters will be judged by whether their output agrees with it. What it cannot establish is speed commensurate with the hardware, because it never speaks the hardware's language. The next three chapters do. Chapter 7 lowers the typed tree to a three-address intermediate representation; Chapter 8 optimises it; Chapter 9 emits RISC-V. The interpreter remains the oracle of correctness throughout.

6.6 Exercises

1. The recursive evaluator of Section 6.1 and the CEK machine of Section 6.4 must agree on every program that does not overflow the host stack. Take the expression `let x = 2 + 3 in x * x`. (a) Trace the recursive `eval`, showing each call and the environment in force. (b) Trace the CEK machine, writing out the state—`Eval` or `Return`, the value or expression, and the full `kont` stack—at every step. (c) Identify, in the CEK trace, the exact step at which the `LetF` frame is pushed and the step at which it is popped, and say what plays that role in the recursive version.

2. Consider `adder` from Section 6.2 and the program `let add5 = adder(5) in add5(10)`. (a) Show the `VClosure` value produced by `adder(5)`: its `param`, its `body`, and the contents of its captured `env`. (b) Explain what would go wrong if the closure captured the caller's environment at *call* time instead of the defining environment at *creation* time. (c) Construct a program for which the two capture strategies give different answers.

3. Take `sum_to` and run it (on paper or by instrumenting `cek.py`) for `n = 3`. (a) Record the length of `kont` at the moment of each recursive call. (b) Confirm it does not grow with `n`, and point to the line in `step_ret` responsible. (c) Now rewrite `sum_to` in non-tail form—`n + sum_to(...)`—and describe precisely which frame is left on the stack at each call, and why the continuation now grows linearly in `n`.

4. Section 6.3 classifies the value as a synthesised attribute and the environment as an inherited one. (a) For `TIfExpr`, state which child receives which inherited attribute, and what determines *which* branch is evaluated at all—is that decision part of the attribute grammar, or outside it? (b) Pattern matching (`TMatchExpr`) binds new names in the matched arm. Describe the inherited and synthesised attributes of a match expression, and explain why the bindings produced by a pattern are most naturally seen as flowing *down* into the arm body.

5. I/O is threaded as the affine `VIO` token (Section 6.4). (a) Write a Lark function that prints two lines, threading the token correctly, and show why the type checker of Chapter 5 rejects the version that reuses the original token for the second `print`. (b) The interpreter could in principle make `print` a direct effect—calling Python's `print` and returning `VUnit`, with no token at all. State two distinct properties the language would lose by doing so, and connect each to a guarantee established in an earlier chapter.

Lark runs. The CEK machine evaluates the typed tree directly, with closures that capture lexical scope, an explicit continuation that delivers proper tail calls, and an affine I/O token that threads effects through a pure language. Its limits are now visible and precise: it walks a structure built for reading, not for executing, and pays for that on every operation. Chapter 7 takes the same typed tree and lowers it to a three-address intermediate representation—linear, explicit, and dull—trading the interpreter's directness for a form a compiler can analyse, optimise, and ultimately turn into the machine code of Part I.

Notes

[1]This chapter treats the CEK machine as an engineering response to a concrete problem. Chapter 10 treats it as a semantic object: a CEK machine is a precise definition of call-by-value evaluation order, derivable from the structural operational semantics, with the SECD machine as its historical predecessor. The same artefact wears two hats; here it is the implementation, there it is the specification.

[2]This handles self-recursion. Mutual recursion across separately written top-level definitions—`is_even` calling `is_odd` where `is_odd` is defined later—requires one extra step: after all top-level closures are built, a backpatch pass adds every top-level function to every other's captured environment. The pedagogical interpreter in `lark/04` omits this; later phases (`lark/07/src/cek.py`) add it. The principle is unchanged: lexical scope is realised by what the closure captures.

[3]Representing the continuation as a fixed set of data constructors—one per kind of deferred work—rather than as a function is *defunctionalization*, the technique John Reynolds introduced in his study of definitional interpreters [Reynolds, 1972]. The frame types below are the defunctionalized continuation; the step loop is the `apply` that interprets them.

[4]This move—from a recursive evaluator to a machine that carries its control state as explicit data—is the arc of Abelson and Sussman's *Structure and Interpretation of Computer Programs* [Abelson et al., 1996]. Their metacircular evaluator is the recursive `eval` this chapter began with; their explicit-control evaluator and register machines turn the control stack into data, exactly as the CEK machine does here; and their environment model of evaluation is the same environment our closures carry.

NOTES

Part IV

Compilation

Chapter 7

Intermediate Representations

The interpreter of Chapter 6 ended at a ceiling, and the ceiling was precise: the CEK machine walks the program's *syntax tree*, and syntax is the wrong shape for a machine to execute. Every step matches on the form of a node, every operand is fetched from a heap of boxes, every function entry copies an environment. The work is real, but almost none of it is the computation the program expresses—it is the overhead of interpreting a structure built for a human to read.

This chapter changes the representation. Between the typed tree and the machine code of Part I sits a third form, deliberately unlike either: a flat sequence of simple operations over explicit locations, called an *intermediate representation*. It is linear where the tree was nested, explicit where the tree was implicit, and dull where the tree was expressive—and each of those is a virtue, because each is what an analysis or a code generator needs. The decision made here propagates the rest of the way down: the optimiser of Chapter 8 rewrites this representation, and the register allocator of Chapter 9 assigns its temporaries to real registers. Getting the IR right is what makes the back end possible.

The reference implementation is Lark's Phase 5 compiler, `lark/05/src/`: `tac.py` defines the IR, `lower.py` translates the typed tree into it, and `cfg.py` recovers its control structure. The interpreter of Chapter 6 does not disappear—it becomes the oracle against which the compiler's output is checked.

A word on what follows. Two of this chapter's topics—static single assignment (Section 7.4) and the value-numbering DAG (Section 7.5)—are techniques Lark deliberately does *not* use. They are here so that the reader can read other compilers, where both are everywhere; each section says plainly where Lark stops and gives the engineering reason. The distinction is worth holding throughout: most of the chapter builds Lark's actual IR, and a clearly marked minority surveys the wider landscape it sits in.

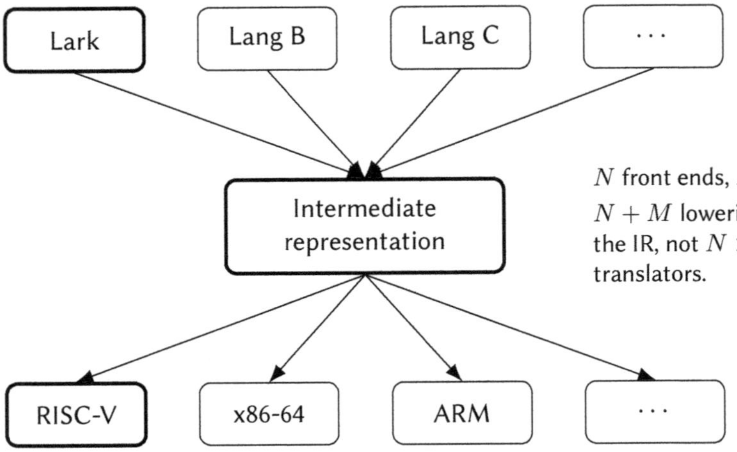

N front ends, M targets: $N + M$ lowerings through the IR, not $N \times M$ direct translators.

Figure 7.1: The hourglass. Every front end lowers *into* one neutral intermediate representation; every back end lowers *out* of it. The waist decouples the two sides: adding a language or a target costs one lowering, not one per pairing. Lark fills exactly one box on each side (highlighted)—which is why it does not strictly need an IR, and why the IR it has is deliberately shaped like neither Lark nor RISC-V.

7.1 The Case for an Intermediate Representation

Why not translate the typed tree straight to RISC-V? It can be done, and for a language this small it would even work. But three forces push a serious compiler to insert a representation in the middle.

The tree is the wrong shape. This is the argument Chapter 6 ended on, now turned from a complaint into a plan. A tree expresses *nesting*—an `if` contains its branches, a + contains its operands—and nesting is exactly what a processor does not have. A processor executes one instruction after another and jumps when it must. To target it, the nesting has to be flattened into a sequence and the control made explicit. Doing that flattening once, into a clean IR, is simpler than doing it tangled together with instruction selection.

Decoupling. A compiler with N source languages and M target architectures needs, in the worst case, $N \times M$ translators. Route every language through one IR and the count drops to $N + M$: each front end lowers to the IR, each back end lowers from it. The IR is the waist of the hourglass (Figure 7.1). Lark has one front end and one target, so it does not need this—but the design is worth stating, because it is why the representation that follows looks nothing like Lark and nothing like RISC-V. It is deliberately neutral.[1]

It is the substrate for everything after. Optimisation and code generation are not done on the tree; they are done on the IR, because the IR is where the relevant facts are visible. Which values are live at once? Which computation is redundant? Which branch is never taken? These are questions about a flat program with explicit control, and the next two chapters are almost entirely about asking them. The IR is not a translation convenience. It is the form in which a program becomes *analysable.*

7.2 Three-Address Code

Lark's IR is *three-address code* (TAC). The name states the shape: every instruction computes a single operation, naming at most three "addresses"—one destination and up to two operands. `x = y + z` is the canonical form; there is no `x = (y + z) * w`, because that is two operations and must become two instructions. The restriction is the entire point. A form in which every instruction does exactly one thing is a form in which every instruction can be reasoned about in isolation.

Values: temporaries and constants. An operand is one of two things: a *temporary*—a named slot holding the result of some earlier instruction—or a compile-time *constant.*

Listing 7.1: TAC values (`lark/05/src/tac.py`)

```
@dataclass(frozen=True)
class Tmp:
    """A named temporary -- result of every computation."""
    name: str

@dataclass(frozen=True)
class Const:
    """A compile-time constant
    (int, float, bool, str, or None for unit)."""
    value: int | float | bool | str | None

Val = Union[Tmp, Const]
```

Temporaries are *unbounded.* The lowerer invents a fresh one (`t0`, `t1`, ...) for every intermediate result, as if the machine had infinitely many registers. It does not, of course; mapping this endless supply of temporaries onto a finite register file is exactly the job of the register allocator in Chapter 9. Until then, pretending registers are free keeps lowering simple—the front end never has to think about the hardware.

The instruction set. Lark's TAC has thirteen instruction forms. They fall into four groups: compute a value, transfer control, call a function, and touch the heap.

Listing 7.2: The TAC instructions, abbreviated (`lark/05/src/tac.py`)

```
# dst = src
@dataclass(frozen=True)
class IAssign:     dst: Tmp; src: Val
# dst = l op r
@dataclass(frozen=True)
class IBinOp:      dst: Tmp; op: str; l: Val; r: Val
# dst = op src
@dataclass(frozen=True)
class IUnary:      dst: Tmp; op: str; src: Val

# label:
@dataclass(frozen=True)
class ILabel:      name: str
# goto label
@dataclass(frozen=True)
class IJump:       label: str
@dataclass(frozen=True)
class ICondJump:
    cond: Val; true_label: str; false_label: str

@dataclass(frozen=True)
class ICall:
    dst: Tmp | None; fn: str; args: tuple[Val, ...]
@dataclass(frozen=True)
class IClosureCall: dst: Tmp; fn: Val; arg: Val
@dataclass(frozen=True)
class IReturn:     val: Val | None

# tagged record
@dataclass(frozen=True)
class IAlloc:
    dst: Tmp; tag: str; fields: tuple[Val, ...]
# read constructor tag
@dataclass(frozen=True)
class IGetTag:     dst: Tmp; src: Val
# read one field
@dataclass(frozen=True)
class IGetField:  dst: Tmp; src: Val; idx: int
@dataclass(frozen=True)
```

```
class IAllocClosure:
    dst: Tmp; fn_name: str; captured: tuple[Val, ...]
```

Three details are worth pausing on, because each is a decision the type system of Chapter 5 made visible. Heap records carry a *tag* (`IAlloc`, `IGetTag`)—the constructor name of an algebraic data type, the thing a `match` dispatches on. A *closure* is built explicitly (`IAllocClosure`) by packaging a lifted function name with the values it captured, and called through (`IClosureCall`) one argument at a time, because Lark's functions are curried. And a *static* call (`ICall`) names its callee directly, because the type checker already resolved which function that is. The IR is untyped, but its shape is the shadow the type system casts.

The two call instructions are where the currying of Chapter 6 meets its exception, and the asymmetry in their shapes records it: `ICall` carries a whole *tuple* of arguments, `IClosureCall` carries a *single* one. Currying remains the meaning, but when the callee is a known top-level function—the common case, including every call to `sum_to`—the lowerer knows its arity exactly and emits one `ICall` that passes all arguments at once, never building the intermediate one-argument functions. Only when the callee is an *unknown* value, a closure applied through `IClosureCall`, does it fall back to applying one argument at a time. The uncurried direct call is the optimisation known arity buys; the curried path is the fallback that always works.

A program is a list of functions. Each `Function` is a flat list of instructions plus a small source of fresh names; a `TAC` program is the functions in definition order.

Listing 7.3: Functions and the program (`lark/05/src/tac.py`)

```
@dataclass
class Function:
    name:   str
    params: tuple[str, ...]
    body:   list[Instr] = field(default_factory=list)

    # fresh temporaries: t0, t1, t2, ...
    def fresh(self, hint: str = "t") -> Tmp: ...
    # fresh labels: .L0, .L1, ...
    def label(self, hint: str = "L") -> str:  ...
    def emit(self, instr: Instr) -> None:
        self.body.append(instr)
```

A first example. Consider the expression $(a \times b) + (c \times d)$—the same one Chapter 1 used to count live values. In TAC it becomes three instructions, two of them naming the products and one combining them:

Listing 7.4: $(a \times b) + (c \times d)$ as three-address code

```
t0 = a * b
t1 = c * d
t2 = t0 + t1
```

The temporaries `t0` and `t1` must both be live when `t2` is computed—which is precisely the observation Chapter 1 asked you to make about that expression on hardware with three registers. The IR has not changed the arithmetic; it has made the demand on registers *explicit and countable.* That countability is what the allocator of Chapter 9 consumes.

7.3 Control-Flow Graphs

Straight-line TAC plus jumps can express any control structure, but a flat list hides it: to see that a loop exists, you must read the jump targets and reconstruct the cycle in your head. Analysis needs the control structure as an *object*, not as something to be inferred. That object is the *control-flow graph* (CFG): nodes are *basic blocks*—maximal runs of instructions with no jump in except at the top and no jump out except at the bottom—and edges are the possible transfers of control between them.

Finding the blocks. The construction is classical and turns on the notion of a *leader*: the first instruction of a basic block. The leaders are the entry, every labelled instruction, and every instruction that *follows* a jump. A block runs from one leader up to (but not including) the next.

Listing 7.5: Leaders, then blocks (`lark/05/src/cfg.py`, abbreviated)

```
leaders = {0}
for i, instr in enumerate(body):
    if isinstance(instr, ILabel):
        leaders.add(i)
    if (isinstance(instr, (IJump, ICondJump, IReturn))
            and i + 1 < len(body)):
        leaders.add(i + 1)
```

With the blocks sliced out, the edges follow from each block's last instruction: an `IJump` has one successor, an `ICondJump` has two, an `IReturn` has none (it leaves the function), and a block that ends without a transfer falls through to the next. Wiring successors gives predecessors for free—a back edge in one direction is a forward edge in the other.

Lark's `sum_to`, as a graph. Recall the tail-recursive summing loop from Chapter 6. Lowered and split into blocks, its CFG has four nodes:

Listing 7.6: The control-flow graph of `sum_to` (from `lark/05/src/cfg.py`; list punctuation trimmed)

```
[__entry__]  preds=[]                  succs=[.then1, .else2]
    t0 = n == 0
    if t0 jump .then1 else .else2
[.then1]     preds=[__entry__]         succs=[.end3]
    r4 = acc
    jump .end3
[.else2]     preds=[__entry__]         succs=[.end3]
    t5 = acc + n
    t6 = n - 1
    t7 = call sum_to(t5, t6)
    r4 = t7
    jump .end3
[.end3]      preds=[.then1, .else2] succs=[]
    return r4
```

The `if` that was a single nested node in the AST is now two edges out of the entry block, rejoining at `.end3`; the branches assign a shared temporary `r4` that the merge block returns. The diamond is the shape of a conditional made explicit. Notice also what the recursive call has become: `t7 = call sum_to(t5, t6)`, an ordinary `ICall`. The interpreter of Chapter 6 took special care that this call, being in tail position, ran in bounded space; in the TAC it is just a call, and it will be Chapter 9's job to notice the tail position again and turn the call into a jump back to `__entry__`. The graph is what makes that "notice" a local check rather than a global search.

7.4 Static Single Assignment

The CFG exposes control. A second transformation exposes *data*, and it is the one that made industrial-strength optimisation tractable. The difficulty it solves is reassignment. When a variable is assigned several times, a use of it is ambiguous about *which* assignment it reads, and an analysis must track the question through every path. *Static single assignment* form (SSA) removes the ambiguity by a brutal simplification: every variable is assigned *exactly once*. A variable reassigned three times becomes three distinct versions, x_1, x_2, x_3, and every use names the version it means.

The interesting case is a merge. If `.then1` defines r_1 and `.else2` defines r_2, what does the merge block `.end3` read? SSA answers with a *ϕ-function*, a pseudo-instruction that selects a version according to the edge control arrived on:

$$r_3 \;=\; \phi(r_1 \text{ from } \texttt{.then1},\; r_2 \text{ from } \texttt{.else2}).$$

The ϕ is not executed—no machine has a "choose by predecessor" instruction—but it makes the data-flow fact explicit for the optimiser, and is removed before code generation by inserting copies on the incoming edges. With every value defined once, questions like "what is the definition reaching this use?" have a one-word answer, because there is only one definition. Constant propagation, dead-code elimination, and common-subexpression elimination all become dramatically simpler over SSA, which is why LLVM and most modern compilers use it as their central form.

What Lark actually does. Lark's Phase 5 compiler does *not* build SSA. It works directly over the CFG, computing *liveness* by backward data-flow analysis (`lark/05/src/liveness.py`) and feeding the result to a linear-scan register allocator (Chapter 9). For a language and a target this size, linear scan is the better engineering trade: most of SSA's benefit is in enabling aggressive optimisation passes that Lark does not perform. SSA is in this chapter because it is the idea you must know to read any serious compiler, and because the companion code (`ch07/04_ssa/`) builds the transform on the same little IR—but the honest statement is that Lark reaches the register allocator by the simpler road.[2]

7.5 Common Subexpressions and the DAG

One more way of looking at a basic block exposes *redundancy*. Consider `(a * b) + (a * b)`. Lowered naïvely, the product `a * b` is computed twice:

Listing 7.7: A redundant computation, before and after sharing

```
t0 = a * b          ;    t0 = a * b
t1 = a * b          ;    t2 = t0 + t0
t2 = t0 + t1        ;
```

If `a` and `b` are unchanged between the two products—and within a single basic block, with values defined once, they are—then `t1` *is* `t0`, and the second multiply is waste. Recognising this is *common-subexpression elimination* (CSE), and the data structure that makes it natural is the *directed acyclic graph* (DAG). Where a syntax tree gives each occurrence of `a * b` its own subtree, a DAG gives the two occurrences *the same node*: identical computations are shared rather than duplicated, and the tree's leaves-to-root structure becomes a graph in which fan-out marks reuse.

The local version is *value numbering*: walk the block giving each distinct computation a number, keyed by its operator and the numbers of its operands; when a computation's key has been seen, reuse the earlier temporary instead of emitting a new instruction. It is a hash table and a single pass. The companion code (`ch07/05_dag/`) builds the DAG for a basic block and reads CSE off it.

Lark's lowerer does none of this: it emits the obvious instruction for every node and leaves redundancy in place. That is deliberate. The lowerer's one job is a faithful, mechanical translation; *improving* the TAC is a separate concern, with its own correctness argument, and it is the subject of Chapter 8. Keeping translation and optimisation apart is what lets each be simple.

7.6 Lowering Lark to TAC

Lowering is the translation from the typed tree to TAC. Its core is one function, `_expr`, which lowers a single expression: it emits instructions into the current function and *returns the `Val` that holds the result.* That return value is the whole interface—a parent expression lowers its children, receives a `Tmp` or `Const` for each, and combines them.

Listing 7.8: The heart of lowering (`lark/05/src/lower.py`, abbreviated)

```
def _expr(
    self, expr: TExpr, fn: Function, env: dict[str, Val]
) -> Val:
    match expr:
        case TLit(value=v):
            return Const(v)  # a literal is already a value
        case TVar(name=n):
            return env[n]  # a variable: look up its slot
        case TBinOp(op=op, left=l, right=r):
            # lower the operands first
            lv  = self._expr(l, fn, env)
            rv  = self._expr(r, fn, env)
            dst = fn.fresh()
            # then emit the operation
            fn.emit(IBinOp(dst, op, lv, rv))
            return dst
        case TLetExpr(name=n, value=v_expr, body=body):
            # lower the bound value
            v = self._expr(v_expr, fn, env)
```

```
        # body sees n -> v
        return self._expr(body, fn, {**env, n: v})
    case TIfExpr(cond=c, then_=t, else_=e):
        return self._lower_if(c, t, e, fn, env)
    ...
```

Two things echo earlier chapters. The order of the `TBinOp` case—lower both operands, *then* emit the combining instruction—is the synthesised attribute of Chapter 6's attribute grammar, now producing `Vals` instead of runtime values. And `TLetExpr` threads an environment exactly as the type checker and the interpreter did, except the environment now maps a name to the *temporary* that holds it, not to a type or a value. The same traversal, a third codomain.

Flattening control. The `if` expression is where flattening is visible. The recursive evaluator returned one branch's value directly; the lowerer cannot, because the machine has no nested `if`. It emits a conditional jump, two labelled blocks that each assign a shared destination, and a merge label—the diamond from Section 7.3.

Listing 7.9: Lowering `if` to jumps (`lark/05/src/lower.py`)

```
def _lower_if(self, cond, then_, else_, fn, env) -> Val:
    cv = self._expr(cond, fn, env)
    l_then, l_else, l_end = (
        fn.label("then"), fn.label("else"), fn.label("end")
    )
    dst = fn.fresh("r")
    fn.emit(ICondJump(cv, l_then, l_else))
    fn.emit(ILabel(l_then)); tv = self._expr(then_, fn, env)
    fn.emit(IAssign(dst, tv)); fn.emit(IJump(l_end))
    fn.emit(ILabel(l_else)); ev = self._expr(else_, fn, env)
    fn.emit(IAssign(dst, ev)); fn.emit(IJump(l_end))
    fn.emit(ILabel(l_end))
    return dst
```

Closures, lowered. A function value cannot be a pointer to code alone, because Chapter 6 established that it must carry the environment it closed over. Lowering makes that environment a heap record. Each `TLambda` is *closure-converted*: its free variables are computed, the lambda body is lifted to a fresh top-level function taking an extra leading `env` parameter, and at the original site an `IAllocClosure` packages the lifted function's name with the captured values. Inside the lifted function, each free variable is reloaded from `env` with `IGetField`. The closure that was an implicit Python dictionary in `lark/04` is now an explicit object with a known layout—one more thing the interpreter left to the host that the compiler must spell out.

Lowering `match`. The interpreter matched a pattern against a value by a recursive search (Chapter 6); the machine cannot search, so lowering must turn the `match` into a *decision*: read the scrutinee's tag, test it, and branch. This is exactly what the `IGetTag` and `IGetField` instructions of Section 7.2 exist for. Each arm becomes a test that either jumps to the arm's body or falls through to the next arm, and the body binds the constructor's fields with `IGetField` before it runs.

Listing 7.10: Lowering a `match` to a chain of tests (`lark/05/src/lower.py`, abbreviated)

```
def _lower_match(self, scrut, arms, fn, env):
    # lower the scrutinee once
    sv    = self._expr(scrut, fn, env)
    dst   = fn.fresh("r")
    l_end = fn.label("match_end")
    for pat, body in arms:
        l_body, l_next = fn.label("arm"), fn.label("next")
        # match? -> body, else next
        self._pat_check(pat, sv, fn, l_body, l_next)
        fn.emit(ILabel(l_body))
        arm_env = dict(env)
        # IGetField for each field
        self._pat_bind(pat, sv, fn, arm_env)
        fn.emit(IAssign(dst, self._expr(body, fn, arm_env)))
        fn.emit(IJump(l_end))
        fn.emit(ILabel(l_next))
    # no arm matched: trap
    fn.emit(ICall(None, "__lark_match_fail", ()))
    fn.emit(ILabel(l_end))
    return dst
```

The test for a constructor pattern is the heart of it: read the tag, compare it to the constructor's name, and conditionally jump.

Listing 7.11: The constructor test (`lark/05/src/lower.py`, abbreviated)

```
case TPCon(name=tag, args=sub_pats):
    tag_tmp = fn.fresh("tag")
    # read the constructor tag
    fn.emit(IGetTag(tag_tmp, sv))
    tag_ok = fn.fresh("tag_ok")
```

```
    fn.emit(IBinOp(tag_ok, "==", tag_tmp, Const(tag)))
    # this arm, or the next
    fn.emit(ICondJump(tag_ok, l_match, l_fail))
    # constructors with fields recurse, checking
    # each sub-pattern by IGetField
```

Run that over area from Section 5.6 and the recursive match of the source comes out as a flat decision in TAC:

Listing 7.12: The match in area, lowered (output of lark/05; pass-through jumps elided and labels renamed for readability)

```
fn area(s):
    tag4 = tag(s)                          ; IGetTag -> tag4
    tag_ok5 = tag4 == 'Rect'
    if tag_ok5 jump .rect else .try_circle
.rect:
    f11 = s[0]                             ; IGetField 0  -> w
    f12 = s[1]                             ; IGetField 1  -> h
    t13 = call __float_mul(f11, f12)
    r0 = t13
    jump .match_end
.try_circle:
    tag16 = tag(s)
    tag_ok17 = tag16 == 'Circle'
    if tag_ok17 jump .circle else .fail
.circle:
    f21 = s[0]                             ; IGetField 0  -> r
    t22 = call __float_mul(3.14159, f21)
    t23 = call __float_mul(t22, f21)
    r0 = t23
    jump .match_end
.fail:
    call __lark_match_fail()               ; no arm matched
.match_end:
    return r0
```

The shape is a *decision tree*, and Lark builds the simplest one there is: a linear chain that tries the arms in source order, one tag-test after another, falling through to the next on a miss. A production compiler for a language with many constructors would do better—balancing the tests, or switching on the tag through a jump table—but for matches of a handful of arms the chain is both correct and clear, and it is the same “simpler road” Lark took past SSA in Section 7.4. Two details earn their place. The float multiply is a call to a runtime helper, `__float_mul`; what matters here is the control structure around it, not the arithmetic. And the final arm falls through to `__lark_match_fail`: this is the non-exhaustiveness of Section 5.6 made concrete—the runtime trap that stands in for the static check Lark does not yet perform, the same failure the CEK machine raised as `non-exhaustive match` in Chapter 6, now compiled in. (When Chapter 13 adds the static check, the trap stays in the emitted code as defence in depth—unreachable, but the IR does not have to trust the frontend to know it.)

The whole of `sum_to`. Putting the pieces together, the lowerer turns the function

Listing 7.13: `sum_to` in Lark

```
fn sum_to(acc : Int, n : Int) : Int =
    if n == 0 then acc else sum_to(acc + n, n - 1)
```

into this TAC—the verified output of `lark/05`, not a hand-translation:

Listing 7.14: `sum_to` lowered (output of `lark/05`)

```
fn sum_to(acc, n):
    t0 = n == 0
    if t0 jump .then1 else .else2
.then1:
    r4 = acc
    jump .end3
.else2:
    t5 = acc + n
    t6 = n - 1
    t7 = call sum_to(t5, t6)
    r4 = t7
    jump .end3
.end3:
    return r4
```

Every construct of the source survives in flattened form: the comparison is one `IBinOp`, the conditional is an `ICondJump` over a diamond, the two arithmetic operations of the recursive case are two more `IBinOps`, and the recursive call is an `ICall`. Nothing has been optimised—`r4` is assigned and immediately returned, a redundancy a single pass would remove— because optimisation is not lowering's job. What lowering produces is a correct, literal, analysable rendering of the program. Chapter 8 will make it faster; Chapter 9 will make it real.

7.7 Running the Intermediate Representation

Lowering is mechanical, but mechanical is not the same as correct. The `_expr` traversal could mis-order two operands, drop a branch, or thread the wrong environment into a `let`, and nothing seen so far would notice. The honest way to find out whether the IR means what the source meant is to *run* it and compare. So we build a small interpreter for TAC—and it turns out to be the register machine of Chapter 2, now reading structured instructions instead of packed bytes.

A frame is a register file and a program counter. Where Chapter 2's register machine had a fixed array `regs = [0]*16`, the TAC VM has a *dictionary* keyed by temporary name—because the IR pretends registers are unbounded, and that pretence is not resolved until the allocator of Chapter 9. Labels replace byte addresses; everything else is the same machine.

Listing 7.15: A TAC frame (`lark/05/src/tac_vm.py`, abbreviated)

```
class Frame:
    def __init__(self, fn, params, globals_):
        self.fn   = fn
        self.pc   = 0
        # temporaries and parameters
        self.regs = dict(params)
        # label name -> body index
        self._labels = {instr.name: i
                        for i, instr in enumerate(fn.body)
                        if isinstance(instr, ILabel)}

    def read(self, v):  # a Val is a Const or a Tmp
        match v:
            case Const(value=x): return x
            case Tmp(name=n):    return self.regs[n]

    def jump(self, label):
        self.pc = self._labels[label]
```

The call stack is explicit. The crucial design choice is that the VM keeps its own call stack as a list, rather than calling itself recursively in Python. Each entry pairs a frame with the destination temporary in the *caller* where this frame's return value belongs. The benefit is the same one Chapter 6 earned for the CEK machine: a program whose recursion runs a million deep is a long loop here, not a Python stack overflow—and the oracle has to survive exactly the deep recursions the compiled code will.[3]

Listing 7.16: The dispatch loop, control flow and calls (`lark/05/src/tac_vm.py`, abbreviated)

```
def _run_fn(self, fn, args):
    frame0 = Frame(fn, args, self._globals)
    # (frame, dst-in-caller / None)
    call_stack = [(frame0, None)]

    while call_stack:
        frame, _ = call_stack[-1]
        instr = frame.fn.body[frame.pc]

        if isinstance(instr, ILabel):
            frame.pc += 1
        elif isinstance(instr, IJump):
            frame.jump(instr.label); frame.pc += 1
        elif isinstance(instr, ICondJump):
            taken = (
                instr.true_label
                if frame.read(instr.cond)
                else instr.false_label
            )
            frame.jump(taken); frame.pc += 1
        elif isinstance(instr, IReturn):
            ret = (
                frame.read(instr.val)
                if instr.val is not None else None
            )
            _, dst = call_stack.pop()
            if call_stack and dst is not None:
                caller, _ = call_stack[-1]
                caller.regs[dst.name] = ret
                caller.pc += 1
        elif isinstance(instr, ICall):
            callee = self._fns[instr.fn]
            argv   = [frame.read(a) for a in instr.args]
            regs   = dict(zip(callee.params, argv))
            new_frame = Frame(callee, regs, self._globals)
            call_stack.append((new_frame, instr.dst))
        else:
            # the value-computing instructions
            self._step(frame, instr)
            frame.pc += 1
```

The control-flow cases are the CFG of Section 7.3 made executable: a jump resets the program counter to a label's index, a conditional jump reads its `cond` and picks an edge, a return pops the call stack and writes the result into the slot the caller named. The value-computing instructions are duller still—one `match` arm each, every arm reading its operands and writing one temporary:

Listing 7.17: Computing instructions; note the tag operations `match` will use (`lark/05/src/tac_vm.py`, abbreviated)

```
def _step(self, frame, instr):
    match instr:
        case IAssign(dst=dst, src=src):
            frame.regs[dst.name] = frame.read(src)
        case IBinOp(dst=dst, op=op, l=l, r=r):
            frame.regs[dst.name] = _binop(
                op, frame.read(l), frame.read(r)
            )
        case IAlloc(dst=dst, tag=tag, fields=fields):
            frame.regs[dst.name] = {
                "__tag__": tag,
                "fields": [frame.read(f) for f in fields],
            }
        case IGetTag(dst=dst, src=src):
            frame.regs[dst.name] = (
                frame.read(src)["__tag__"]
            )
        case IGetField(dst=dst, src=src, idx=idx):
            frame.regs[dst.name] = (
                frame.read(src)["fields"][idx]
            )
```

A tagged record is just a dictionary with a `"__tag__"` and a list of fields; `IGetTag` reads the tag and `IGetField` reads a field by index. These are the runtime half of the algebraic data types the type checker admitted in Chapter 5—and `IGetTag` in particular is the operation a `match` dispatches on, the point where a decision tree reads which constructor it is looking at.

Three machines, one meaning. The TAC VM is not the point on its own; its point is to be a second opinion. Lark can run the same program three ways, at three different altitudes:

- the **CEK machine** of Chapter 6 walks the typed tree directly—the meaning of the source, taken as given;

- the **TAC VM** of this section runs the lowered IR—the meaning after `lower.py`;
- the **RV32 emulator** `riscv_vm.py` executes the actual machine code of Chapter 9—the meaning after instruction selection and register allocation.

Each arrow between them is a translation that is supposed to preserve meaning. So the test is blunt and total: run the same program on all three and demand *byte-identical* output. If the CEK machine and the TAC VM agree but the emulator dissents, the bug is in code generation; if the tree and the IR already disagree, the bug is in lowering. A divergence does not merely signal an error—it localises it to a stage. This *differential oracle* is the spine of the two chapters ahead: every optimisation in Chapter 8 must leave all three outputs identical (that is what makes it an optimisation and not a rewrite of the program's meaning), and the soundness argument of Chapter 11 is this same demand, stated once and for all instead of checked example by example.

7.8 Exercises

1. Lower the expression `(a + b) * (a + b)` to TAC by hand, following the `_expr` rules of Section 7.6—emit the obvious instruction for every node, as Lark's lowerer does. (a) How many `IBinOp` instructions result? (b) Apply local value numbering (Section 7.5) and give the reduced sequence. (c) State the precise condition under which the reduction is sound, and explain why it always holds *within* a single basic block but not necessarily across two.

2. Take the `sum_to` TAC of Section 7.6. (a) Identify every basic block and confirm the leader rule of Section 7.3 produces exactly those four blocks. (b) Draw the CFG. Does it contain a *back edge*—a cycle that would make the function a loop? Explain why the recursive call `t7 = call sum_to(…)` creates none at this stage, and name the transformation in Chapter 9 that introduces one. (c) The `if`-result is assigned to `r4` in both branches and returned at the merge block. Explain why this cannot be collapsed by a local rewrite that replaces `return r4` with `return t7`—name the branch on which that rewrite would be wrong—and describe the non-local change to the control flow that *would* remove `r4` and the merge block altogether. (Chapter 8 takes this up as copy propagation and its limits.)

3. Rewrite `sum_to` into SSA form (Section 7.4). (a) Give each assignment to `r4` its own version. (b) Write the ϕ-function that `.end3` needs and name the version it selects on each incoming edge. (c) Explain why the parameters

`acc` and `n` need no ϕ-function, connecting your answer to the absence of a back edge you established in Exercise 2.

4. The `TLetExpr` case in `_expr` extends the environment with `{**env, n: v}` and lowers the body in the extended environment, but emits *no* instruction for the binding itself. (a) Explain why a `let` needs no TAC instruction of its own. (b) Contrast this with the recursive evaluator of Chapter 6, which built a new environment dictionary at run time for each `let`. Where did that run-time cost go?

5. Lark's lowerer closure-converts every `TLambda` (Section 7.6). Consider `fn adder(n : Int) : Int -> Int = fn(x : Int) => n + x`. (a) Identify the free variables of the inner lambda. (b) Sketch the `IAllocClosure` emitted at the definition site and the `IGetField` loads at the top of the lifted function. (c) Explain what goes in the closure's captured list when `adder(5)` is evaluated, and why this is the explicit form of the `dict(env)` capture from Chapter 6.

The typed tree is now a flat, explicit, analysable program: a list of three-address instructions whose control structure is a graph and whose every temporary is a countable demand on the registers to come. That flatness was bought on purpose, because it is the form in which a program can be improved and in which it can be matched to a machine. Chapter 8 takes the first of those: it reads the TAC and the CFG and rewrites them—folding constants, eliminating dead code and common subexpressions, removing the very redundancies this chapter left in place—each rewrite justified by a fact the IR made it possible to see, and each held to the differential oracle that this chapter, at last, made concrete.

Notes

[1]The hourglass is the organising idea of LLVM, whose intermediate representation (LLVM IR) is the shared waist for dozens of languages and dozens of targets. The same idea, a generation earlier, drove the use of *p-code* as a portable target for Pascal compilers. A neutral IR is the single most leveraged engineering decision in a production compiler.

[2]The construction of SSA—in particular, the minimal placement of ϕ-functions using the *dominance frontier*—is due to Cytron, Ferrante, Rosen, Wegman, and Zadeck (1991). The algorithm is elegant and entirely skippable for a compiler that is not going to exploit it, which is the position Lark is in. Knowing when *not* to adopt a technique is part of engineering judgement.

[3]The explicit stack avoids *Python's* recursion limit; it does not make recursion run in bounded space. The TAC VM still pushes a frame for every call, including tail calls. Turning a tail call back into a jump—so that `sum_to` runs in constant space—is a code-generation concern, taken up in Chapter 9. The VM's job is to be obviously correct, not fast.

Chapter 8

Optimization

The three-address code of Chapter 7 is correct and analysable, and it is also wasteful. The lowering was deliberately literal: it folded nothing and shared nothing. An expression like `2 + 3` was emitted as an addition to be performed at run time rather than the constant it plainly is; `sum_to` carried its `if`-result through a merge variable that no local rewrite can collapse. This chapter is about such waste—which of it a compiler can remove, which it can only defer, and which it should deliberately leave.

Optimization is the one phase of a compiler that is defined by a constraint rather than a goal. A code generator must produce *some* machine code; an optimizer must produce *better* code that means *exactly the same thing*. The improvement is the easy half. The hard half—the half this chapter keeps returning to—is the guarantee that meaning is preserved, because a "faster" program that computes a different answer is not an optimization but a bug. That guarantee is what ties optimization to everything before it: the IR makes the rewrites *visible*, the interpreter of Chapter 6 defines the meaning that must be *preserved*, and the differential testing of this phase's snapshot, `lark/06`, is what *checks* that it was.

A second theme runs underneath, and the chapter ends on it. Most of the transformations here are ones Lark's compiler does *not* perform. That is not an omission to apologise for; it is a decision, and Section 8.6 is the argument for it.

8.1 What Optimization Is

An optimization is a transformation T on programs such that, for every program p, the meaning of $T(p)$ equals the meaning of p—and, one hopes, $T(p)$ runs faster or smaller. Everything turns on what "meaning" is. For Lark it is fixed and concrete: the meaning of a program is the value (and the sequence of outputs) the CEK machine of Chapter 6 produces. The interpreter is not just one way to run Lark; it is the *definition* of what running Lark means, and every later stage is judged against it.

This gives optimization an exact correctness condition: a rewrite is legal if and only if it changes no observable behaviour for any input. Proving that in general is undecidable, so a real compiler does the next best thing—it restricts itself to rewrites that are *justified by a fact the IR makes plain*, and it *tests* aggressively that meaning survived.

The fact-and-check discipline. Each optimization in this chapter rests on a property that is true of the program text and visible in the IR: that an operand is a constant, that a value is never used, that a block is unreachable, that a computation does not change across a loop. The control-flow graph and the flat instruction sequence of Chapter 7 are what make those properties local and checkable rather than matters of guesswork.

The oracle. Checking is not optional. Lark's compiler is validated by *differential testing*: every acceptance program is run through all three backends—the CEK interpreter, the TAC virtual machine, and the RV32 machine—and their outputs must be byte-for-byte identical.

Listing 8.1: The meaning-preservation oracle (`lark/06/tests/diff_test.py`)

```
BACKENDS = [
  ("CEK", CEK), ("TAC", TAC_VM), ("RV32", RV32_VM)
]
# Run each test through every backend;
# assert the outputs agree.
# Any divergence is reported with the
# backend names and a unified diff.
```

If an optimization in the lowerer or the back end ever changed a program's behaviour, some backend's output would drift and the harness would fail. This is why the interpreter is kept alive long after it stops being the way Lark runs: it is the reference answer against which every transformation is checked. An optimization you cannot check is one you cannot safely ship—a point Section 8.6 makes decisive.

8.2 Constant Folding and Propagation

The simplest optimization evaluates at compile time what would otherwise be evaluated at run time. *Constant folding* replaces an operation on constant operands with its result; *constant propagation* substitutes a known constant value forward into later uses, exposing more folding. The two alternate until nothing changes.

Consider `let x = 2 + 3 in let y = x * x in …show(y)`. Lark lowers it literally:

Listing 8.2: Naive TAC: nothing folded (as lowered by `lark/05`)

```
t0 = 2 + 3
t1 = t0 * t0
t2 = call show(t1)
```

Every fact needed is on the page. `t0`'s operands are the literals 2 and 3, so `t0 = 5` (fold). `t1`'s operands are now both the constant `t0 = 5`, so `t1 = 5 * 5`, then `t1 = 25` (propagate, then fold). `show` is then applied to a constant:

Listing 8.3: After folding and propagation

```
t2 = call show(25)
```

Two arithmetic instructions have vanished, replaced by a constant computed once, at compile time, by the compiler instead of repeatedly at run time by the machine. The companion code builds this as two co-operating passes, `ch08/02_constant_folding/constant_fold.py` and `ch08/02_constant_folding/propagator.py`, which iterate to a fixed point over a basic block.[1]

What Lark already does, and does not. Lark's lowerer performs *no* folding—the `t0 = 2 + 3` above is exactly what it emits. But it is not entirely naive about constants. In the same program, a binding `let dead = 99 in …` that is never used produces *no instruction at all*: a constant bound to an unused name is simply never materialised, because lowering returns the constant as a value and emits code only where one is needed. Lark thus gets a sliver of dead-code elimination for free from the shape of its lowering (Section 8.3), while leaving genuine folding on the table.[2]

8.3 Dead Code Elimination and Reachability

Two different notions of "dead" code travel under one name. A computation is *dead* if its result is never used; a block of code is *unreachable* if no path of control ever arrives at it. Both can be removed, and the IR of Chapter 7 makes both detectable.

Useless computations. The simplest case is a temporary that merely renames another:

Listing 8.4: A redundant copy

```
t1 = a + b
t2 = t1
t3 = t2 * t2
```

`t2` holds nothing but a copy of `t1`. *Copy propagation* replaces each use of `t2` with `t1`; `t2` is then assigned but never read, and *dead-assignment elimination* deletes it:

Listing 8.5: After copy propagation and dead-assignment removal

```
t1 = a + b
t3 = t1 * t1
```

Knowing that the assignment to `t2` is dead is exactly a question of *liveness*—is the variable used on any path after this point?—which Chapter 9's register allocator already computes by backward data-flow over the CFG. The same analysis that decides which values need registers decides which assignments are dead. One analysis, two consumers.

Not every redundant-looking copy yields to a local pass. In `sum_to` (Chapter 7) the `if`-result is assigned to a temporary in *each* branch and returned at the merge block; because that temporary is defined on two paths, no local copy propagation may replace the return with either branch's value—collapsing it would require *sinking* the return into both branches, a non-local rewrite. The redundancy is real, but it is not the local kind this section removes.

Unreachable blocks. Reachability is a graph property: a block is live code only if there is a path to it from the entry block. A traversal of the CFG from the entry marks the reachable blocks; everything unmarked is unreachable and can be deleted. The companion code (`ch08/03_dead_code/reachability.py`, `ch08/03_dead_code/dead_code.py`) implements both the traversal and the use-count elimination on the little IR.

The honest note here matches the last section's. Lark prunes unused constant bindings as a side effect of lowering, but it runs no general dead-code or copy-propagation pass over its TAC. What redundancy lowering leaves—the merge-variable copy in `sum_to` among it—the back end absorbs instead: the register allocator gives a copied temporary and its source the same register (the move coalescing of Chapter 9), so the copy costs nothing at run time even though no instruction was deleted from the IR. The redundancy is paid off late and cheaply, not early and explicitly.

8.4 Expression Simplification

Beyond constants lie the *algebraic identities*: facts true of an operation for *all* values, which let the compiler rewrite an expression into a cheaper equivalent without knowing its operands.

$$x + 0 = x, \quad x \times 1 = x, \quad x \times 0 = 0, \quad x - x = 0, \quad x \times 2 = x + x.$$

The last is *strength reduction*: replacing a costly operation with a cheaper one of equal effect (a multiply by a power of two becomes a shift). Each identity is a small theorem about the operation's algebra, and the companion `ch08/04_simplification/expression_simplifier.py` applies a table of them to an expression tree.

Where the algebra is a trap. These identities are sound over the integers and the reals, but a machine's types are neither. Over Lark's 32-bit `Int`, `x + 1` can overflow, so a rewrite must preserve the wrapping behaviour the target defines (behaviour Chapter 13 later promotes from the target's habit to the language's own definition); and integer division truncates toward zero rather than flooring, so a rewrite touching / must respect the hardware's sign rule, not the floor rule of Python's // that Chapter 2's teaching VMs use as a deliberate simplification. Worse, over 32-bit `Float` the familiar laws *fail*: `x + 0.0` is not `x` when `x` is negative zero, and `x * 0.0` is not `0.0` when `x` is `NaN` or infinity. An optimizer that applies real-number algebra to floating-point silently changes results. This is precisely why Section 8.1's oracle insists on *bit-identical* output across backends, and why `lark/06` fixes `Float` to 32-bit IEEE semantics everywhere: without an exact definition of what a float operation means, you cannot tell a sound simplification from a corrupting one.[3]

8.5 Loop-Invariant Code Motion

The optimizations so far are local to a basic block. The most valuable class of optimizations is not: it concerns *loops*, because a saving inside a loop is multiplied by the number of iterations. *Loop-invariant code motion* (LICM) finds a computation inside a loop whose operands do not change from one iteration to the next, and *hoists* it out, so it runs once before the loop instead of once per pass.

The enabling fact is, again, a property of the CFG: a loop is a cycle, a *back edge* from a block to one that dominates it; a computation is invariant if every operand is defined outside the loop or is itself invariant. Both are graph properties the IR exposes.

Why Lark has nothing to hoist. Here the chapter's honesty becomes structural. Chapter 7 observed that `sum_to`, though it *recurses*, compiles to a CFG with *no back edge*: its recursive call is an ordinary `ICall`, and the control-flow graph is acyclic. Lark has no loops at the TAC level at all—iteration is recursion, and recursion is a call. The back edge that makes `sum_to` a genuine loop appears only in Chapter 9, when tail-call optimization rewrites the self-call as a jump back to the function's entry. Loop-invariant code motion therefore has no object to act on in Lark's IR; it would become possible only *after* the back end introduces the loop it needs, by which point the compiler has stopped optimizing. LICM is in this chapter because it is the canonical loop optimization and the reader must know it; it is absent from Lark because Lark's loops do not exist where LICM would look for them.

8.6 The Diminishing Returns of Optimization

It is now time to be plain about a fact the chapter has admitted section by section: Lark's compiler implements almost none of the optimizations it has just described. There is no constant folder, no algebraic simplifier, no dead-code pass, no code motion. The IR is lowered, the register allocator coalesces copies and the assembler eliminates self-tail-calls (Chapter 9), and that is the whole of it. This is a deliberate stopping point, and defending it is the most useful thing this chapter can do.

The shape of the returns. Optimization has steeply diminishing returns, and the steps are wildly unequal in size. The largest single improvement in this entire book is not an optimization pass at all: it is the move from interpreting a tree to compiling to native code, the jump from Chapter 6's CEK machine to Chapter 9's RISC-V—two or three orders of magnitude. Against that, constant folding and dead-copy elimination are rounding error, and on the small, recursion-driven programs Lark runs, the two optimizations the back end does perform—keeping values in registers across calls, and turning tail recursion into a loop—capture most of what is left. The third pass and the thirtieth pass of a production compiler are chasing a thin margin that matters enormously at Google's scale and not at all at Lark's.

The cost of a pass. Each optimization is not free to possess. It is code that runs on every compile, it is a new place for the compiler to be wrong, and it is a new obligation to prove—or at least test—that meaning was preserved. The float-simplification trap of Section 8.4 is the cautionary case: an "obvious" rewrite that silently corrupts results. Every pass added is a surface where a miscompilation can hide, and a miscompilation is the worst kind of bug, because it makes correct source code do the wrong thing with no error anywhere.

Measuring honestly. The discipline that decides when to stop is measurement, not intuition. The honest questions are: does this pass make a program a reader will actually run measurably faster, and can its correctness be demonstrated? Lark answers the second with the differential oracle of Section 8.1 and the first by observing that, for its workload, the answer is mostly no. A compiler that adds a pass it cannot measure a benefit from, or cannot verify the safety of, has confused activity with progress. Knowing where that line falls—and stopping at it deliberately rather than drifting past it—is not a failure of ambition. It is the same engineering judgement that chose affine over linear types and linear scan over graph colouring: take the guarantee you can keep and the gain you can prove, and decline the rest.

8.7 Exercises

1. Take the naive TAC for `let x = 2 + 3 in let y = x * x in y + x`. (a) Write it out as Lark would lower it (no folding). (b) Apply constant folding and propagation to a fixed point, showing each intermediate step and which instruction triggers the next fold. (c) State the property that has to be true of `+` and `*` for every step to be meaning-preserving, and explain why it holds for 32-bit `Int` but would need care for `Float`.

2. In `sum_to` (Chapter 7) the `if`-result is assigned to a temporary in both branches and returned at the merge block. (a) Explain why *local* copy propagation cannot replace the return with either branch's value—name the property of the merge variable that makes the rewrite unsound. (b) Describe the non-local rewrite (sinking the return into both branches) that does remove the temporary and the merge block, and sketch the resulting two-exit function. (c) Lark performs neither, leaving the temporary for the register allocator's move coalescing (defined in Section 9.3 of Chapter 9). What does coalescing achieve here that the IR-level rewrite does not, and vice versa?

3. Reachability is a graph traversal from the entry block. (a) Give a small Lark function whose lowered CFG contains a block that can never execute at run time, and identify it. (Hint: an `if` whose condition is a constant, such as `if true then …else ….`) (b) Explain why Lark's lowerer emits this dead block *anyway*—connect your answer to the fact that it folds no constants, so it lowers the condition to a real conditional jump with both targets. (c) A plain reachability pass does *not* remove the block, because the conditional jump still gives it an incoming edge. Show how constant folding (Section 8.2) must run *first*—turning the jump unconditional—before reachability can see the branch as dead and delete it.

4. Section 8.4 claims `x + 0.0 = x` is unsound for floating point. (a) Identify the value of `x` for which it fails and state both results. (b) Explain how the

differential oracle of Section 8.1 would catch a compiler that applied this rewrite. (c) The identity `x + 0 = x` *is* sound for `Int`. What is the difference between the two cases?

5. Section 8.6 argues that the interpreter-to-compiler jump dwarfs any single optimization pass. (a) For `sum_to(0, n)`, explain in terms of work-per-iteration why the CEK machine is orders of magnitude slower than the compiled loop, naming three costs the compiled code does not pay. (b) Argue either for or against adding constant folding to Lark, using the two criteria of Section 8.6—measurable benefit and demonstrable correctness—rather than aesthetics.

Optimization, taken seriously, is the discipline of changing a program's form while swearing an oath about its meaning—and of knowing when the oath costs more than the change is worth. Lark keeps the oath by changing little: it folds nothing and hoists nothing, trusting the interpreter as its definition of truth and the differential oracle as its proof. What improvement it does take, it takes at the boundary with the machine, where the gains are largest and the checks are cheapest. Chapter 9 reaches that boundary. It takes the three-address code—unoptimised, explicit, and honest—assigns its temporaries to the thirty-two registers of RISC-V, turns its tail calls into jumps, and emits the instructions that finally run on silicon.

Notes

[1]Iterating an analysis to a fixed point—here within a basic block, but in general across the whole control-flow graph over a lattice of dataflow facts—is the method Gary Kildall unified [Kildall, 1973].

[2]The asymmetry is instructive. Dropping an unused binding falls out of a lowering that emits nothing for a pure value that no instruction consumes; it costs no code. Constant folding, by contrast, requires a dedicated pass that recognises constant operands and evaluates the operation with the same overflow and rounding behaviour the target would use—which for floats means reproducing 32-bit IEEE semantics exactly (Section 8.4). The cheap optimization is taken; the one with a correctness obligation is deferred.

[3]The standard industrial compromise is a flag. A compiler offers "fast math" that assumes real-number algebra and runs faster, off by default, with the warning that it may change results. The existence of the flag is an admission that these "optimizations" are not meaning-preserving in the technical sense—they trade the correctness condition of Section 8.1 for speed. Lark has no such flag,

and no float simplification, by the same conservative instinct that chose affine types: a guarantee you cannot keep is not worth making.

Chapter 9

Code Generation

The three-address code of Chapter 7 is everything the back end needs and nothing it can run. Its temporaries are unbounded, as though the machine had an inexhaustible supply of registers; its operations are target-neutral, named but not yet chosen; its calls assume a convention no one has written down. This chapter closes the last gap in the book. It selects real RISC-V instructions for each operation, assigns the endless temporaries to the thirty-two registers the hardware actually has, fixes the contract by which functions call one another, and—the moment the whole book has been building toward—turns the tail call of `sum_to` into the jump that Chapter 6 promised and Chapter 7 deferred. At the end of it, a Lark program is machine code, and it runs on silicon.

The reference implementation is `lark/05`: `regalloc.py` allocates registers by linear scan, `asm.py` selects instructions and lays out frames, `riscv_asm.py` assembles the result, and `runtime/` links it for a Raspberry Pi Pico 2/2W. The interpreter of Chapter 6 does not run any of this code—but it judges all of it, because the generated program is correct exactly when its output agrees with what the interpreter said the program means.

9.1 From Intermediate Representation to Instructions

The distance from TAC to RISC-V is three problems wearing one name. The first is *instruction selection*: each TAC operation must become one or more real machine instructions. The second is *register allocation*: the unbounded supply of temporaries the lowerer invented must be mapped onto a fixed, small set of physical registers, spilling the overflow to memory. The third is the *calling convention*: a contract, invisible in the IR, governing where arguments go, where results come back, and which registers a call may destroy.

None of the three is hard for Lark in isolation, because Chapter 7 chose a three-address code that already resembles a register machine. That was deliberate. The IR was shaped, from the start, so that this chapter would be a translation rather than a reinvention: every TAC instruction is close to one RISC-V instruction, modulo getting its operands into registers. The decision made two chapters ago pays out here.

9.2 Instruction Selection

Instruction selection answers "which machine instructions compute this IR operation?" The principled general technique is *tree matching*: the IR operation is a small tree, the machine's instructions are tree patterns with costs, and the selector tiles the operation tree with the cheapest patterns that cover it—*maximal munch*. Tree matching earns its keep on complex instruction sets, where one instruction can fold an address computation, a load, and an arithmetic operation into a single tile.

Lark's selector does none of this, and is right not to. RISC-V is a load-store RISC: its instructions are simple and orthogonal, and TAC was built to mirror them. So selection is a near one-to-one table. An `IBinOp` addition becomes `add`; a comparison `n == 0` becomes a subtract followed by `seqz` (set-if-equal-zero); an `ICondJump` becomes a conditional branch and an unconditional jump; an `ICall` becomes `call`. The cost of such simplicity is verbosity: the selector loads each operand into a fixed scratch register before operating, so a comparison expands to a small run of moves.

Listing 9.1: `n == 0` selected naïvely (from the emitted `sum_to`)

```
mv   t0, s10          # t0 <- n     (operand into scratch)
li   t1, 0            # t1 <- 0
sub  t2, t0, t1       # t2 <- n - 0
seqz t2, t2           # t2 <- (t2 == 0)
mv   s9, t2           # store the result
```

Five instructions for what one comparison-and-branch could nearly do. The `mv` chains are exactly the redundancy a peephole pass (Chapter 8) would collapse, and their survival is the visible price of the optimizations Lark chooses not to run. The code is correct, literal, and a little fat—the same honest bargain the lowerer struck.

9.3 Register Allocation

Register allocation is the heart of code generation and the one genuinely hard problem in it. The lowerer wrote code as if temporaries were free; the hardware has thirty-two registers, several of them spoken for. Lark allocates from the eleven callee-saved registers `s1–s11`; every temporary must be assigned one, or *spilled* to a stack slot and loaded back when needed.

The difficulty. Two temporaries may share a register if and only if they are never live at the same time. Phrased as a graph—a node per temporary, an edge between any two simultaneously live—this is graph colouring with as many colours as registers, and graph colouring is NP-complete. Optimal allocation is, in general, intractable.

Two practical answers. Production compilers approximate. *Graph colouring* (Chaitin's algorithm and its descendants [Chaitin, 1982]) builds the interference graph and colours it heuristically, spilling when a node cannot be coloured; it allocates well but is comparatively slow. *Linear scan* [Poletto and Sarkar, 1999] is the faster answer, and the one Lark uses: it represents each temporary as a *live interval*—the span between its first and last use in the linearized instruction stream—and sweeps the intervals in order of their start.

Listing 9.2: Linear scan: the core sweep (`lark/05/src/regalloc.py`, abbreviated)

```
# Process intervals in order of increasing start point.
for iv in sorted(intervals):

    # Free the registers of intervals
    # that have already ended.
    for a in active:
        if a.end < iv.start:
            free.append(reg_assign[a.name])

    active = [a for a in active if a.end >= iv.start]

    # No register is available:
    # decide which interval to spill.
    if not free:

        # Choose the active interval that ends latest.
        spill_cand = max(active, key=lambda a: a.end)

        # If the current interval ends sooner,
        # keep it in a register and spill the
        # longer-lived interval instead.
```

```
        if spill_cand.end > iv.end:
            reg_assign[iv.name] = reg_assign.pop(
              spill_cand.name
            )
            spill_slots[spill_cand.name] = next_slot()
        else:
            spill_slots[iv.name] = next_slot()

    # A register is available: assign to current interval.
    else:
        reg_assign[iv.name] = free.pop()
        active.append(iv)
```

The rule when registers run out is the algorithm's one clever stroke: spill the interval that ends *latest*, because it is the one most likely to keep a register tied up while others come and go. The sweep is a single pass, near optimal in practice, and fast enough to run on every compile.

`sum_to`, **allocated.** The allocator assigns the function's seven temporaries with room to spare:

Listing 9.3: Linear-scan allocation of `sum_to` (output of `lark/05/src/regalloc.py`)

```
Allocation 'sum_to'  7 reg  0 spill
  regs_used=[s6,s7,s8,s9,s10,s11]
  acc     -> s11    [0,10]
  n       -> s10    [0,10]
  r4      -> s9     [2,12]
  t0      -> s9     [0,1]
  t5      -> s8     [6,8]
  t6      -> s7     [7,8]
  t7      -> s6     [8,9]
  verify: OK
```

Two things are worth seeing. There are *zero spills*: the function fits entirely in registers, which is the everyday case on a machine with thirty-two of them and the heart of what "compiler-friendly" means (Section 9.4). And `t0` and `r4` *share* `s9`—their intervals `[0,1]` and `[2,12]` do not overlap, so the same physical register holds first one and then the other (Figure 9.1). The register reuse that the IR's unbounded temporaries made invisible is recovered here, exactly, by the interval test. A *verifier* confirms the result: no two interfering temporaries were given the same register. This is where Chapter 8's move coalescing also lives—when

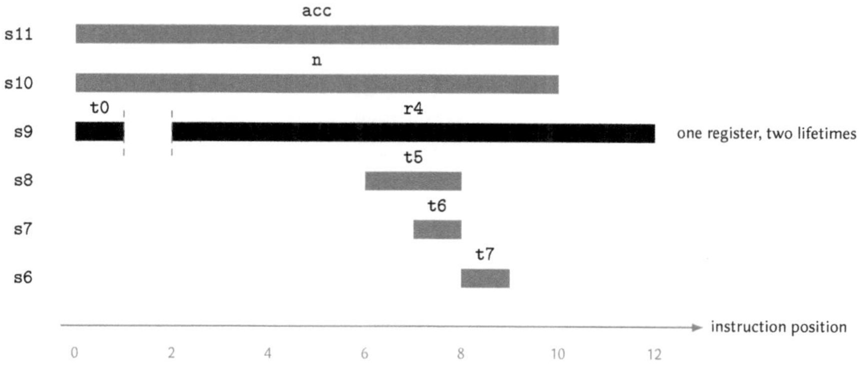

Figure 9.1: Linear-scan allocation of `sum_to`'s seven temporaries, drawn as live intervals on the instruction stream. Each bar spans a temporary's first to last use; its row is the physical register the sweep assigned. `t0` dies at position 1 and `r4` is not born until position 2 (the dashed gap), so their intervals do not overlap and both are placed in `s9`—the reuse the interval test recovers. Nothing spills: seven temporaries fit comfortably in the callee-saved registers.

a temporary is a copy of another, the allocator prefers to give them the same register, so the copy disappears at no cost.

9.4 Targeting RISC-V

RISC-V was introduced in Chapter 1 as the modern target; here it receives Lark. Two of its properties shape the generated code.

Load-store discipline. Arithmetic happens only between registers. Memory is touched only by `lw` (load word) and `sw` (store word). A value that lives on the stack—a spill, a saved register—must be loaded before use and stored after definition. This is why register allocation matters so much: every temporary that does not fit a register becomes load-store traffic.

The calling convention. A convention invisible in the IR becomes concrete machine code. Arguments arrive in `a0`–`a7`; a result leaves in `a0`; the return address is in `ra`; `sp` is the stack pointer and `s0` the frame pointer. The registers split into *caller-saved* (clobbered freely across a call) and *callee-saved* (`s1`–`s11`, which a function must preserve). Lark allocates only callee-saved registers, so a temporary's value survives a call with no save-around-call code at all—the cost is paid once, in the prologue and epilogue, for the registers the function actually uses.

This explains the two roles registers play in the emitted code, and why the scratch `t0`–`t2` of Section 9.2 are not a contradiction of "allocate only `s`-registers."

The `t` registers are caller-saved, and that is precisely why they are never allocated: each lives only *within* a single instruction's expansion—load the operands into `t0` and `t1`, compute into `t2`, store the result back to the destination's allocated home—and is dead again before the next instruction begins, let alone before any call. They are fixed plumbing, not values with lifetimes, so the allocator never sees them. The callee-saved `s`-registers are the opposite: they hold a temporary's value across instructions and across calls, which is exactly the property the allocator exists to manage.

Listing 9.4: The frame of `sum_to`: prologue and epilogue (emitted by `lark/05`)

```
sum_to:
  addi sp, sp, -32    # open a 32-byte frame
  sw   ra, 28(sp)     # save return address
  sw   s0, 24(sp)     # save caller's frame pointer
  addi s0, sp, 32     # establish this frame's pointer
  sw   s6, -12(s0)    # save callee-saved registers we use
  ...                 #   (s7 .. s11)
  mv   s11, a0        # move args into allocated registers
  mv   s10, a1
  ...
.sum_to_end3:
  mv   a0, s9         # result into a0
  lw   s6, -12(s0)    # restore callee-saved registers
  ...
  lw   ra, 28(sp)     # restore return address
  addi sp, sp, 32     # close the frame
  ret
```

What compiler-friendly buys. The phrase from Chapter 1 now has a measurable meaning. Thirty-two orthogonal registers mean most functions never spill—`sum_to` did not. A regular, three-operand instruction format means TAC maps almost directly onto it. A load-store design means the cost model is simple enough that an allocator can reason about it. The abundance is not luxury; it is what lets a small, simple code generator produce decent code. The assembler that finishes the job, `riscv_asm.py`, is a conventional two-pass design: it resolves label addresses, expands pseudo-instructions (`la` into an `auipc`/`addi` pair, `li` of a large constant into `lui`/`addi`), and emits the runtime stubs that `print` and `show` call.

9.5 The 6502 as Contrast

To see what RISC-V's abundance is worth, return to the machine Chapter 1 set beside it. The 6502 has three working registers—an accumulator `A` and two index registers `X` and `Y`—and they are not interchangeable; most arithmetic must pass through `A`. On such a machine, register allocation is not the question "which of thirty-two?" but the question "what cannot possibly fit?"—and the answer is almost everything. Linear scan over three non-orthogonal registers would spill on nearly every interval.

A 6502 code generator is therefore organised around memory, not registers. It leans on the *zero page*—the first 256 bytes of memory, which a special short addressing mode reaches in fewer cycles—and treats those locations as a pool of pseudo-registers, shuttling values between them and the accumulator. `sum_to`, which compiled to a tidy register loop with zero spills on RISC-V, would on the 6502 become a sequence of zero-page loads and stores, the accumulator a turnstile every value passes through. This is the concrete form of the question Chapter 1 asked about $(a \times b) + (c \times d)$: with three working registers, the compiler is forced to spill intermediates to memory that on RISC-V would simply sit in `s`-registers.

Lark targets RISC-V only; the 6502 is not a second back end but the contrast that makes the first one legible. Constrained hardware makes invisible costs visible—which is exactly why Chapter 1 kept it in view.

9.6 Tail-Call Elimination in Generated Code

Now the loop closes. Chapter 6 showed that a purely functional language must implement iteration as tail recursion, and that the CEK machine ran tail calls in bounded space by passing the continuation onward unchanged. Chapter 7 observed that in the TAC, `sum_to`'s recursive call was an ordinary `ICall` and its control-flow graph had no back edge—no loop. The loop was promised to this chapter. Here it is made.

The recognition. A self-tail-call is a call to the current function whose result flows directly to the function's return, with nothing computed in between. The code generator detects it by following the call's result temporary forward through copies and jumps; if it reaches an `IReturn` of that value, the call is in tail position.

Listing 9.5: Detecting a self-tail-call (`lark/05/src/asm.py`, abbreviated)

```
def reaches_return(instructions, live):
  for instr in reversed(instructions):
```

```
        # the call's result is `live`;
        # does it flow straight to a return?
        if isinstance(instr, IReturn):
          return (
            instr.val is not None
            and instr.val.name == live
          )
        if (
          isinstance(instr, IAssign)
          and instr.src.name == live
        ):
          live = instr.dst.name  # follow the copy
          continue

  return False
```

The transformation. When a function contains such a call, the generator emits a label `.`*fn*`_loop` just after the prologue, and compiles the tail call not as `call` but as: move the new arguments into the parameter registers, then `jump` back to that label. No new frame, no `call`, no return—the function reuses its own activation and begins again.

Listing 9.6: `sum_to`'s tail call, compiled to a loop (emitted by `lark/05`)

```
.sum_to_loop:               # <- the back edge, introduced here
  ...
.sum_to_else2:
  mv   t0, s11              # acc
  mv   t1, s10              # n
  add  t2, t0, t1           # acc + n
  mv   s8, t2
  mv   t0, s10
  li   t1, 1
  sub  t2, t0, t1           # n - 1
  mv   s7, t2
  mv   a0, s8               # new arg 0: acc + n
  mv   a1, s7               # new arg 1: n - 1
  mv   s11, a0              # reload the parameter registers
  mv   s10, a1
  j    .sum_to_loop         # tail call == jump.
                            # no frame is pushed.
```

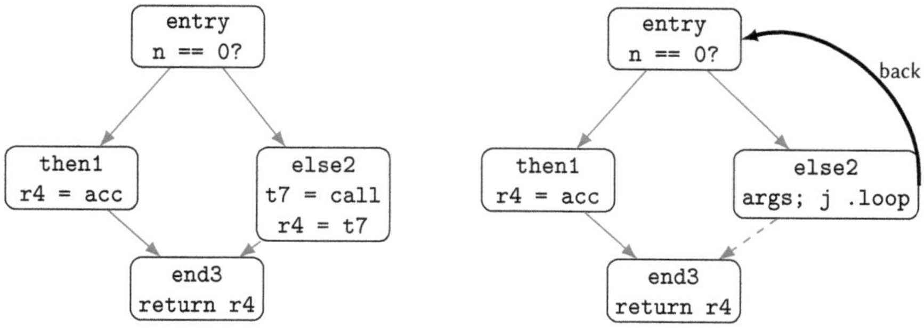

Before (Ch. 7): acyclic   **After** (Ch. 9): a loop

Figure 9.2: `sum_to`'s control-flow graph, before and after tail-call elimination. In the TAC of Chapter 7 (left) the recursive call lives *inside* block `else2` as an `ICall`; it is not a control edge, so the graph is acyclic. Compiling the tail call to a jump (right) replaces that call with a *back edge* to `entry`—the cycle that makes `sum_to` a real loop—and leaves the old `else2`→`end3` path unreachable.

This is the back edge Chapter 7 said the code generator would introduce. The control-flow graph of the *generated* code has a cycle where the TAC's did not, and `sum_to(0, 1000000)` now runs in a single stack frame—a true loop, executing on the hardware as iteration, even though the source and the interpreter both expressed it as recursion. Proper tail-call elimination, promised by the CEK machine and realised in machine code.

One honest detail completes the picture. Just after the `j .sum_to_loop` sit a few unreachable instructions—the original, non-tail return path, now bypassed forever by the jump above it. They are dead code, of exactly the kind Chapter 8 described, and Lark does not remove them, because Lark runs no dead-code pass. The compiler is correct and unpolished, and it has never pretended otherwise.

One scope note keeps the slogan honest. What is optimised here is the *self*-tail-call: a tail call to the *current* function, rewritten to a jump to its own entry label. A *mutual* tail call—`is_even` tail-calling `is_odd`, which tail-calls back—is left as an ordinary `call` and still grows the stack; turning it into a jump would need a shared entry protocol or a trampoline (Exercise 4c). "A tail call is a jump" is thus a promise about self-recursion, which is exactly the case iteration needs.

9.7 The Program on Silicon

The assembly is assembled, linked against a small runtime (`lark/05/runtime/`: a bump-pointer heap, the `print` and `show` stubs, a bare-metal entry point), and flashed to a Raspberry Pi Pico 2/2W—an `RV32IMAC` core costing a few dollars. There, with no operating system beneath it, a Lark program runs as native machine code: the `sum_to` loop iterates in registers, the affine `IO` token threads through real serial output, and the answer appears.

It is worth pausing on the length of that chain. Source text became tokens (Chapter 3), tokens became a tree (Chapter 4), the tree was given types and an ownership discipline (Chapter 5), the typed tree was evaluated to define its meaning (Chapter 6), lowered to a flat intermediate form (Chapter 7), left deliberately unoptimised (Chapter 8), and is now thirty-two registers and a stack frame on a chip. Every link was a decision, and the decisions constrained one another the whole way down—`Copy` as a trait made the affine token, the affine token let the code generator emit no ownership checks, the flat IR let the tail call become a jump. That propagation, from a choice in the type system to an instruction on silicon, is the subject the Introduction named. The compiler is complete.

9.8 Exercises

1. The comparison `n == 0` compiled to five instructions (Section 9.2): two `mv`, a needless `li` of zero, a `sub`, and a `seqz`. (a) Rewrite the fragment by hand into the fewest RISC-V instructions that compute the same result and branch, using `beqz` and the hardwired zero register `x0`. (b) Which optimization from Chapter 8 would remove the `mv` chain, and at which stage—IR or instruction selection—would you choose to run it, and why?

2. In the allocation of `sum_to`, `t0` and `r4` share register `s9` (Section 9.3). (a) Write out their live intervals and confirm they do not overlap. (b) Construct a small function whose temporaries cannot all fit in `s1–s11`, forcing a spill, and identify which interval linear scan would spill and why. (c) State the exact condition under which two temporaries may share a register.

3. Linear scan spills the latest-ending interval when registers run out (Section 9.3). (a) Explain why "latest-ending" is a better choice than "earliest-ending" or "the current interval." (b) Give a sequence of intervals on which linear scan produces a worse allocation than optimal graph colouring would, and say how many registers each uses.

4. `sum_to`'s tail call became `j .sum_to_loop` (Section 9.6). (a) Trace what the stack pointer does across one million iterations, and contrast it with what `call` would have done. (b) The recursive evaluator of Chapter 6 overflowed the host stack on this program; explain why the compiled code does not, in terms of the back edge. (c) Mutual tail recursion—`is_even`

tail-calling `is_odd`—is *not* optimized by this transformation. Why not, and what would a general tail-call optimization have to do instead?

5. On the 6502, `sum_to` cannot stay in registers (Section 9.5). (a) Sketch how the loop body (`acc + n, n - 1`) would be compiled using the accumulator and zero-page locations for `acc` and `n`. (b) Count the memory accesses per iteration and compare with the RISC-V version's zero. (c) What property of the 6502 forces this, and what general lesson does it carry about the relationship between an instruction set and the compiler that targets it?

Lark is now a compiler: source text in, RISC-V machine code out, running on a microcontroller with no interpreter beneath it. The journey from silicon to semantics has been walked once in each direction—up, from the fetch-decode-execute loop to a type system that reasons about ownership; and down, from that type system to thirty-two registers and a tail call that is a jump. What remains is not more machinery but a change of view. Chapter 10 returns to the CEK machine, not as the interpreter it has been but as a formal object—an operational semantics—and asks what it was, exactly, that the compiler had to preserve. The implementation is finished; the account of why it is correct begins.

Notes

[1]Iterating an analysis to a fixed point—here within a basic block, but in general across the whole control-flow graph over a lattice of dataflow facts—is the method Gary Kildall unified [Kildall, 1973].

[2]The asymmetry is instructive. Dropping an unused binding falls out of a lowering that emits nothing for a pure value that no instruction consumes; it costs no code. Constant folding, by contrast, requires a dedicated pass that recognises constant operands and evaluates the operation with the same overflow and rounding behaviour the target would use—which for floats means reproducing 32-bit IEEE semantics exactly (Section 8.4). The cheap optimization is taken; the one with a correctness obligation is deferred.

[3]The standard industrial compromise is a flag. A compiler offers "fast math" that assumes real-number algebra and runs faster, off by default, with the warning that it may change results. The existence of the flag is an admission that these "optimizations" are not meaning-preserving in the technical sense—they trade the correctness condition of Section 8.1 for speed. Lark has no such flag, and no float simplification, by the same conservative instinct that chose affine types: a guarantee you cannot keep is not worth making.

NOTES

First Interlude: One Program, All the Way Down

The compiler is complete. Every stage has been built and explained, but each in its own chapter, with its own running fragments. One example has travelled the whole distance—`sum_to`, the function that sums the integers from one to n—and it has earned a single continuous view. This interlude follows it from the characters a programmer types to the instructions a processor runs, with every intermediate form on one path. Nothing here is new; it is the book assembled.

The source. Two lines of Lark, recursive, with an explicit type signature.

Listing 9.7: The program

```
fn sum_to(acc : Int, n : Int) : Int =
    if n == 0 then acc else sum_to(acc + n, n - 1)
```

Tokens (Chapter 3). The lexer's single left-to-right pass turns the signature's characters into a flat stream of tokens, discarding whitespace and classifying each lexeme by kind:

Listing 9.8: The signature, lexed

```
FN NAME LPAREN NAME COLON UPPER COMMA NAME COLON
UPPER RPAREN COLON UPPER ASSIGN ...
```

Syntax tree (Chapter 4). Recursive descent consumes the token stream and builds an abstract syntax tree. The flat sequence becomes nested structure—the `if` contains its condition and both branches, the recursive call is an `Apply` node, and the body is the value of the declaration:

Listing 9.9: The body, parsed (abbreviated)

```
FnDecl(name='sum_to',
  params=[('acc', Int), ('n', Int)],
  body=IfExpr(
    cond = BinOp('==', Var('n'), Lit(0)),
    then_= Var('acc'),
    else_= Apply(Var('sum_to'),
                 [BinOp('+', Var('acc'), Var('n')),
                  BinOp('-', Var('n'),   Lit(1))])))
```

Type (Chapter 5). Hindley–Milner inference checks the tree. Because the function is recursive, the checker first binds `sum_to` to a fresh type variable, then infers the body against it: the comparison forces `n : Int`, the additions force `acc : Int`, and the recursive call unifies cleanly with the variable it was given. The result is a single principal type.

Listing 9.10: The inferred type

```
sum_to : Int -> Int -> Int
```

Meaning (Chapter 6). The CEK machine *defines* what running this program means. It is the reference answer every later stage is checked against. Evaluated directly on the typed tree:

Listing 9.11: The meaning, computed by the interpreter

```
sum_to(0, 100)  ==>  5050
```

Intermediate representation (Chapter 7). The lowerer flattens the tree into three-address code over a control-flow graph of four basic blocks. The nesting is gone; control is explicit jumps; every intermediate value has a name. Crucially, the recursive call is an ordinary `call`, and the graph has *no back edge*—no loop, yet.

Listing 9.12: Lowered to TAC over a four-block CFG

```
[__entry__]                   # t0 = n == 0
    t0 = n == 0
    if t0 jump .then1 else .else2
[.then1]                      # the base case
    r4 = acc
    jump .end3
[.else2]                      # the recursive case
    t5 = acc + n
```

```
    t6 = n - 1
    t7 = call sum_to(t5, t6)
    r4 = t7
    jump .end3
[.end3]                     # the merge
    return r4
```

Optimization (Chapter 8). Here Lark does almost nothing, and that is the honest part of the story. It folds no constants and runs no dead-code pass; the merge variable `r4`, assigned in both branches and returned at `.end3`, survives untouched because no *local* rewrite can soundly collapse it. The two real optimizations Lark performs both live in the back end: move coalescing and the tail-call rewrite below.

Register allocation (Chapter 9). Linear scan maps the seven temporaries onto the callee-saved registers, with room to spare. Two intervals that never overlap—`t0` and the merge variable `r4`—share `s9`, and nothing spills.

Listing 9.13: Allocation: zero spills; `t0` and `r4` share `s9`

```
acc -> s11    n  -> s10    r4 -> s9     t0 -> s9
t5  -> s8     t6 -> s7     t7 -> s6     (0 spill)
```

Machine code (Chapter 9). Instruction selection emits RISC-V, and the moment the whole book was building toward arrives: the recursive tail call is recognised and compiled not as `call` but as a `jump` back to the function's own entry. The back edge the CFG did not have appears here, in the generated code. `sum_to` runs as a true loop, in a single stack frame.

Listing 9.14: The recursive case, compiled (the tail call is a jump)

```
.sum_to_else2:
  mv    t0, s11
  mv    t1, s10
  add   t2, t0, t1      # acc + n
  mv    s8, t2
  ...
  mv    a0, s8          # new arguments
  mv    a1, s7
  mv    s11, a0
  mv    s10, a1
  j     .sum_to_loop    # tail call == jump
```

Silicon (Chapter 9). Assembled, linked against a small runtime, and loaded onto a Raspberry Pi Pico 2/2W, the program runs on a real RISC-V core and prints its answer—the same 5050 the interpreter computed back at the start, now produced by hardware.

This is the spine of the book in one figure-of-eight. Read downward, each stage is a translation that gives up some abstraction for some executability: the tree loses its nesting to become linear TAC; the unbounded temporaries lose their freedom to become thirty-two registers; the recursive call loses its frame to become a jump. Read the other way, every shape was *decided from below.* The tail call could become a jump only because the type checker established `sum_to`'s arity; the temporaries fit in registers only because the IR made their lifetimes visible; the whole chain is sound only because one definition—the interpreter's—fixed what 5050 had to be and held every stage to it. That is the propagation the book has been tracing. Part V turns back to ask what, formally, was just built—and the second interlude, overleaf, makes that turn once in miniature before the chapters make it in earnest.

Second Interlude: One Theorem, All the Way Down

The interlude before this one followed one program down through the machines. This one follows one *claim* down through the proofs. The claim is Milner's—well-typed programs do not go wrong—and Part V will spend four chapters making it precise, proving it, opening the instrument that checked the proof, and then attacking everything just built. Before that begins, here is the whole journey once, in miniature: a single tiny program, taken from source text to a machine-checked certificate that it cannot get stuck, one page per idea. Nothing is proved in generality here; it is Part V performed once, by hand, at half speed. (The notation ahead is the subject of Appendix C; this interlude is a good place to have it open.)

The program. Almost nothing, which is the point—small enough that every layer stays visible on one page.

Listing 9.15: The program

```
(fn(x : Bool) => if x then 1 else 2)(true)
```

The claim, for this one program: it has a type, `Int`; running it reaches a *value* of that type; and at no point does the machine face a state it has no rule for. Every layer below is that same sentence, at a lower altitude and a higher standard of evidence.

The type, as a question (Chapter 5). The checker's verdict is one judgement—under no assumptions, the expression has type `Int`:

$$\vdash\ (\texttt{fn}(x:\texttt{Bool}) \Rightarrow \texttt{if}\ x\ \texttt{then}\ 1\ \texttt{else}\ 2)(\texttt{true})\ :\ \texttt{Int}$$

So far this is only a claim. What makes it *true* is the next layer.

The evidence, as a tree (Chapter 5). The judgement holds because a derivation exists—one rule application per bar, axioms at the leaves. Derivations outgrow the page almost immediately, so use the working convention and name the `if`'s subtree first:

$$\mathcal{D} \;=\; \frac{x{:}\texttt{Bool} \vdash x : \texttt{Bool} \qquad x{:}\texttt{Bool} \vdash 1 : \texttt{Int} \qquad x{:}\texttt{Bool} \vdash 2 : \texttt{Int}}{x{:}\texttt{Bool} \;\vdash\; \texttt{if}\ x\ \texttt{then}\ 1\ \texttt{else}\ 2 \;:\; \texttt{Int}}$$

Three premises, one per subexpression, each an axiom. On top of $\mathcal{D}$, two rules finish the proof: the lambda rule closes over x, and the application rule meets the argument:

$$\frac{\dfrac{\mathcal{D}}{\vdash\ \texttt{fn}(x{:}\texttt{Bool}) \Rightarrow \texttt{if}\ x\ \texttt{then}\ 1\ \texttt{else}\ 2 \;:\; \texttt{Bool} \to \texttt{Int}} \qquad \dfrac{}{\vdash\ \texttt{true} : \texttt{Bool}}}{\vdash\ (\texttt{fn}(x{:}\texttt{Bool}) \Rightarrow \texttt{if}\ x\ \texttt{then}\ 1\ \texttt{else}\ 2)(\texttt{true}) \;:\; \texttt{Int}}$$

Read the pair as `infer`'s call tree—seven frames, one per rule, the leaves returning without recursing—because that is what it is: when the checker of Chapter 5 accepts this program, it *builds* this tree on the Python call stack and throws it away. The rest of the interlude is about not throwing it away.

The meaning, one step at a time (previewing Chapter 10). Part V's first move is to write evaluation as a relation: $e \to e'$, one step of computation. This program takes exactly two.

$$\begin{array}{lll} & (\texttt{fn}(x{:}\texttt{Bool}) \Rightarrow \texttt{if}\ x\ \texttt{then}\ 1\ \texttt{else}\ 2)(\texttt{true}) & : \texttt{Int} \\ \to & \texttt{if true then}\ 1\ \texttt{else}\ 2 & : \texttt{Int} \quad (\beta) \\ \to & 1 & : \texttt{Int} \quad (\textit{if-true}) \end{array}$$

Look at the right-hand column, because the theorem is already visible in it. After each step the result still has type `Int`—that is *preservation*, witnessed twice. And at each line that is not yet a value, some rule applied—that is *progress*, witnessed twice. Two observations about one program; Chapter 11 proves them about every program.

The tree, kept (previewing Chapter 11). The derivation the checker discarded can instead be built as *data*—a value of the intrinsically typed `Expr`, in which only well-typed programs can be written down at all. Here is this program's derivation, as it checks in the kernel (wrapped for the page):

Listing 9.16: The call tree, reified (checked by `lcore`)

```
choose   = ELam empty TBool TInt
             (EIf (ext TBool empty) TInt
               (EVar (ext TBool empty) TBool
```

```
                  (here empty TBool))
             (ELitInt (ext TBool empty))
             (ELitInt (ext TBool empty)))
program = EApp empty TBool TInt choose
          (ELitBool empty true)
              -- program : Expr empty TInt
```

Same tree, third form: each constructor is one bar of the derivation above, and the kernel accepting `program : Expr empty TInt` is the same verdict the type checker gave—now held in the hand rather than implied by a call stack. (One honesty: the model keeps shapes and types, not numbers—`ELitInt` carries no `1`. The theorem being chased says the program reaches *an integer value*; which integer is the interpreter's business, and the first interlude's.)

The steps, kept too (previewing Chapter 11). The two arrows are also data—constructors of the `Step` relation, whose type only *connects* expressions of the same type, so a step that changed the type could not be written:

Listing 9.17: The two steps, as checked evidence

```
after1 = EIf empty TInt (ELitBool empty true)
         (ELitInt empty) (ELitInt empty)

step1 : Step TInt program after1          -- the beta step
step1 = StepBeta TBool TInt body
        (ELitBool empty true)

step2 : Step TInt after1 (ELitInt empty)  -- if-true
step2 = StepIfTrue TInt (ELitInt empty)
        (ELitInt empty)
```

A detail worth a pause: `step1`'s stated reduct `after1` is the *result of the substitution*, and the kernel checks the claim by *computing* the substitution and comparing. The β-step tracked by hand a page ago is here performed by the proof checker, inside a type.

The theorem, applied (previewing Chapter 12). Chain the two steps and the run itself becomes evidence: an `Eval` value, the whole trace as one object. And to evidence, theorems apply. The main theorem of Part V—`eval_produces_val`, evaluation soundness, a three-line recursion the reader will meet in Chapter 12—applied to this run, of this program:

Listing 9.18: The certificate (checked by `lcore`)

```
runs : Eval TInt program (ELitInt empty)
runs = EvalStep TInt program after1 (ELitInt empty)
         step1
         (EvalStep TInt after1 (ELitInt empty)
            (ELitInt empty) step2
            (EvalDone TInt (ELitInt empty) ValInt))

answer_is_value = eval_produces_val TInt program
                    (ELitInt empty) runs
   -- answer_is_value : IsVal TInt (ELitInt empty)
```

Run the proof files and this line through the kernel and it answers: `answer_is_value : IsVal TInt (ELitInt empty).` Read the type aloud, because it is the claim from the top of the interlude, kept every step of the way down: *the program's result is a value, of type `Int`.* Not observed on one run of one interpreter—*derived*, from a typing derivation, two step derivations, and a theorem, each an object a machine has checked.

This is the twin of the first interlude's figure-of-eight, drawn in the other ink. Read downward, nothing was computed and everything was *kept*: the judgement became a tree, the tree became data, the run became evidence, and the claim at the top became a type inhabited at the bottom. Each form is the one above it with less left to trust—from "the checker printed no error" to "here is the object, check it yourself." What remains is everything this page waved through. What exactly does the arrow mean, and why these rules? Chapter 10. Do preservation and progress hold for *every* program, not just this one? Chapter 11. What is the machine that checked `answer_is_value`, and why should its word count? Chapter 12. And when the whole edifice stands, who checks the checker? Chapter 13, which asks it with planted lies. One program went all the way down to the silicon; one theorem is about to go all the way down to the kernel. Part V begins.

Part V

Foundations

Chapter 10

Abstract Machines and Operational Semantics

The compiler is finished. Chapter 9 turned Lark into machine code, and from Chapter 6 onward the CEK machine has served quietly as the oracle—the reference answer every later stage was checked against. This chapter changes nothing about the implementation and everything about how to see it. It asks what the CEK machine *is*. The answer is that it is not an implementation trick but a *definition*: a precise, executable statement of what it means to run a Lark program. Seen that way, the interpreter was never merely one way to run the language; it was the language's meaning, written in a form that happens to compute.

To make the claim land, the chapter does three things. It places the CEK in a lineage, after the SECD machine that came first. It shows the sense in which such a machine *is* an operational semantics, derivable from the evaluation rules rather than invented apart from them. And it sets the whole functional story against a contrast—the Warren Abstract Machine and the logic programming it serves—to show that an abstract machine is always a paradigm's commitments made concrete. The moral, stated at the end, is that every implementation choice is a semantic claim.

A note on reading. These last theory chapters ask a little more than the implementation chapters did, so it helps to know what is load-bearing. The chapter's one essential idea is that an abstract machine *is* an operational semantics; it is carried by the SECD-to-CEK lineage (Sections 10.2, 10.3) and the derivation in Section 10.4. The Warren Abstract Machine and its miniature Prolog (Sections 10.5, 10.6) are a deliberate contrast, not a second syllabus: read them for how differently a machine can be shaped, not to master their internals.

10.1 What an Abstract Machine Is

There is a ladder of ways to say what a program means, and each rung trades abstraction for executability.[1]

Table 10.1: Levels at which a program's meaning can be stated

Form of semantics	Level of abstraction
Denotational	mathematical meaning
Structural operational	language-level steps
Abstract machine (SECD, CEK, WAM)	execution-level steps
Real hardware	physical execution

Denotational semantics maps each program to a mathematical object—a function, a value in a domain—and says nothing about steps. *Structural operational* semantics (SOS) defines meaning as a relation $e \to e'$: how one expression rewrites to the next. *Real hardware* is the bottom rung, where a step is a clock cycle. An *abstract machine* sits between the middle two. It is concrete enough to run—a state and a transition function, executable as written—but abstract enough to reason about, free of registers, caches, and calling conventions.

Formally an abstract machine is a *transition system*: a set of states and a *step relation* that takes each state to its successor. The CEK machine of Chapter 6 is exactly this—two kinds of state and a `step` function from one to the next—which is why a single `while` loop could run it. The value of the layer is that it makes evaluation *order* explicit and inspectable without descending into hardware: you can see, in the state, precisely what has been computed and what remains.

10.2 The SECD Machine

The first abstract machine for a functional language was Peter Landin's SECD machine (1964), built to evaluate expressions of the lambda calculus; Landin soon used it to define ISWIM (1966), the language from which the functional lineage descends. Its name is its state: four registers.

S — **Stack** holds intermediate values as expressions are evaluated.

E — **Environment** binds variables to values.

C — **Control** is the list of instructions still to execute.

D — **Dump** saves a whole S/E/C triple so it can be restored after a function call returns.

The Dump is the machine's defining idea: the call stack made into an explicit register. To call a function, the machine pushes the current Stack, Environment, and Control onto the Dump, installs the function's body as the new Control, and begins again; to return, it pops the Dump and restores what it saved. Evaluation is a sequence of small transitions over these four registers, each one mechanical and inspectable. The SECD machine showed, for the first time, that a higher-order functional language could be given a fully explicit, stepwise execution model—that "apply this function to this argument" could be reduced to register shuffling without losing its meaning.

10.3 The CEK Machine

Lark's machine is the CEK machine of Felleisen and Friedman (1986): *Control, Environment, Kontinuation.* It is the SECD machine's successor, and the two differences are exactly what a language with first-class closures needs.

First, the environment is not a global register but a *value.* A closure carries its own environment (Chapter 6), so there is no single E to save and restore; each function value already holds the bindings it needs. Second—and this is the heart of it—the Dump is replaced by an explicit *continuation*: a first-class data structure representing "what to do next." Where SECD saved opaque machine triples, the CEK machine carries a list of *frames*, each a small, named piece of deferred work.

The machine has two states, as Chapter 6 built them:

Listing 10.1: The CEK machine's two states (`lark/04/src/cek.py`)

```
@dataclass
# reduce expr
class Eval:    expr: TExpr;  env: dict;  kont: list[Frame]

@dataclass
# deliver a value
class Return:  val:  Value;  kont: list[Frame]
```

`Eval` reduces an expression in an environment; `Return` delivers a finished value to the first pending frame. The step relation moves between them, and the program's result is the value that meets an empty continuation. Two properties of this design were already cashed out in earlier chapters and are worth naming again as *semantic* facts. Because the continuation is explicit data, a tail call hands it onward unchanged and the machine reuses its state— proper tail calls, which Chapter 9 compiled to a jump, are a property of the *semantics*, not an optimization bolted on. And because the environment is a value threaded through the states, the affine ownership of Chapter 5 is clean: there is no hidden mutable store for a resource to escape into, only values passed from one state to the next.

The same machine exists twice in the repository. The Python version (`lark/04/src/cek.py`) is the readable definition; the C version (`lark/07/src/cek.c`) is the same transition system written to run on bare metal, the abstract machine made physical on the Pico 2/2W. That they agree—step for step, output for output—is not a coincidence but the point: the machine is a specification, and both are implementations of it.

10.4 Machines as Operational Semantics

Here is the chapter's central claim, made precise. The CEK machine is not an implementation that *approximates* some separate, truer semantics. It *is* the semantics, in executable form, and it can be derived from the evaluation rules by a systematic process [Ager et al., 2003].

Start with structural operational semantics [Plotkin, 1981] for a call-by-value language. Meaning is a relation $e \to e'$ defined by rules, written with the same horizontal bar as the typing rules of Chapter 5 and read the same way—premises above, conclusion below (Appendix C decodes the notation, and flags the one trap here: between *expressions*, the arrow is a step of evaluation, not the function type it builds between *types*). Two kinds appear. *Congruence* rules say where evaluation may happen next:

$$\frac{e_1 \to e_1'}{e_1\ e_2 \ \to\ e_1'\ e_2} \qquad \frac{e_2 \to e_2'}{v\ e_2 \ \to\ v\ e_2'}$$

the first evaluating the function, the second—only once the function is a value v—evaluating the argument. And a *reduction* rule says what a redex becomes:

$$(\lambda x.\, e)\ v \ \to\ e[x := v] \qquad (\beta\text{-reduction})$$

substitution of a value for a bound variable.[2] Conditionals and `let` add their own rules in the same shape—a congruence rule to evaluate the scrutinee, a reduction rule to choose the branch.[3]

The congruence rules hide a structure. "Evaluate e_1 in the position $[\cdot]\ e_2$" names an *evaluation context*—a term with a hole marking where the next step occurs. The systematic derivation of the CEK machine is the observation that these contexts can be *reified*: the hole's surroundings, instead of being rediscovered by re-traversing the term at each step, are stored as an explicit stack. That stack is the continuation, and each context frame is one congruence rule turned into data. The `ApplyFnF` frame of Chapter 6—"evaluating the function, with these arguments still to come"—*is* the context $[\cdot]\ e_2$. The machine and the semantics are the same definition seen from two distances: the rules say *which* steps are legal; the machine says how to find the next one without searching. This is why the interpreter could be the oracle. "The meaning of a Lark program" and "what the CEK machine computes" are not two things that happen to agree—they are one thing, and the compiler's correctness is the claim that its output computes it too.

10.5 The Warren Abstract Machine

An abstract machine encodes a paradigm's commitments, and the clearest way to see that is to change the paradigm. Logic programming does not evaluate expressions to values; it *searches* for proofs. Its canonical machine, David Warren's WAM (1983), is built from utterly different parts than the CEK, because it answers a different question.

Two mechanisms define it. *Unification* replaces evaluation: instead of reducing a redex, the machine makes two terms equal by binding their variables, or fails. *Backtracking* replaces sequential control: where the CEK has a continuation for what to do *next*, the WAM has *choice points* for what to try *instead.* A choice point records the machine's state and an alternative to attempt; a *trail* records the variable bindings made since, so they can be undone when a search path fails and the machine returns to the last choice point. The WAM's instructions are not arithmetic and jumps but unification steps and choice-point management. The machine is the shape of the paradigm: relations rather than functions, search rather than reduction, success-or-failure rather than a returned value.

10.6 A Miniature Prolog

Beneath the WAM is a semantics as definite as the CEK's: *SLD-resolution* over Horn clauses. A program is facts and rules; a query is a goal; computation is the systematic attempt to satisfy the goal by unifying it against clause heads and recursively solving the bodies. The companion code (`ch10/06_prolog/`) implements this directly.

Listing 10.2: Facts, a rule, and a query in the miniature Prolog (`ch10/06_prolog/`)

```
parent(john, bob).
parent(bob, ann).
grandparent(X, Y) :- parent(X, Z), parent(Z, Y).

?- grandparent(john, W).        % W = ann
```

To solve `grandparent(john, W)`, the interpreter unifies the goal with the rule's head—binding `X = john`, `Y = W`—and is left with the body `parent(john, Z), parent(Z, Y)`. It solves `parent(john, Z)` by unifying against the first fact (`Z = bob`), then `parent(bob, W)` against the second (`W = ann`). The result is a *search*, and its shape is a tree: each goal branches over the clauses whose head might match, and the interpreter walks the tree *depth-first*, backtracking—undoing bindings—whenever a branch fails.

That depth-first walk is a *design commitment*, not a detail. Depth-first search is incomplete: a program can descend an infinite branch and never reach a solution that breadth-first search would have found. Prolog accepts this in exchange for a predictable, stack-shaped execution that the WAM implements efficiently—and it gives the programmer a lever over the search, the *cut* (`!`), which discards choice points and prunes the tree. The companion interpreter implements cut precisely because backtracking is the language's central mechanism, and controlling it is half of writing Prolog. Where Lark's affine discipline is a commitment about *resources*, Prolog's depth-first search is a commitment about *time*: both are paradigm choices visible in the machine.

10.7 What Abstract Machines Teach

Set the two machines side by side and the lesson is plain. The CEK machine has a continuation because Lark evaluates expressions in order; the WAM has choice points because Prolog searches for proofs. Neither structure is arbitrary, and neither is "just" an implementation. Each is a *semantic claim* in machine form—a precise answer to "what does it mean to run a program in this language?"—and the implementation is that claim carried out.

This is the deepest sense in which the book's title runs in both directions. A choice at the top—call-by-value rather than call-by-name, reduction rather than search, affine resources rather than a garbage-collected heap—propagates all the way down to the structure of the machine that runs it, and the machine, in turn, is a statement about the meaning at the top. Choosing the CEK over the SECD is a claim about how closures and continuations relate; choosing depth-first resolution is a claim about how a logic program spends its time; choosing call-by-value fixes which of the SOS rules fire and when. The abstract machine is the one place where "what a program means" and "how it runs" are written as the same sentence.

For Lark, that sentence is the CEK machine. It defined the language in Chapter 6, judged the compiler from Chapter 7 onward, and stands here revealed as what it always was: the operational semantics of the language, executable. What remains is to prove that the claim holds—that the machine never gets stuck on a well-typed program, and that the meaning it defines is one the type system guarantees. That proof is the last chapter.

10.8 Exercises

1. Table 10.1 lists four levels at which meaning can be stated. (a) For the Lark expression `let x = 2 + 3 in x * x`, say what the meaning is at each level—what a denotational account would assign, what an sos derivation would do, what the CEK machine would do, and what the hardware of Chapter 9 would do. (b) Which two levels are "the same definition seen from two distances," and why?

2. The SECD machine saves a whole S/E/C triple on the Dump at every call; the CEK machine pushes a frame. (a) For a *tail* call, what does each machine do, and why does only the CEK machine reuse its state without growing? (b) Relate your answer to the jump that Chapter 9 emitted for `sum_to`.

3. Section 10.4 claims the `ApplyFnF` frame *is* the evaluation context $[\cdot]\ e_2$. (a) Write the small-step sos derivation of `(f x) + 1` far enough to see the context $[\cdot]\ x$ appear. (b) Trace the CEK machine on the same expression and identify the frame that reifies that context. (c) State, in one sentence, what it means to say the machine and the semantics are "the same definition."

4. In the miniature Prolog, the query `grandparent(john, W)` succeeds with `W = ann`. (a) Draw the search tree, marking each unification and each backtrack. (b) Add a fact `parent(john, carol).` and a second grandchild; show how depth-first search orders the solutions. (c) Where would a `cut` go to commit to the first grandparent found, and which choice points would it discard?

5. Section 10.7 claims every implementation choice is a semantic claim. (a) Call-by-name (evaluate the argument only when used) changes one of the two congruence rules of Section 10.4; which, and how? (b) Give a Lark-like expression whose result or termination would differ under call-by-name, and explain what observable difference the changed rule produces. (c) Why is Lark's choice of call-by-value visible in the CEK machine's `ApplyArgF` frame?

The CEK machine, which ran Lark from the start and judged every compiler stage that followed, turns out to have been the language's meaning all along—an operational semantics that happens to compute. Beside it, the Warren machine showed that a different paradigm carries its commitments in a different machine, and that an abstract machine is always a semantics made executable. What has not yet been done is to prove the central claim on which the whole edifice rests: that a well-typed Lark program cannot go wrong—cannot reach a state the machine has no rule for. Chapter 11 makes the type system and the machine confront each other formally, and shows, in machine-checked detail, that the types were telling the truth.

Notes

[1]The systematic textbook treatment of these levels—operational semantics in both its big-step (*natural*) and small-step (*structural*) forms, denotational semantics, and the axiomatic semantics this book does not pursue—is Nielson and Nielson's *Semantics with Applications* [Nielson and Nielson, 2007]. This chapter samples the operational rungs and the abstract machine between them; that book develops the whole ladder.

[2]The λ-calculus that these rules tame is older and wilder than any machine. In its pure form, β-reduction may fire at any redex in any order; the Church–Rosser theorem guarantees that if a normal form exists it is unique, however one reaches it. Barendregt's *The Lambda Calculus: Its Syntax and Semantics* [Barendregt, 1984] is the standard reference for that theory. A machine must choose an order, and the congruence rules above are that choice made concrete: call-by-value, leftmost redex first, the argument reduced only once the function is a value.

[3]These are exactly the constructors of the step relation in Lark's machine-checked semantics: congruence rules for application, `if`, and `let`, and reduction rules for β-redexes, the two `if` branches, and `let`-binding. The mechanisation, and the proof that well-typed programs do not get stuck, is the subject of Chapter 11.

Chapter 11

Correctness

Chapter 10 ended on a debt. The CEK machine, it argued, is Lark's operational semantics—the definition of what a program means—and the whole edifice rests on a claim that was stated but not shown: that a well-typed Lark program cannot get stuck, cannot reach a state for which the machine has no rule. This chapter pays the debt. It shows, in machine-checked detail, that the types were telling the truth.

But "correct" is a word that hides at least three different claims, and the chapter separates them before arguing any one. Then it takes them in turn: the contract a single program promises (Hoare logic), the soundness of the type discipline itself (progress and preservation, mechanically verified), the specification that says what Lark *is* before anyone argues it behaves, the testing that guards the parts no proof reaches, and finally the affine types that let the checker enforce a kind of correctness most languages leave to runtime or to luck. It is the last chapter, and it closes the book's circle: from the fetch-decode-execute loop of Chapter 1, a language was built up to a type system and a semantics, and here that semantics is proved sound.

11.1 What "Correct" Means

There is no single property called correctness. There are at least three, and confusing them is the source of much wasted argument.

The program meets its contract. A particular program does what its author intended—sorts the list, returns the right answer. This is correctness *relative to a specification of that program*, and it is what most people mean by "a correct program." It says nothing about the language; a perfectly type-sound language is full of programs that compute the wrong thing correctly.

The type discipline is sound. The language's own promise—that a well-typed program will not commit a type error at runtime, will not add an integer to a function or branch on a string—actually holds. This is a property of the *language*, not of any one program, and it is the one this chapter proves. It does not say programs are bug-free; it says a whole class of bugs has been ruled out by construction.

The implementation matches the language. The compiler in front of you actually implements the language the type system describes—the lowering, the register allocator, the code generator faithfully preserve meaning. This is a property of the *implementation*, and no type-soundness proof touches it: a sound language can have a buggy compiler. It is guarded by testing.

These are independent. The rest of the chapter takes one after another, and the reader should keep them apart: a contract is about a program, soundness is about a language, and faithful implementation is about a compiler.

11.2 Hoare Logic

The oldest formal account of the first kind of correctness is Hoare logic (1969). Its unit is the *triple*

$$\{P\}\, c\, \{Q\}$$

read: if the precondition P holds before the command c runs, then the postcondition Q holds after. A specification is a pre/post pair; verifying the program is showing the triple is valid. The rules compose over the structure of the program—a rule for sequencing, one for conditionals, one (with a loop *invariant*) for iteration—so that a proof of the whole is assembled from proofs of the parts, exactly as a type derivation is.

Listing 11.1: A Hoare triple as an executable contract

```
{ x >= 0 }
  y := x;   z := 0;
  while y > 0 do   z := z + 1;   y := y - 1   end
{ z == x }
```

The companion code (`ch11/02_hoare/`) annotates programs with preconditions, postconditions, and loop invariants, and generates the *verification conditions*—the logical obligations that, if true, make the triple valid. That generator is the heart of a program verifier: it reduces "does this program meet its contract?" to "are these logical formulas true?"—which a theorem prover, or a careful reader, can then discharge.

Hoare logic was designed for imperative programs full of mutable state, where the hard part is tracking how an assignment changes what is true. Lark has no mutable state, which makes the logic almost trivial—a pure function's postcondition is just a statement about its return value—but removes none of the point. Specifying what a program should do, in a language precise enough to check, is the discipline; the absence of mutation only makes it easier. Contracts are about *programs.* The next sections are about the *language.*

11.3 Type Safety: Progress and Preservation

The slogan is Robin Milner's: *well-typed programs do not go wrong.* The content behind the slogan is two theorems, due in their modern form to Wright and Felleisen, about the relationship between a type system and an operational semantics.

Preservation (also called subject reduction): if an expression has type τ and it takes a step, the result still has type τ. Evaluation never changes a term's type.

$$\text{if } e : \tau \text{ and } e \to e', \text{ then } e' : \tau.$$

Progress: a well-typed, closed expression is not stuck—it is either already a value, or it can take a step.

$$\text{if } e : \tau \text{ and } e \text{ is closed, then } e \text{ is a value or } e \to e'.$$

Together they give safety by induction. A well-typed program starts well-typed; preservation keeps it well-typed through every step; progress guarantees that at each step it is either finished or able to continue. It can therefore never arrive at a non-value with no rule to apply—a *stuck* state, which is exactly what "going wrong" means. The program runs to a value of its type, or runs forever; it never reaches nonsense. If the two displays above read as a blur, notice that each is a single sentence relating the book's two judgements—typing ($e : \tau$, Chapter 5) and stepping ($e \to e'$, Chapter 10)—and that noticing this is most of the work. Appendix C builds its method for reading formal statements on precisely this example, and this chapter, which leans on both judgements at once from here on, is where that appendix earns its keep.

Lark's proof, and a trick that makes preservation disappear. Lark's type safety is not asserted; it is machine-checked, in a proof (`lark/formal/proof/lark/`) verified by a small dependent-type-theory kernel. The proof uses an *intrinsic* encoding, and the encoding is worth seeing, because it turns one of the two theorems into something you cannot even state wrongly.

In the encoding, a well-typed term is not an expression that happens to satisfy the typing rules—it *is* a typing derivation. The datatype of expressions is indexed by a context and a type:

Listing 11.2: Intrinsically-typed terms (simplified from `lark-typing.lcore`)

```
data Expr : Ctx -> Ty -> Type where
  EApp : Expr g (TFn a b) -> Expr g a -> Expr g b
  ELam : Expr (ext a g) b -> Expr g (TFn a b)
  EIf  : Expr g TBool -> Expr g t -> Expr g t -> Expr g t
  ...
```

Read `EApp`: an application is well-typed *only* when the function has type `TFn a b` and the argument has type `a`, and then the result has type `b`. There is no way to build an ill-typed application—the constructor will not accept the arguments. The type checker of Chapter 5 has become the constructors of a datatype; an `Expr g t` is a proof that some term has type `t` in context `g`.

Now the reduction relation:

Listing 11.3: The step relation preserves type *by its type* (`lark-step.lcore`)

```
Step : Expr empty t -> Expr empty t -> Type
```

A step relates a closed term—the `empty` context, a whole program—to another term *of the same type t*. Preservation is therefore not a theorem to be proved—it is built into the type of `Step`. One cannot even write down a reduction rule that changes the type, because the constructor would not typecheck. The eight rules of the relation—β-reduction, the two `if` branches, `let`-binding, and the four congruences—are exactly the small-step semantics of Chapter 10, and each corresponds, line for line, to a case of the CEK machine in `cek.py`. Preservation, the harder of the two classical theorems, costs nothing here: the price was paid once, in choosing an encoding where ill-typed intermediate states are unrepresentable.[1]

What remains is progress, in the form the proof actually establishes: *evaluation soundness.* Big-step evaluation is defined as a sequence of steps ending in a value, and the theorem is that it always does end in one:

Listing 11.4: Evaluation soundness (`lark-preservation.lcore`)

```
eval_produces_val : Eval t e v -> IsVal t v
```

If a closed, well-typed term `e` evaluates to `v`, then `v` is a value of type `t`. A well-typed Lark program does not get stuck. This is the claim Chapter 10 made and deferred, now discharged: the CEK machine, on a well-typed program, always either delivers a value or takes another step. The proof is checked by `lcore`, a Martin-Löf type-theory kernel of some eight thousand lines of C—the entire trusted base—and it passes with no errors.[2]

The scope, stated plainly. It would be easy to let "well-typed programs do not go wrong" stand as an unqualified slogan, and the qualification belongs in the body, not the fine print. Lark *as fully specified* is not yet sound, and the reason is a deliberate language-design choice rather than a flaw in the compiler. Trait dispatch is dynamic (Section 5.8): a bound such as `[Describe a]` is parsed but not enforced, and a well-typed call to a trait method on a type with no `impl` is *accepted by the checker* and then gets stuck at run time with `no impl of ...`. By the three meanings of Section 11.1 this is a gap in *language soundness*—the language admits a well-typed program that goes wrong—not a bug in the *implementation*; the compiler faithfully runs the dynamic dispatch the language asks for. The proven-sound fragment is the functional core, and it excludes exactly the two features whose checking is incomplete: trait dispatch and the affine discipline. This is not a confession to be buried. A book whose thesis is that types rule out whole classes of failure owes the reader a precise statement of where that guarantee currently stops—and the honest border makes the guarantee on the core mean more, not less.

11.4 Formal Specification

A proof is only as meaningful as the specification it proves something about. To say "well-typed programs do not go wrong" is empty until "well-typed" and "go wrong" are pinned down with no room for interpretation. That pinning-down is *formal specification*, and it is logically prior to everything in this chapter: before you can argue an implementation is correct, you must state, in mathematics, what it is supposed to do.

Lark's specification (`lark-formal.tex`) does this completely. It gives the types and contexts; the typing rules as inference rules; the substitution that β-reduction performs; the small-step and big-step semantics; and, beyond the verified core, the affine discipline, the trait system, the module system, and the surface grammar. Crucially, every formal construct is tied by an explicit *correspondence table* to the line of Lark source it describes—`TFn` to `ty.py`'s function type, `ELam` to `infer.py`'s lambda case, `StepBeta` to `cek.py`'s application step. The specification is not a separate idealization hovering above the code; it is a precise account *of this implementation*, with the map between them written down. That map is what makes the proof about Lark, and not about some prettier language that merely resembles it.

11.5 Testing a Compiler

The proof secures the type system. It does not secure the compiler. The lowerer, the register allocator, and the code generator of Chapters 7–9 are thousands of lines that no part of the mechanised proof touches, and a sound language with a miscompiling back end is no comfort at all. What guards that territory is testing—and the three kinds Lark uses are complementary, each catching what the others miss.

Differential testing runs every program through all three back ends—the CEK interpreter, the TAC virtual machine, and the RV32 machine—and demands byte-identical output (`lark/06/tests/diff_test.py`). It is the oracle of Chapter 8: because the interpreter *defines* the meaning, any back end that disagrees with it has a bug, and the harness names which one. Differential testing finds the place where two implementations of the same specification diverge.

Property-based testing generates programs and checks that stated *invariants* hold over all of them (`lark/06/tests/gen.py`, using Hypothesis): that an affine resource used twice is always rejected, that type-checking is idempotent, that a `Copy` value may be used freely. Where differential testing compares implementations, property testing checks a single implementation against a property the author believes—on hundreds of inputs the author never thought to write by hand.

Fuzzing feeds malformed and random input and checks only that the compiler fails gracefully rather than crashing. It finds robustness bugs in the parts that face untrusted text—the lexer and parser—where the question is not "is the answer right?" but "does the program survive the question?"

Proof and testing are not rivals; they divide the labour. Proof gives *certainty* about a small, formal core. Testing gives *confidence* about the large, real implementation that surrounds it. A serious language wants both, and knows which it is relying on where. This section describes the machinery as it stands here; Chapter 13 escalates all three kinds—whole well-typed programs manufactured by the thousand, the fuzzers themselves validated with planted bugs—and reports, bug by bug, what the escalation found.

11.6 Trusting Code You Did Not Write

The machinery of the last two sections answers a question the Introduction raised and the rest of the book has been quietly preparing: how do you trust a compiler pass you did not write by hand? The question is no longer hypothetical. A great deal of code—including code in compilers, and including parts of Lark's own development—is now drafted by language models, and a generated pass arrives with no author to vouch for it and no guarantee that its plausible-looking shape does what it claims.

The discipline that answers the question is exactly the discipline already built, and it does not change with the source of the code. A pass, however written, is an *assertion*: "this transformation preserves meaning." Three things in this chapter turn that assertion into something accepted or rejected on evidence rather than trust. Differential testing (§11.5) runs the suspect pass against the interpreter that *defines* the meaning and reports the first program on which they disagree. Property-based testing checks that the language's stated invariants—affine resources used once, `Copy` values used freely—survive the pass on inputs no author chose. And the type-safety theorem (§11.3) bounds in advance what any well-typed transformation is permitted to do. None of these asks who, or what, wrote the code; they interrogate the code itself.

This is the modern form of an old point. The reason to understand a compiler completely is not that you will type every line of it—you may not—but that *understanding is the specification against which any line, yours or a machine's, is judged.* A generator can produce the pass; it cannot produce the oracle that tells you the pass is correct, because that oracle is the meaning of the language, and the meaning is the thing this whole book has been building. The ability to check is what does not transfer to the machine, and it is precisely what these chapters teach.

11.7 Affine Types: Correctness the Checker Enforces

Type safety rules out a fixed class of errors—the type confusions. But a type system can be made to enforce far more, and Lark's affine types are the book's glimpse of how far. Recall from Chapter 5 that an affine value may be used at most once, and that `IO` is affine. The consequence is that a property which in most languages is a runtime bug or a hand-maintained discipline—do not write to a closed handle, do not use a freed resource, do not reorder effects—becomes, in Lark, a *compile-time guarantee.* The checker proves it, for every program, before the program runs.

This is correctness of a different order than type safety. Type safety says the program will not commit a category error; affine typing says a *resource* will not be misused, and it says so statically, by the same mechanism. It is a small step into a large country. The type system that can enforce "used at most once" is on the same road as the type system that can enforce "this list is non-empty," "this index is in bounds," "this function returns a sorted permutation of its input."

That road leads to *dependent types*, where the type checker and the proof checker become the same program—the `lcore` kernel that verified this chapter's proof is exactly such a checker. Lark stops short of that rung, at Hindley-Milner with affine ownership and traits. Chapter 12 opens that kernel up and walks what lies beyond, through the systems—Idris, Agda, Lean—that live there. Affine types are the first place in this book where the type system stops merely classifying values and starts *proving things*, and that is the note the language ends on: a checker that does not just accept programs, but vouches for them. A promise this strong deserves hostility, and Chapter 13 supplies it: the attack finds the one program this section's rule does not see, and the discipline that comes back is both repaired and, at last, machine-checked.

11.8 Exercises

1. Section 11.1 distinguishes three meanings of "correct." For each of the following defects, say which of the three notions it violates, and which it leaves intact: (a) a sorting function that returns its input unchanged; (b) a register allocator that assigns two interfering temporaries the same register; (c) a language in which `1 + true` type-checks and crashes at runtime.

2. State the preservation and progress theorems precisely (Section 11.3). (a) Give a term in an untyped language that is *stuck*—a non-value with no applicable rule—and explain which theorem rules it out in a typed language. (b) Lark's encoding makes preservation "disappear." Explain in what sense it is still true, and what work the disappearance shifts onto the definition of `Expr`.

3. The `Step` relation has type `Expr g t -> Expr g t -> Type` (Section 11.3). (a) Write, in this style, the type signature a reduction relation would need if it were allowed to *change* a term's type, and explain why no constructor of the eight-rule relation could inhabit it. (b) Relate this to the differential-testing oracle: what does preservation guarantee that testing can only sample?

4. Section 11.5 assigns each testing method a distinct job. (a) Construct a compiler bug that differential testing would catch but property testing would not, and one for which the reverse holds. (b) Explain why neither could replace the type-safety proof, and why the proof could not replace either.

5. Section 11.7 claims affine typing enforces resource correctness statically. (a) Write a Lark program that misuses the `IO` token and identify the exact rule that rejects it. (b) Describe a property *stronger* than "used at most

once"—for example, "used exactly once"—and say what would change in the type system to enforce it. (c) Why is "used exactly once" (linear) a heavier burden on the programmer than "at most once" (affine), and why did Lark choose the lighter one?

The debt is paid. A well-typed Lark program cannot get stuck—not by assertion, but by a proof a machine has checked, about the very semantics that ran every example in this book. The type system was telling the truth. With that, the construction is complete: a language carried from the fetch-decode-execute loop of a real processor, up through a scanner and a parser, a type checker and an interpreter, an intermediate form and a code generator that reaches genuine silicon, and back down through the abstract machine that defines its meaning to the proof that the meaning is sound. What is left is to understand the instrument that checked this very proof—a small type checker reached for to vouch for the larger one, and left, in a book that explains everything twice, unexplained. The next chapter opens it: the idea that a type is a proposition and a program its proof, made exact, and Lark's own soundness argument read back as a program in a language rich enough to state it. Chapter 12 takes it up.

Notes

[1]Splitting type soundness into *progress* (a well-typed term is a value or can step) and *preservation* (a step preserves the type), proved syntactically over a small-step reduction relation, is the method of Wright and Felleisen [Wright and Felleisen, 1994]—now the standard recipe for mechanised soundness, and the shape of the proof here, even though the encoding makes preservation hold by construction.

[2]The honest scope of the mechanised proof is the *functional core*: the simply-typed lambda calculus with Lark's base types, functions, `let`, and `if`. The affine discipline, traits, and the module system are specified formally (Section 11.4) but their soundness is argued on paper rather than fully machine-checked. This is the usual state of affairs even for industrial languages: a verified core, a specified periphery, and honest signposting of where the one becomes the other. Extending the mechanisation outward is exactly the kind of work the `proof/` kernel exists to support.

Chapter 12

Types as Proofs

Chapter 11 proved that a well-typed Lark program cannot get stuck. But it proved it with a tool it never explained. The soundness argument was checked by `lcore`—"a Martin-Löf type-theory kernel of some eight thousand lines of C," the chapter said, and moved on. That is a strange omission in a book whose method has been to explain everything twice: once as theory and once as the code that implements it. The book built a lexer and explained lexers, built a parser and explained parsing, built a type checker and explained type systems—and then, at the very end, it reached for a second, smaller type checker to vouch for the first, and left it a black box.

This chapter opens the box. It is not a chapter about going beyond Lark; it is a chapter about the instrument the book already used. The `.lcore` files in `lark/formal/proof/` are the proof; `lcore` is the program that checked it; and both rest on a single idea, promised as far back as Chapter 5 and used without ceremony in Chapter 11: that a type is a proposition and a program is its proof. Make that idea exact and the proof checker stops being mysterious—it is just a type checker, of the kind built in Chapter 5, for a type system rich enough that the propositions worth proving fit inside it. The chapter then reads Lark's own soundness proof as what it is—a program in such a language—and closes by asking how far up this road a working language should travel, and where it should stop.

A note on reading. This is the most abstract chapter in the book and the one with the most optional depth, so it is worth saying who it is for. The argument—a type is a proposition, a program is its proof, and Lark's soundness proof is a program in a language rich enough to say so—stands on its own. The machinery that makes it exact (Martin-Löf's dependent types, the `indrec` eliminator, normalisation by evaluation, de Bruijn indices) is shown because the proof is real and genuinely uses it, but a reader who follows the argument and skims the mechanics will still arrive at the chapter's point. It is written for the reader who wants to know what the instrument of Chapter 11 was; it does not ask that reader to become a type theorist. It does ask fluency in the judgement-and-rule notation, and a reader whose grip on it is loose should keep Appendix C open beside this chapter: its one-page symbol table covers everything used here, Π and Σ included, and its four-move reading method is built for displays as dense as this chapter's.

12.1 Curry–Howard Made Exact

Chapter 5 introduced the slogan and deferred the substance: the Curry–Howard correspondence, it said, makes the connection between types and propositions exact. Here is the exactness.

The observation, made independently by Haskell Curry and William Howard, is that two things mathematicians had treated as unrelated are in fact the same thing under two names. On one side, the rules of constructive logic: how to prove an implication, a conjunction, a disjunction. On the other, the rules of a typed lambda calculus: how to give a type to a function, a pair, a tagged union. Line them up and they coincide exactly—not by analogy, but rule for rule.[1]

Logic	**Type theory**	**In a program**
proposition	type	a type
proof of P	term of type P	a value
$A \Rightarrow B$	$A \to B$	function type
proof of $A \Rightarrow B$	a function	a function
modus ponens	application	a function call
$A \wedge B$	$A \times B$	a pair / tuple
$A \vee B$	$A + B$	a tagged union
$\top$ (true)	unit type	()
$\bot$ (false)	empty type	no value exists
$\forall x.\, P(x)$	$\Pi(x{:}A).\, P(x)$	dependent function
$\exists x.\, P(x)$	$\Sigma(x{:}A).\, P(x)$	dependent pair

Table 12.1: The Curry–Howard correspondence, rule for rule.

Read the table as a dictionary. To prove $A \Rightarrow B$ is to give a method that turns any proof of A into a proof of B—which is exactly a function from type A to type B. To prove $A \wedge B$ you must exhibit both a proof of A and a proof of B—a pair. To prove $A \vee B$ you must exhibit one or the other, tagged with which—a value of a sum type, the ADTs of Chapter 5. The proposition with no proof, falsehood, is

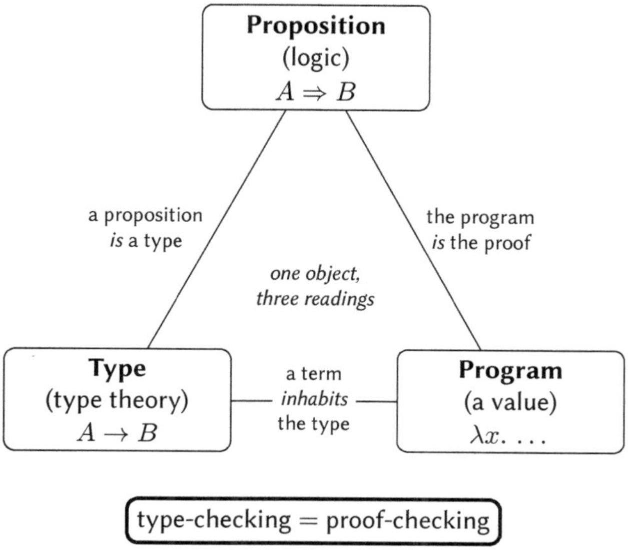

Figure 12.1: The Curry–Howard correspondence as one object seen three ways. A proposition, the type whose values are its proofs, and a program of that type are not three analogous things but the same thing under three vocabularies. The corollary that drives the chapter sits at the bottom: because a program of type P *is* a proof of P, confirming a program has its type *is* confirming a proof establishes its proposition.

the type with no value: the empty type. And *modus ponens*—from $A \Rightarrow B$ and A, conclude B—is function application, the `EApp` of every chapter since the parser.

The consequence is the one that matters for this book. If a type is a proposition and a program of that type is a proof, then *type-checking is proof-checking*. The work the type checker of Chapter 5 does—read a term, confirm it has the claimed type—is, viewed through the dictionary, exactly the work a proof checker does: read a proof, confirm it establishes the claimed proposition. They are not similar activities. They are one activity, described in two vocabularies (Figure 12.1). Lark's `infer.py` and the `lcore` kernel that checked Chapter 11's proof are the same kind of program; they differ only in how expressive a logic their types can state.

12.2 What Dependent Types Add

The correspondence as stated already covers the propositional logic of $\wedge$, $\vee$, $\Rightarrow$. The interesting propositions, though, quantify: *for all* lists, reversing twice is the identity; *there exists* an index at which the value occurs. The last two rows of Table 12.1 are the new machinery the quantifiers demand, and they are what a Hindley–Milner system like Lark's does not have.

A dependent type is a type that mentions a *value*. In Lark's type system, `Int` and `Int -> Bool` are types and `3` and `true` are values, and the two worlds never mix: no type contains a number, no value names a type. Dependent type theory erases that wall. It allows a type like `Vec n`—the type of vectors of *exactly n elements*, where n is an ordinary runtime number appearing inside the type. It allows a function whose *result type depends on its argument's value*: give it n, get back `Vec n`; give it a proof that `x > 0`, get back a value whose type records that fact.

Two type formers generalise the function and pair of the previous section to span the wall:

- The *dependent function* $\Pi(x{:}A).\,B(x)$ generalises $A \to B$: the return type B may now mention the argument x. When B ignores x it collapses to the ordinary $A \to B$. Read as logic, it is $\forall x.\,B(x)$: a proof is a method producing, for every x, a proof of $B(x)$.
- The *dependent pair* $\Sigma(x{:}A).\,B(x)$ generalises $A \times B$: the second component's type may mention the first. Read as logic, it is $\exists x.\,B(x)$: a proof is a witness x together with a proof of $B(x)$.

With these, a type can state a proposition about specific values, and so a function signature can carry a genuine specification. A type checker for such a system was used twice in Chapter 11 without comment: the soundness proof's central object, the relation `Step`, is exactly a Π-type over the type being preserved, and the progress predicate `NotStuck` is a sum of the two outcomes whose "can take a step" case is a Σ-type—a witness e' paired with a proof that the term steps to it. The book has been writing dependent types since the last chapter; it simply did not name them.

12.3 The Proof Kernel `lcore`

`lcore` is the program that turns the previous two sections into something a machine can check. It is a checker for Martin-Löf type theory [Martin-Löf, 1984]—intuitionistic type theory with Π, Σ, inductive datatypes, a universe hierarchy, and an equality type—written in roughly eight thousand three hundred lines of

C, in lark/formal/proof/code/core/. That figure is the whole trusted base. If those eight thousand lines are correct, every proof they accept is correct; no other component of the Lark project needs to be trusted for the soundness result to hold. Keeping the kernel small is therefore not tidiness but the entire strategy: it is the surface a careful reader must audit, and nothing else is.

A user of lcore works with three kinds of declaration. The first introduces an inductive datatype with its constructors—the same mechanism as Lark's type declarations, but the result type may be an indexed family:

Listing 12.1: Datatypes in lcore: an ordinary type and an indexed family (schematic)

```
data Ty : Type where
  TInt : Ty
  TFn  : Ty -> Ty -> Ty

-- an indexed family:
-- indexed by a context and a type
data Expr : Ctx -> Ty -> Type where ...
```

The second is the dependent function, written with Π or as a lambda, exactly the Π-type of the previous section. The third, and the one without a counterpart in Lark, is the *eliminator*. To use a value of an inductive type—to compute with it, or to prove something about it—one applies indrec, the induction-recursion principle for that type. indrec takes a *motive* (what you are trying to produce, as a function of the value) and one case per constructor, and it is simultaneously the way to write a recursive function and the way to write a proof by induction. Under Curry–Howard those are the same act: structural recursion on a term and structural induction on a derivation are one operation.

The conversion check at the kernel's heart is *normalisation by evaluation* [Berger and Schwichtenberg, 1991]. To decide whether two types are equal—whether Vec (2 + 2) and Vec 4 are the same type, so that a value of one may be used where the other is expected—the kernel evaluates both to a normal form and compares. Type-checking a dependent program therefore *runs* parts of it at check time; the boundary between checking and execution, sharp in every earlier chapter, softens here. This is why Chapter 11's proof could write sub_ground … inside a type and have the kernel confirm the step's target: lcore normalised the substitution during checking and saw that it produced exactly the expected term.

The intrinsic encoding of Chapter 11 can now be named for what it is. data Expr : Ctx -> Ty -> Type is a dependently typed datatype: a family of types indexed by a context and a type, so that Expr g t is *the type of proofs that some term has type* t *in context* g. Building a term of that type is discharging a typing derivation. The trick that made preservation vanish was not a trick at all—it was ordinary dependent-type programming, and `lcore` is the language it was written in.

12.4 Lark's Soundness Proof, Read

The proof lives in four files, each a layer on the one before: `lark-typing.lcore` (the intrinsic syntax), `lark-subst.lcore` (substitution), `lark-step.lcore` (reduction), and `lark-preservation.lcore` (the theorem). Read in order, they retrace the whole back half of this book in the language of Section 12.3.

Syntax as derivations. The context is a de Bruijn list—a binding is identified by how many enclosing binders sit between its use and its introduction, not by a name. Variable references are themselves a dependent family:

Listing 12.2: Variables as typed de Bruijn indices (simplified from `lark-typing.lcore`)

```
data Var  : Ctx -> Ty -> Type where
  here   : Var (ext t g) t
  there  : Var g t -> Var (ext s g) t
```

`here` names the innermost binding—the most recent `let` or parameter; `there` steps one binder outward, exactly the environment-lookup walk of `infer.py` and the CEK machine of Chapter 6. A `Var g t` cannot point outside its context: the type forbids it. On top of `Var` sits the intrinsic `Expr` of Chapter 11, every constructor of which encodes one of `infer.py`'s typing rules.

Substitution and a primitive the kernel needs. β-reduction substitutes an argument for a parameter, and substitution under the intrinsic encoding must produce a *well-typed* result—it cannot merely rewrite syntax, it must rewrite a derivation into another derivation of the same type. Most cases go through by recursion. The lambda case does not, and the reason is instructive. Substituting under a binder requires lifting every environment entry into a context with one more binding—*weakening*:

Listing 12.3: Weakening, a kernel primitive (`lark-subst.lcore`)

```
weaken : Expr g t -> Expr (ext a g) t
```

Written as an ordinary recursion inside the kernel, `weaken`'s lambda case needs the two contexts `ext a (ext b g)` and `ext b (ext a g)` to be *the same type*. They are equal as propositions but not by the kernel's definitional computation, and so the recursion will not typecheck. The proof's resolution is honest about the seam: `weaken` is provided as a kernel primitive (`TM_WEAKEN` in `eval.c`), implemented by shifting de Bruijn indices directly on the underlying value with a cutoff, so the result has the right type without appeal to any commutativity equation. It is the one place where the proof reaches below the type theory into the C that implements it—and the specification (`lark-formal.tex`) documents exactly why. Read that arrangement with suspicion, because the book will: an exercise below asks whether trusting the primitive is acceptable, and Chapter 13 answers by discharging it—a checked proof replaces the C, and the replacement catches the primitive in an error.[2]

Reduction that cannot change a type. The step relation was shown in Chapter 11; the point to add here is the shape of its type.

Listing 12.4: The step relation, a Π-type over the preserved type (`lark-step.lcore`)

```
data Step : (t : Ty) -> Expr empty t -> Expr empty t -> Type
  where ...   -- 8 constructors
```

`Step` is a Π-type quantifying over the type `t`, and both terms it relates are `Expr empty t`—closed, and of the *same* `t`. Preservation is the proposition $\forall t.\, \forall e\, e'.\, e \to e' \Rightarrow (e : t \Rightarrow e' : t)$, and that proposition is precisely the type written above. Its proof is the eight constructors: each one, by being accepted by `lcore`, is a checked proof of one reduction rule's type-preservation. There is no separate theorem because there is nothing left to prove—the dependent type stated the proposition, and inhabiting it proved it.

The theorem, as a recursion. What does require a genuine inductive proof is evaluation soundness: if a closed term evaluates to a value, the result really is a value of the right type.

Listing 12.5: Evaluation soundness, proved by induction (`lark-preservation.lcore`)

```
eval_produces_val : Eval t e v -> IsVal t v
eval_produces_val = indrec Eval
   (\t e v _. IsVal t v)      -- motive: the proposition
   (\t v iv. iv)              -- EvalDone: value, return it
   (\t e e' v s ev ih. ih)  -- EvalStep: pass the IH through
```

This is the whole proof, and it is a three-line recursion. The motive states the proposition—*for any evaluation, the result is a value.* The `EvalDone` case is handed the witness directly. The `EvalStep` case takes a step and an evaluation of the reduct, and passes through the induction hypothesis. Curry–Howard at work: a proof by induction on the structure of an evaluation *is* a recursive function over the `Eval` datatype, and `lcore` checks it by the same machinery it would use to check any recursive program. Run the four files through the kernel—once Chapter 13 has discharged the weakening primitive, its lemma loads between the first two—and it reports every definition checked and no errors. That run is what Chapter 11 stood on. The companion `ch12/bridge/` makes the correspondence concrete from the other end: it lifts individual Lark programs—`fn f(x:Bool):Bool = x` and its kin—to their `lcore` terms and runs the kernel, which assigns each its type and rejects an ill-typed one, so that type-checking a Lark program and checking an MLTT proof are seen to be a single act.

12.5 The Road From Lark

Lark sits at a definite point on a ladder, and the chapters have climbed to it rung by rung. It is worth seeing the whole ladder at once, because each rung buys a class of guarantees and charges a price in checking and in annotation.

Hindley–Milner, Lark's footing (Chapter 5). Types classify values; inference is complete, so a program needs almost no annotations and the checker always terminates with a yes or a no. The price is expressiveness: no type can mention a value, so "non-empty list" or "sorted" is unsayable.

Affine and trait extensions, Lark's actual position. Affine types (Chapter 5, Chapter 11) add a resource discipline: a value used at most once, checked statically. Traits add bounded polymorphism. Both stay decidable and mostly inference-friendly. This is as far as Lark goes, and the choice was deliberate—everything here can be checked without the programmer writing a single proof.

Bidirectional checking, the next structural step. Splitting the checker into a mode that *infers* a type and a mode that *checks* against an expected one lets annotations carry information inference cannot recover, and is the standard route by which systems grow past full inference toward richer types.[3]

Full dependent types, the top rung. Types may mention values without restriction; the type checker is a proof checker in the full sense of Section 12.1, and a function's type can specify it completely—`sort : (xs : List) -> SortedPermutationOf xs`. The languages that live here are *Idris*, *Agda*, and *Lean*, and the `lcore` kernel of this book is a small one of the same family. The guarantee is total: a checked program meets a specification as precise as the programmer cares to write.

The affine types of Chapter 11 were the book's one step off the Hindley–Milner rung—the first place a Lark type stopped classifying a value and started *proving* something about its use. The road from there to the top is continuous. It is the same idea, Curry–Howard, allowed to range over richer and richer propositions, paid for in checking that grows harder at every rung.

12.6 The Limit

The price has a ceiling, and it is the reason Lark stops where it does. Once types may state arbitrary propositions, checking a program means checking arbitrary proofs—and that is, in general, *undecidable.* There is no algorithm that takes any dependently typed program and always answers, in finite time, whether it type-checks; the question subsumes provability in arithmetic. Practical dependently typed languages stay usable only by demanding that the programmer supply the hard proofs by hand and confining the checker to verifying them, which it can do because checking a given proof is decidable even when finding one is not.

This is the trade the ladder charges. At the Hindley–Milner rung, inference is complete and free: the compiler finds the types and the programmer writes none. At the dependent rung, the guarantee is total but the proofs are the programmer's burden, and a specification like "returns a sorted permutation" may cost more effort to prove than the function cost to write. In between lies a spectrum of engineering judgments about how much guarantee is worth how much annotation, and no point on it is the right answer for every language.

Lark answered for itself. It chose the rung where the checker still works alone—Hindley–Milner, plus an affine discipline whose proofs are cheap enough to stay invisible, plus traits. It refused the rung where the programmer becomes a prover, not because that rung is wrong but because Lark's purpose was to be a language one could implement and understand completely, and a proof assistant is a different and larger thing. The book built the smaller `lcore` only to vouch for the language, not to become the language. Knowing where to stop on this ladder is itself a design decision—the last and quietest of the decisions this book has been about.

12.7 Exercises

1. Using Table 12.1, translate each logical statement into a type, and say whether it is inhabited (provable): (a) $A \Rightarrow A$; (b) $A \Rightarrow (B \Rightarrow A)$; (c) $(A \land B) \Rightarrow A$; (d) $A \lor (A \Rightarrow \bot)$. For the one that is *not* inhabited in constructive logic, explain what term you would need and why you cannot write it.

2. Section 12.2 distinguishes Π from $\to$ and Σ from $\times$. (a) Write the type of a function that takes a natural number n and returns a vector of exactly n zeros, using Π. (b) Write the type "there exists an index into `xs` holding

the value v," using Σ. (c) Explain why neither type can be written in Lark's Hindley–Milner system.

3. Chapter 11 called the vanishing of preservation a "trick." Section 12.3 calls it "ordinary dependent-type programming." (a) Explain how `data Expr : Ctx -> Ty -> Type` being an *indexed family* is what makes ill-typed terms unrepresentable. (b) The `Step` relation is indexed by a single type `t` shared by both endpoints. Write the type a step relation would have if it were allowed to change the type, and explain why no constructor could inhabit it.

4. The `weaken` primitive (Section 12.4) is the one place the proof drops below the type theory into C. (a) State the definitional equation a recursive `weaken` would require and why it does not hold for free. (b) Why is it acceptable, for the trustworthiness of the result, to implement `weaken` in the kernel rather than prove it in the object theory? (c) What would be lost if *every* difficult lemma were handled this way?

5. Section 12.6 says full dependent type checking is undecidable. (a) Explain why "decidable to *check* a given proof" and "undecidable to *find* a proof" are consistent, and which one a dependently typed compiler relies on. (b) Lark chose to stop below this rung. Give one guarantee Lark therefore cannot make that Idris or Agda can, and one cost Lark avoids that they must pay. (c) Argue, for a language of your choosing, where on the ladder of Section 12.5 it should sit, and why.

The box is open. The checker that vouched for Lark's soundness is no longer a black instrument invoked at the end; it is a type checker like the one built in the middle of this book, for a logic rich enough that the proposition "well-typed programs do not go wrong" fits inside it as an ordinary type. The same idea ran the whole length of the construction—Curry–Howard, types as propositions—surfacing first as a slogan, then as the affine discipline, then as the proof that closed the book's circle, and here at last as itself. But a construction this tall now rests on a great many instruments of trust—the compiler, the tests, the allocator's oracle, this very kernel—and every one of them has so far been taken at its word. The book's last chapter takes none of them at their word. It attacks the finished construction with manufactured programs and planted lies, instrument by instrument, and what it finds—in the compiler, in the affine checker, and inside the kernel this chapter just opened—is the reason the attack was owed. Chapter 13 takes it up.

Notes

[1]Curry first noticed the correspondence in combinatory logic; Howard extended it to first-order logic in a 1969 manuscript, eventually published as *The Formulae-as-Types Notion of Construction* [Howard, 1980]. Wadler's *Propositions as Types* [Wadler, 2015] is a modern and unusually readable account of how far the correspondence reaches.

[2]The obstacle is that `ext` σ (`ext` τ_λ Δ) and `ext` τ_λ (`ext` σ Δ) are propositionally but not definitionally equal in the kernel; a recursive `weaken` would need them interchangeable for free. Implementing weakening as a de Bruijn shift on the `VL_INDCON` tree sidesteps the equation entirely. The remark on stuck `weaken` terms in the specification shows the conversion checker still compares such terms soundly when their arguments are neutral.

[3]Lark's own checker is pure synthesis—a single inference pass, not the infer/check split—as Chapter 5 noted. Bidirectional structure is what a language reaches for first when it wants types too expressive to infer completely; it is the architecture beneath most practical dependently typed checkers, including the elaborator in front of `lcore`.

NOTES

Chapter 13

The Adversary

Chapter 11 ended with a debt paid, and Chapter 12 with an instrument explained. Between them they may have left an impression that this chapter must now correct: that the story of Lark's correctness is a story of safety accumulating—tests, then theorems, then a checked proof, each layer quietly underwriting the last. The record says otherwise. Everything this chapter describes was built *after* the soundness proof was green, and nearly every piece of it found something wrong. The language with the machine-checked soundness proof was found to miscompile a one-line program on one of its three back ends. The affine checker—the subject of the previous chapter's proudest section—was found to accept a program that duplicates the `IO` token. And the proof kernel that vouched for the soundness proof was found to accept false evidence in three distinct ways, the last of which made it logically inconsistent: it could be talked into proving `Empty`.

None of this is an embarrassment to the book's method. It *is* the book's method, entering its final register. A proof secures exactly what it states, about exactly the artifact it describes; everything else—the thousands of lines the proof never mentions, the gap between the rules on paper and the rules as implemented, the checker of the proof itself—is secured by nothing until something attacks it. This chapter is the attack. It turns the machinery of Chapter 11 around and points it at every instrument of trust the book has built, including the instruments of trust themselves: the compiler is fuzzed with manufactured programs, the fuzzer is tested with planted bugs, the register allocator's answers are independently certified, the affine discipline is re-derived inside the proof kernel, and the kernel is caught, three times, extending credit it had no right to extend. The chapter's one principle, earned repeatedly, is this: *a guarantee is worth exactly as much as the adversary it has survived.*

A note on reading. The first four sections stay in the concrete register of Chapter 11's testing sections—real programs, real diagnostics, real bugs—and every formal display is decoded in Appendix C. The graded typing of Section 13.5 and the kernel forensics of Section 13.6 use the machinery of Chapter 12; each opens with its bug, and a reader who follows the bugs and skims the derivations loses none of the argument. What should not be skimmed is the pattern: every section is the same move—find the thing being trusted, and make it earn it—applied one level deeper than the section before.

13.1 Making the Language Attackable

The first bug is a quiet one, and it lived in the test suite. For most of the book's construction, Lark's differential harness carried a small table of excuses: `RV32_XFAIL` entries for programs whose integer arithmetic overflowed 32 bits, skip lists for the C machine on the same inputs. Each entry recorded a divergence between back ends that was *expected*—the interpreter computed in Python's unbounded integers, the RV32 machine in hardware's 32 bits, and where they disagreed the harness looked away. This is a common and comfortable state for a language to be in, and it is fatal to everything this chapter wants to do. An adversary works by finding divergences; a specification with exceptions cannot lose an argument. Before the compiler could be attacked, the language had to be made *attackable*: every program's behaviour defined, so that every divergence is a bug and every bug is adjudicable.

Three changes did it, and they are worth seeing as one act.

Every integer operation defined. `Int` became, by definition, a wrapping two's-complement 32-bit integer, with even the traditional undefined corners pinned down by adopting the RISC-V M extension's division rules: $x/0 = -1$, $x \bmod 0 = x$, and $\text{INT\_MIN}/{-1} = \text{INT\_MIN}$.[1] The interpreter, the TAC machine, the C machine, and the RV32 back end all implement the same arithmetic, and every excuse-table in the test suite was deleted—the overflow tests now expect the wrapped values, everywhere. The point is not that wrapping is good arithmetic; it is that *agreed* arithmetic is the precondition for differential testing meaning anything.

Every match checked. Chapter 5 left match exhaustiveness to a runtime trap: a `match` with a missing case compiled, and failed if the missing value arrived. The trap became a static check (`08/src/exhaust.py`), using Maranget's usefulness algorithm [Maranget, 2007]: compute whether a wildcard row would still be *useful* after the written patterns, and if it would, the algorithm's own working produces the counterexample, which becomes the diagnostic:

Listing 13.1: The non-exhaustiveness witness is the error message

```
error: non-exhaustive match:
```

```
pattern 'Cons(Err(_), Nil)' not covered
```

The runtime trap remains in the lowerer as defence in depth, and is now unreachable. For this chapter's purposes the witness matters as much as the check: a generator about to manufacture thousands of programs with `match` expressions needs the language to state, precisely, which of them are legal.

Termination, where it is claimed. The third change is opt-in: a function may be declared `fn total`, and the checker (`08/src/total.py`) then requires structural descent—some fixed argument position must shrink, by pattern-matching depth, at every recursive call, with the function's callees checked in turn across the call graph. Most Lark functions do not carry the modifier; the ones that do have a guarantee the type system alone cannot give. The detail that earns this feature its place in the chapter is an interaction. The totality checker *refuses* to accept `n - 1` as descent on an integer argument, and the diagnostic says why: `Int` is a wrapping i32, so subtraction is not well-founded—below `INT_MIN` lies `INT_MAX`, and a "decreasing" loop can run forever. Recurse on data, the error advises, not on integers. Two features from the same phase, each individually sensible, met and produced a constraint neither was designed for—the defined semantics reached into the totality checker and removed a rule that every textbook example of termination checking takes for granted. This is the Introduction's propagation again, turned sideways: a semantic decision propagating not down the pipeline but across, into a sibling analysis. Hold on to the question of what totality is *for*; it returns, with force, at the end of Section 13.6.

13.2 Manufacturing Adversaries

Here is the first real catch, exactly as the machinery of this section found and shrank it:

Listing 13.2: The program that broke the RV32 back end (shrunk; the core of `errors/15_ambig_op.lark`)

```
fn main(io : IO) : IO =
  print(io, (let f = (fn(x) => (x + x)) in f("uh oh")))
```

Run it on the CEK interpreter: `uh ohuh oh`. On the TAC machine: `uh ohuh oh`. On the RV32 machine: garbage—the bytes that happen to lie at an address no one meant to compute. A silent miscompilation, in a language whose type system had a machine-checked soundness proof, found within the first few hundred generated programs.

The diagnosis is a lesson in where soundness proofs end. Lark's operators are ad-hoc polymorphic: + works on `Int` as addition and on `String` as concatenation. Inside the lambda, `x` is unannotated, so Hindley–Milner generalises it and `x + x` is typed at a type *variable.* The interpreter and the TAC machine are untroubled—they look at the value at run time and dispatch. But `lower.py` must commit at compile time: it selects `__str_concat` when the static type is `String`, and its fallthrough case—reached because a type variable is neither `String` nor `Int`—emits an integer `add`. On the RV32 machine that adds the two string *pointers* and prints whatever lies at their sum. Nothing in the soundness proof touches this: the proof secures the typing rules and the small-step semantics, and both interpreters honour them perfectly. The bug lives in the gap between a dynamic dispatch and a static one—exactly the territory Chapter 11 said testing must guard, in the paragraph that warned "a sound language with a miscompiling back end is no comfort at all." The warning came true, verbatim, and the machinery that caught it is this section's subject.

Inverting the rules. Random text does not find such bugs: a program must first survive the lexer, the parser, and the type checker before it can reach the lowerer, and random text does not survive the lexer. The tool that works is a *well-typed program generator* (`09/tests/gen_prog.py`), built by running the typing rules backwards [Pałka et al., 2011]. Where the checker of Chapter 5 takes an expression and asks "what type does this have?", the generator takes a *type* and asks "what expressions have this type?"—pick a goal type, pick a typing rule whose conclusion produces that type, recurse into the rule's premises as new goals. Every inference rule read top-down by `infer` is read bottom-up by the generator; the two are the same table of rules traversed in opposite directions, and Appendix C's reading of a rule as a function clause works for both.[2]

Generation must respect every discipline the checker enforces, and the disciplines earn their keep by making that hard. The generator threads the affine state through generation just as `infer.py` threads its tracking map—an `IO` token used linearly, non-`Copy` values consumed at most once—so the programs are affine-legal by construction. Helper functions form an acyclic call graph, so every generated program terminates by construction (Section 13.1's groundwork: terminating, defined, exhaustive programs are the only ones whose outputs can be demanded to agree). Two properties then close the loop: **P6**, every generated program typechecks—which tests the *generator* against the checker—and **P7**, every generated program produces byte-identical output on all three back ends—which tests the *compiler* against itself, with the differential oracle of Chapter 8 as judge.

P6 looks like bookkeeping and is not. Its very first counterexample was `let f = (fn(a) => show(a)) in f(0)`: the generator assumed `show` on a lambda parameter was fine because the call site pins `a` to `Int`—and the checker rejected it, correctly, because the `Show`-bound pass of Chapter 5 runs on the generalised body, before any call site is consulted. The generator's author had inverted the rules he believed Lark had; P6 forced him to invert the rules Lark *has*. The generator now tracks *groundedness*—which expressions may still carry a free type variable—alongside the affine state, and the lesson generalises: a generator built from the rules-as-implemented is itself a test of your understanding of your own language, and its failures are documentation.

The fix is the best part. A compiler bug of this shape invites a compiler patch: teach `lower.py` to refuse the fallthrough. Lark's fix went higher. The real defect is that the program's meaning depended on information no back end could be sure of at compile time; so the *language* now rejects it. A monomorphism restriction on operators was added to `infer.py`: if, when a declaration is generalised, the operand type of an operator inside it is still an unresolved variable, that is a type error—`ambiguous operator type`, add an annotation. All three back ends now agree *by rejection*; no back end ever sees a program it would miscompile; and error test 15 pins the diagnostic so the rule cannot silently regress. Notice the direction of travel. The Introduction's thesis was that decisions propagate *down*—a type-system choice becomes a constraint on the register allocator. Here a bug propagated *up*: a code-generation defect, found by fuzzing, repaired in the type system, where the repair protects every back end at once, including ones not yet written. Propagation runs both ways, and a language under adversarial pressure uses both directions.

13.3 Validating the Validator

The generator now guards the compiler. What guards the generator? The question is not rhetorical, and this section opens with the bug that makes it concrete—a bug that was *not caught.*

As a check on the new machinery, a bug was planted—the old discipline of mutation testing [DeMillo et al., 1978], aimed here at the test system rather than the tested: the TAC machine's division was quietly altered to return -2 on division by zero, in violation of Section 13.1's defined semantics. P7 should catch this instantly—the interpreter says -1, the TAC machine says -2, divergence, alarm. Three hundred generated programs ran. Nothing. The planted bug sailed through, because under uniform random generation a division whose right operand happens to be zero almost never occurs; the guard was aimed at the whole space of programs and the bug lived in a corner of it. The remedy was to bias the corner: the generator's divisors are now drawn from the edge set $\{0, 1, -1\}$ half the time, and with that change the planted bug was caught and shrunk to `show((0 / 0))` in about a second. The fuzzer had a blind spot the size of the exact semantics Section 13.1 worked hardest to define, and nothing but a deliberate lie would have revealed it.

Validate the validator. A guard that has never caught anything is a hope, not a tool—its silence is compatible with both "nothing is wrong" and "I am not looking." The only way to tell the two apart is to make something be wrong, on purpose, and watch. This book ends up applying the principle four times: a planted miscompilation proves the differential fuzzer can see (this section); planted undefined behaviour proves the sanitizers are awake (below); a planted false claim, `(star : Empty)`, proves the proof kernel checks what it is handed; and a planted "proof" of `Empty` via `fix` proves the kernel's logic is closed (Section 13.6). Every validator in this chapter was itself validated by a lie, and the two that had never been lied to turned out to be broken.

The frontend, fuzzed the old way. The generator attacks the back half of the compiler with well-typed programs; the front half faces untrusted text and must be attacked with garbage. Property **P8** states the frontend's whole obligation: for *any* input text, the pipeline from lexer through every checker pass either succeeds or raises a positioned diagnostic—a Python traceback is a bug. Four input distributions probe it: random unicode, token soup, well-typed programs mutated until they are not, and pathological shapes (expressions nested hundreds deep, operator chains hundreds long). Three crashes fell out. Deep input blew the recursive-descent parser's stack—fixed with a *node budget* (a parser that has built 2,000 AST nodes inside one declaration stops and says so), backed by a recursion-limit raise applied at call time rather than at import, because the test harness itself restores the interpreter's limit around each example—a fuzzing-harness subtlety worth one sentence of anyone's time. And two one-character lexer crashes: the superscript digit ^{2} passes Python's `isdigit` test but not its `int()` conversion, and a numeric literal longer than 4,300 digits trips CPython's integer-conversion limit. Both are now positioned `LexErrors`. Bugs of this class are humble and their lesson is not: the frontend's robustness contract is a *property*, statable in one line and checkable by the thousand, and it held only after it was enforced.

The C machine, under instruments. The CEK machine exists twice, Chapter 10 noted: the readable Python definition, and its C twin that runs on bare metal. The twin is written in C, and C fails in ways no exit code reports—a buffer overrun or a signed overflow can corrupt memory and still print the right answer. `make santest` rebuilds the entire corpus under AddressSanitizer and UndefinedBehaviorSanitizer [Serebryany et al., 2012] with recovery disabled, and—the detail that matters—a sanitizer report *fails the test even when the output agrees*, so an instrumented crash cannot hide behind an expected rejection. The result was zero findings, and the zero was purchased in Section 13.1: the decision to compute wrapping arithmetic in `uint32_t` means the corpus contains no signed overflow for UBSan to find. A semantic decision made for differential testability turned out, one chapter later, to be a memory-safety decision too. And per the boxed principle, the zero was not taken on faith: undefined behaviour was planted and compiled with the same flags, and the sanitizers duly went off. A clean run means something only once a dirty run has been seen.

13.4 The Certificate

Chapter 11 asked how to trust code you did not write. This section asks the harder version: how to trust code you *did* write, when it is two hundred lines of interval bookkeeping that no proof touches and that every compiled program depends on—the linear-scan register allocator of Chapter 9. The bug this section opens with is not in the allocator. It is in the thing that was supposed to watch the allocator, and it is a bug of *architecture*, present from the day it was written. The allocator ships with a checking oracle, `verify()`; that oracle derives interference from `cfg.py` and `liveness.py`—the same modules the allocator itself uses. If the shared liveness analysis is wrong, the allocator makes a wrong assignment and the oracle, seeing the same wrong facts, approves it. The judge was reading the defendant's own brief. No failure had yet resulted; none needed to. An oracle correlated with its subject is not an oracle, and the point of this chapter is to notice such things before the failure arrives.

The replacement (`09/src/regcheck.py`) is a *certificate checker*, and its design principle is independence by construction. It shares exactly one artifact with the allocator—the TAC instruction set, which is the specification—and re-derives everything else, differently: it works on the flat instruction list rather than the basic-block graph, builds its own successor map from labels, defines its own per-instruction def/use sets, and runs its own backward fixpoint to per-instruction liveness. On that independent ground it checks five things:

Listing 13.3: The certificate, from `regcheck.py`'s contract

```
R1  completeness -- every Tmp mentioned has a location
R2  unambiguity  -- register or spill slot, never both
R3  exclusivity  -- live Tmps in distinct registers,
                    and no dead def clobbers a live one
R4  the same two conditions, for spill slots
R5  slot indices lie within the allocated frame
```

The checker runs inside `asm.gen()` on *every* compilation, of every test and every fuzzed program—which means the differential fuzzer of Section 13.2 now stress-tests the certificate for free. A failure raises `RegAllocCertificateError`, and one design decision there carries the section's weight: the error is deliberately *not* in the compiler's diagnostics tuple. A user diagnostic means "your program is wrong"; a certificate failure means "the compiler is wrong," and a compiler that could ever confuse the two would be lying to exactly the person able to fix it.

Two ideas from the research literature meet here, scaled to teaching size. This is *translation validation* [Pnueli et al., 1998, Necula, 2000]: instead of proving the transformation correct once and forever—for linear scan, a serious mechanisation project—check each *output*, which is cheap, and which keeps working when the allocator is rewritten. And the checker itself was held to the boxed principle, in both directions. Mutations were planted in the allocator—an everything-in-one-register bug, a register released while its value was still live—and the certificate caught both, naming the clobbering instruction. Then the opposite test, which most validation schemes skip: a mutation was planted that is *semantically safe*—an interval allowed to expire one instruction early, where the last read and the next write abut—and the certificate, correctly, stayed quiet. A checker that flags safe code is merely paranoid, and paranoid checkers get disabled; precision is what keeps a certificate switched on. R3's odd second clause ("no dead def clobbers a live one") shows the grain of care the checks demand: a definition whose value is never used still *writes* its register, so an exclusivity check phrased only in terms of live values would let a dead def share a register with a live one and silently destroy it.

13.5 The Hole in the Affine Wall

Chapter 11 closed its argument with the affine discipline: "the checker proves it, for every program, before the program runs." Here is the program that made that sentence false:

Listing 13.4: Accepted by the checker; duplicates the IO token (`errors/16_affine_capture.lark`)

```
fn f(io : IO) : (IO, IO) =
  let g = fn(x : Int) => io in
  (g(1), g(2))
```

The name `io` appears once in the body of `f`, so the affine tracker—which counts uses per scope—was satisfied. But the one appearance is *inside a lambda*, and a lambda is a value: it can be called twice, and each call hands back the same captured `IO` token. `(g(1), g(2))` is a pair of two aliases of one affine resource. The rule of Chapter 5, "an affine value is used at most once," was being enforced on names and evaded by closures; the checker's lambda case simply copied the tracking map and looked no further. This is a soundness hole in the discipline the book was proudest of, it survived every differential and property harness the book had built—no back end disagrees about a program all of them run happily—and it was found not by any harness but by the oldest tool in the book: a hostile re-reading of the rules, asking of each "what would break this?" (the fourth move of Appendix C, pointed at the language itself).

The immediate fix is a new rule, chosen for enforceability: *a lambda may not capture an affine variable at all.* Closures in Lark are `Copy`, so even a single capture is a potential duplication; the diagnostic tells the programmer to pass the resource as a parameter instead, which moves the use to the call site where the tracker can see it. Error test 16 pins the rule, property P1 now generates capture-shaped programs, and the generator of Section 13.2 was taught to stop producing the newly illegal forms.

Why a fix is not enough. The unsettling part is not the hole but its provenance. The affine rules existed in three places—the specification's tracking rules, `infer.py`'s implementation, and the book's own prose—and all three agreed, because all three came from the same author thinking the same incomplete thought. Testing could not catch it: every back end implements the *same* scope-counting, so there is nothing to diverge. Against an error of shared understanding the only defence is a fourth party that does not share it—a mechanised model, where "the rules have no hole" is not an impression but a theorem. That is what `formal/proof/lark/lark-affine.lcore` builds, in the language of Chapter 12, and capture is not a patch there but the load-bearing case.

The model assigns every binding a *grade* from the set $\{0, 1, \omega\}$: unusable, usable at most once, unrestricted. Grades form a small semiring—$1 + 1 = \omega$ is the whole affine story in one equation, two demands on one binding exceed "at most once"—placing the model in the tradition of graded and quantitative type theories [McBride, 2016, Atkey, 2018]. The judgement is *leftover typing*: `GExpr g t g'` says the expression has type `t`, consumes from context `g`, and leaves behind `g'`—the residue after its uses are spent. This is `infer.py`'s tracking map, made into an index: where the implementation mutates `tracked` as it walks, the model threads the context through, and one can check, rule against code, that they move in step. Using an affine variable is the rule that spends:

Listing 13.5: Consuming lookup: using an affine binding erases it (simplified from `lark-affine.lcore`)

```
data GVar : GCtx -> Ty -> GCtx -> Type where
  gv_here1 : GVar (gext t G1 g) t (gext t G0 g)   -- 1->0
  gv_herew : GVar (gext t GW g) t (gext t GW g)   -- free
  gv_there : GVar g t g'
          -> GVar (gext s q g) t (gext s q g')
```

Read `gv_here1` with the appendix's eyes: looking up an affine (`G1`) binding is only possible if the leftover context records it as `G0`. And now the crucial absence: *there is no rule for looking up a `G0` binding.* An erased binding cannot be referenced, not because a check forbids it but because no constructor builds such a derivation—the same trick that made preservation unstatable-wrongly in Chapter 11, here making double-use underivable. The capture bug's twin lives in the lambda rule: `GELam` checks its body not in the enclosing context g but in `demote g`—the context with every grade-1 binding knocked down to 0. Inside a lambda, the enclosing affine world is *erased.* The counterexample program above now fails at proof level for a computable reason: the kernel evaluates `demote` of the context, `io`'s grade goes to 0, and the body's reference to `io` needs the `GVar` rule that does not exist. Three theorems, checked by the kernel, pin the discipline: `no_use_in_erased` (nothing in a fully demoted context can be referenced), `capture_rejected` (error test 16, replayed as a proof), and `no_second_use` (property P1, replayed as a proof: the leftover context of a first use admits no second). And per the boxed principle, the model was lied to: a planted false semiring law and a planted use of a grade-0 binding are both rejected by the kernel.

One theorem closes the circle and one observation opens the next book. The closing theorem is an *erasure functor*: every graded derivation maps to the plain intrinsically-typed `Expr` of Chapter 11 with the grades stripped away, so graded programs inherit the entire dynamics—the step relation, evaluation, and soundness—that the earlier proof already established (`graded_eval_sound` is literally the composition of the old theorem with erasure). Affinity needs no dynamics of its own: programs that would duplicate a resource do not exist to be run. The observation is what the grades reveal in hindsight. Lark's `Copy` analysis, built in Chapter 5 as engineering, is exactly the $\{1, \omega\}$ fragment of this semiring, and the 0 grade—the one Lark's surface never mentions—entered the system through `demote`, forced by the capture rule. The language had been a fragment of quantitative type theory all along, without knowing it; the full system, where grades meet the dependent types of Chapter 12, is the next rung of that chapter's ladder, and it is where any sequel to this book would begin.

13.6 Who Checks the Checker

Everything so far leaned on `lcore`. The affine model of the last section, the soundness proof of Chapter 11, the theorems replayed from error tests—all of them are claims *checked by the kernel*, and their entire force is the kernel's word. This section is the record of pointing the chapter's one move at the kernel itself, and it found three failures, in ascending order of severity. A reader keeping score should recall Chapter 12's exercise that asked whether trusting the `weaken` primitive was acceptable. The exercise was more loaded than its author knew.

First failure: the trusted primitive was wrong. Chapter 12 was honest about the seam: `weaken`, the lemma that lifts a term into an extended context, was implemented as a C primitive (`TM_WEAKEN`) because the natural recursion needs two contexts that are equal as propositions but not by computation, and the kernel will not identify them. The discharge of that debt starts from a change of statement. Do not weaken at the head of the context; weaken at a *position*, computed by a recursive function:

Listing 13.6: Weakening at a position: the equation becomes computation (`lark-weaken.lcore`)

```
insert pz     a g         = ext a g         -- at the head
insert (ps n) a (ext s g) = ext s (insert n a g)

wk_expr   : Expr g t -> (n : Pos)
                     -> Expr (insert n a g) t
weaken_1 : Expr g t -> Expr (ext a g) t    -- at pz
```

Under a binder, the recursion simply moves to position `ps n`, and the context equation that blocked the naive proof now holds *definitionally*—`insert` computes it. The generalisation dissolves the obstacle rather than overcoming it, a move worth stealing: when a proof needs an equation the system cannot see, restate the theorem so the equation is the unfolding of a function. With `weaken_1` checked, the substitution lemma was rewired to use it, and *no proof in the stack depends on the primitive at all.*

That would be a satisfying tidy-up; what makes it a section of this chapter is what the discharge exposed. With both implementations in hand, they could be compared—and on variables, they disagreed. The C primitive, shifting the innermost variable at cutoff zero, built the result in the *unextended* context: evidence whose type mentions a context one entry too short, which the kernel's own type checker would reject—if it ever saw it. It never did. Primitive outputs were trusted by definition, never re-checked, so every earlier proof run that weakened a variable had been silently passed ill-typed evidence, and the green light at the end reflected none of it. The kernel bug was found not by testing the kernel but by *doing the proof the primitive had excused everyone from doing*—the answer to Chapter 12's exercise turned out to be: no, it was not acceptable, and the only way to learn that was to stop accepting it. The C is fixed, the kernel's self-tests pin it, but the structural repair is the real one: the trusted base shrank by one primitive, and the seam Chapter 12 documented is gone.

Second failure: the front door. The kernel's job description is "check claims," and it turned out to have a mode that did not. A bare term at the top level—not bound with `:let`, just written—was *normalised without being type-*

checked: the planted claim `(star : Empty)` did not produce an error but a normal form, the annotation taken on faith. The proof stack was sound only by discipline—every real claim happened to go through `:let`, which does check—and discipline is exactly what this chapter refuses to accept as a mechanism; indeed the stack was carrying nineteen bare demonstration lines that had never been checked at all. The kernel now infers a type for every term before normalising it, untyped normalisation survives only behind an explicit escape hatch, and any failed line makes the whole run exit non-zero—so "the proof stack is green" is now a fact a build script can enforce, not an impression from scrolling. Machine-checkably green, where before it was eyeball-green.

Third failure: the kernel could prove `Empty`. The last bug was found by a design question, not a test. The kernel core is shared by `llang`, the small programming language built on it, and `llang` has `let rec`, which needs general recursion—the `fix` combinator. Asking where `fix` should live revealed that it lived in the *shared* core: parser and type checker both accepted it, for everyone. So the proof kernel accepted this:

Listing 13.7: The kernel, proving falsehood (rejected after the gate)

```
:let bad = (fix (\x. x) : Empty)
bad : Empty
```

`fix (\x. x)` inhabits every type, including `Empty`, the type with no values—the proposition *false*. Under Curry–Howard this is not a quirk; it is the end of the world. From a proof of `Empty`, the eliminator derives anything: every theorem in the seven-file stack, and every falsehood too, all provable, all green. The kernel was *logically inconsistent as shipped*, and had been for the book's entire final act; every checked result so far was trustworthy only because nobody had happened to write `fix`. Soundness by absence of temptation. The repair is a gate: `core_allow_fix`, default off, guarding both the parser and the checker's two `fix` rules; `llang` switches it on at startup, because `llang` is a *programming* language, where general recursion is a feature and `Empty` is just an empty type—no proof claim flows through it. A planted `fix`-proof of `Empty` now reddens the run, per the boxed principle.

Step back, because the three failures compose into the chapter's deepest point. Why is `fix` fatal to `lcore` and harmless in `llang`—and harmless in Lark, whose `let rec` the book celebrated? Because a proof checker's guarantee *is* totality: a proof is a program that must be total, or the "proof" of `Empty` is just an infinite loop wearing an annotation. The boundary between the total world and the partial world is where logical consistency lives, and the third failure happened because that boundary was drawn in documentation rather than in code.

It is the same boundary Section 13.1 drew at the surface with `fn total`— there as an opt-in prover's discipline inside a partial language, here as the non-negotiable wall around a logic. The book's first chapter and its last are holding the two ends of one line: which layer is allowed to be partial is a *design decision*, and this chapter's addendum is that it must be a *checked* one, because an unchecked boundary is exactly where the adversary walks in.[3]

13.7 What the Adversary Leaves Standing

The chapter can now be read as a single structure. Every instrument of trust in the book was given a guard, and every guard was given a guard, and the discipline was applied until it reached the floor:

The trusted thing	What now guards it	What it caught
back ends (Ch. 7–9)	generated programs + oracle	RV32 miscompile
the fuzzer itself	planted miscompilation	its own blind spot
frontend robustness	the no-traceback property	three crashes
the C machine	sanitizers (planted UB)	nothing—credibly
register allocator	independent certificate	planted mutations
the certificate itself	mutations, both directions	a missing clause
affine checker	mechanised graded model	(after the capture hole)
kernel primitive	discharged, then compared	ill-typed evidence
kernel front door	planted `(star : Empty)`	unchecked claims
kernel logic	`fix` gate, planted proof	inconsistency

Table 13.1: Every guard, guarded. The right column is the chapter's argument that the discipline is not ceremony: nearly every act of verification found something, and the two guards that had never been tested were broken.

What remains at the floor is what every such structure has: a residue of things believed without a guard. The kernel's eight thousand lines of C, partially excused by its self-tests and by the discharge having shrunk what they are trusted *for*. The Python interpreter, the C compiler, the operating system, and the silicon of Chapter 1, believed on reputation. Thompson's lecture (see the endnote) proves the regress has no bottom; this chapter's reply is that the regress can be *narrowed*—trust is not eliminated but concentrated, into a kernel small enough to actually read, cross-checked by proofs it did not expect, guarded at its own front door. The honest final statement of what the book has built is not "Lark is correct." It is: here is the complete list of things Lark's correctness rests on, each named, most of them attacked, the attacks recorded, and the list shorter than it was a chapter ago. No larger claim survives contact with this chapter's evidence, and no smaller one does the work justice.

13.8 Exercises

1. Section 13.1 argues that defined semantics is a precondition for differential testing. (a) Explain precisely why an `XFAIL` table poisons a differential oracle, in terms of what a divergence can then mean. (b) Prove that `n - 1` is not a well-founded descent on wrapping i32 integers, by exhibiting the infinite descending chain. (c) Propose an alternative rule that would let the totality checker accept integer countdown loops, and state exactly what it must verify.

2. The generator of Section 13.2 inverts the typing rules. (a) Explain why "generate random ASTs, keep the ones that typecheck" fails in practice for a language with affine types. (b) The planted division bug survived uniform generation. Name another semantic corner of Lark (Section 13.1 defines several) that uniform generation would under-sample, and design the edge bias that covers it. (c) The generator excludes `Float`. Describe a class of back-end bugs this scope decision makes invisible, and what must be unified before the scope can grow.

3. Section 13.4 rejects an oracle that shares its liveness analysis with the allocator. (a) Construct a concrete liveness bug and trace how it fools both the allocator and the correlated `verify()`, but not `regcheck`. (b) Explain why the dead-def clause of R3 is necessary: exhibit an allocation that passes plain exclusivity but miscomputes. (c) Compare certifying each output against proving the allocator correct once: which guarantee is stronger, and which survives a rewrite of the allocator?

4. The lambda rule of Section 13.5 demotes the enclosing context. (a) Write the graded derivation showing `fn(x : Int) => x + x` is well-graded (recall `Int` is `Copy`). (b) Show where the derivation for the capture counterexample gets stuck, naming the missing `GVar` rule. (c) Lark's fix bans *all* affine capture, though a lambda called at most once would be safe. What grade would such a lambda need, and why is "called at most once" harder to check than "captures nothing"?

5. Section 13.6 reports three kernel failures. (a) The intrinsic encoding makes ill-typed *terms* unrepresentable; explain why it nonetheless could not protect against the `weaken` bug. (b) State what logical inconsistency means for a proof checker, and show how a single inhabitant of `Empty` makes every proposition provable. (c) Thompson's lecture argues the trust regress

has no bottom. Lay out Lark's remaining trusted base after this chapter, and argue which single element you would attack next, and how.

This is the book's last constructive act, and it ends in a change of temperament rather than a change of subject. The chapters built a language; this one taught it suspicion—of its compiler, of its tests, of its proofs, of the checker of its proofs—and the suspicion paid, every time, in bugs that twelve chapters of good faith had left standing. The construction is now not merely finished but hardened, and the claims it makes come with the receipts of their survival. What remains is to step back from the whole: to ask what it has meant to carry one language from silicon to semantics and back, guard every layer against the layers above and below it, and end holding a short, explicit list of what is still taken on faith. The Conclusion takes that up.

Notes

[1]The choice of the RISC-V rules over, say, trapping is the same style of decision as Chapter 9's: the RV32 back end gets them from the silicon for free, so defining the language to match makes the lowest layer trivially correct and moves all the work to the interpreters—which are easier to change. The C machine computes in `uint32_t` and converts, because *signed* overflow is undefined behaviour in C; that decision is repaid with interest in Section 13.3.

[2]The generator is driven by Hypothesis, the property-testing library Chapter 11 introduced, in the QuickCheck lineage [Claessen and Hughes, 2000]; the inherited superpower is *shrinking*—a failing program is automatically reduced to a minimal failing program, which is why the catch above is one line rather than the forty-line monster the generator actually produced. The technique of hammering a compiler with generated programs against an oracle is differential testing [McKeeman, 1998], and its most famous industrial instance, Csmith, found hundreds of bugs in production C compilers [Yang et al., 2011]—by, exactly as here, defining away undefined behaviour so that every divergence is a bug.

[3]The classic statement that this regress has no comfortable bottom is Thompson's Turing-award lecture [Thompson, 1984], which constructs a compiler that inserts a back door into programs it compiles—including into compilers, including itself, leaving no trace in any source. The constructive reply, argued in [Pollack, 1998], is the one this chapter enacts: you cannot eliminate trust, but you can concentrate it in an artifact small enough to read, cross-check it against independent implementations, and make it check its own inputs. De-correlating the guards—a certificate that shares nothing with its allocator, a proof model that shares nothing with its implementation—is the practical form of the reply.

Conclusion

The Language That Survives

Lark is finished—not as a product, which it was never meant to be, but as an argument. Every part has been named, connected to its neighbours, and in several places measured. A character stream became tokens, the tokens a tree, the tree acquired types, the typed tree a meaning given by a machine, that meaning was lowered to an intermediate form, the form compiled to instructions a real processor runs, and the whole construction finally proved sound against the very semantics that ran every example along the way—then attacked, instrument by instrument, with manufactured programs and planted lies, until every guard had a guard and the claims came with the receipts of their survival. The book set out to carry one language from the silicon to the semantics and back, and the circle is closed.

What held the circle together was not any single technique but a thesis about how the techniques relate. The Introduction called it *propagation*: a decision made at one level becomes a constraint at every level below it. The book spent twelve chapters making that claim concrete. The affine discipline of Chapter 5 was not a local feature of the type checker; it reappeared in Chapter 9 as the threading of an `IO` token through generated code, and again in Chapter 11 as a property the checker could prove. The tail call that Chapter 7 could only leave as an ordinary call became, in Chapter 9, the jump that lets a recursive function run in constant stack space. A choice about what a type should be able to say propagated all the way down to the register allocator, exactly as promised. This is the through-line, and it is what distinguishes understanding a compiler from having read about its passes.

What Was Left Undone

A teaching language earns its clarity by leaving things out, and Lark left out a great deal on purpose (Appendix A catalogues the omissions). Each is a real subject a reader who has come this far is now equipped to study.

Garbage collection. Lark's runtime is a single bump-pointer arena, never reclaimed until the program exits. Real languages reclaim memory during execution, and the design space—reference counting, mark-and-sweep, generational and concurrent collectors—is deep. The affine discipline of this book governs *safety*, not storage; the two meet in languages like Rust, and that meeting is where to look next.

Just-in-time compilation. Lark compiles ahead of time. A JIT compiles at run time, using information—which branches are hot, which types actually occur—that is unavailable until the program runs. It is the same code generation this book taught, performed later and with more knowledge, and it reuses every idea in Chapter 9.

Separate compilation and modules. Lark compiles a whole program at once. Languages that scale compile pieces independently and link them, forcing real questions about interfaces, name resolution across boundaries, and binary compatibility that a whole-program compiler never faces.

Concurrency, mutation, exceptions. Lark is pure, sequential, and total in its surface intent. Each omission is a semantics in its own right—shared state and its memory model, effect handlers, non-local control—and each would change the operational semantics of Chapter 10, worth studying precisely because Lark shows what their absence buys.

The point of naming these is not to apologize. It is that each omission is now legible: the reader can see the shape of the hole and knows what kind of thing fills it.

Where the Ladder Leads

Chapter 12 already climbed the rung above Lark and looked over the top. Lark sits at Hindley–Milner inference with affine ownership and trait-bounded polymorphism; the next rung is dependent types, where the type checker and the proof checker become one program, and the systems that live there—Idris, Agda, Lean, F*—let a type state a full specification. The book's own `lcore` kernel is a small member of that family, and its `proof/` and research kernels (now gathered in the companion's `ch12/`) are the immediate next landmarks for a reader who wants to keep climbing. The ladder simply has no top the way it has a bottom. Chapter 1 began at the silicon, which is a floor; the type-theory ceiling recedes as you climb toward it.

Form and Meaning

Underneath the engineering ran a quieter thread, the one the Introduction admitted was partly philosophical: the relationship between *form* and *meaning*. A program is a piece of syntax—marks arranged by grammatical rules—and yet it *means* something: a computation, a value, in the limit a proposition with a proof. The book's recurring discovery is that form constrains meaning, and deliberately so. A lexical grammar decides what can even be said; a type system decides which sayable things are admissible, and a good one is designed so that the inadmissible things are exactly the meaningless ones. By the time the argument reached Curry–Howard in Chapter 12, form and meaning had become two views of a single object: a well-typed term *is* a proof, and checking its form *is* verifying its meaning. That a syntactic discipline can guarantee a semantic property—that "well-typed programs do not go wrong" is a theorem and not a hope—is the deepest thing this book has to teach, and it is why the construction had to go all the way down to a machine-checked proof to be complete.

The Question Underneath

The Introduction put a question first and promised the book would return to it once the reader could see the answer rather than be told it. This is the return. If a language model can generate a lexer, a parser, even a register allocator on request, why spend the months it takes to learn to build them by hand? The honest answer is not a denial: a capable model can produce most of the code in this book, and produce it quickly. Pretending otherwise would be the one claim this book is least entitled to make.

The answer is that the value was never in the typing. It is in the reasoning the construction forces, and that reasoning is precisely what is required to *use* a generator well rather than be used by it. A model will, asked confidently enough, produce a constant-folding pass that is unsound on floating point, a copy-propagation that silently breaks a variable assigned on two branches, a claim that a control-flow graph has a back edge where it has only a call. These are not hypothetical; they are the exact mistakes the later chapters taught the reader to catch, because they were among the mistakes made and corrected while the book was built. To catch them you must hold the same hierarchy of abstractions in mind that building the thing installs there. A generated compiler is an assertion, and an assertion you cannot evaluate is not knowledge—it is a hope with good syntax.

This is the sense in which understanding does not get outsourced. The thing a model cannot do for you is not write the code; it is hold the *intent*. The specification—what this language should mean, which constraints are safety and which limitation, where on the ladder to stop—is yours, and so is the judgment that decides whether what came back actually meets it. Chapter 11 made the point formally: a proof is only as meaningful as the specification it is about, and writing the specification is the part no proof, and no generator, performs for you. You can delegate the production of something that means what you intend. You cannot delegate the intending, and you cannot check the result without the understanding that building one, once, by hand, is the surest way to acquire.

So the book trades throughput for that understanding deliberately, and does not pretend the trade is free. What it claims is that the trade is worth making at least once, because the capability it produces—to specify a system precisely, to reason across its levels, to know when an artifact is wrong and why—is the capability directing a powerful tool requires, and the one reading the tool's output will never supply.

What Survives

The title of this conclusion is not about Lark. Lark is a teaching language; it will not survive, and was not built to. What survives is the smaller, more durable thing it was a vehicle for: the ideas, and the habit of mind that holds them together. Instruction sets and memory models, the regular and context-free hierarchies, Hindley–Milner inference and the affine discipline, abstract machines as operational semantics, progress and preservation, Curry–Howard—these outlast any particular language, toolchain, or era's way of producing code. They are what is left when the syntax is forgotten.

And there is one further thing, harder to name: the experience of having built something small enough to understand completely—of having followed a single language from the fetch-decode-execute loop of a real processor to a proof that its meaning is sound, with no level left as a black box. That experience is rare, and becoming rarer. A reader who has had it once knows what complete understanding of a system feels like, and will recognize, ever after, the difference between understanding a thing and merely being able to summon it. That recognition is the most valuable thing this book can leave behind. It is what survives.

Chapter A

The Lark Language

The chapters of this book build Lark a layer at a time and argue each choice where it is made. This appendix stands apart from that progression: it describes the language as a finished object—what it is, what it deliberately is not, and, for reference, its grammar and its surface in full. It is meant to be read on its own, or kept open while reading the chapters.

A.1 What Lark is

Lark—Lambda Affine Resource Kernel—is a small, purely functional language with a modern type system. Six properties define it:

Purely functional. There is no mutable state, no assignment, no reference cell. A function is a mathematical mapping from arguments to result, and computing the same call twice gives the same answer. Iteration is recursion.

Hindley-Milner inference. Types are inferred, not required. A program may carry no annotations at all and still be fully checked; annotations are written where they aid the reader, not where the compiler needs them (Chapter 5).

Algebraic data types. Values are built from sum and product constructors declared with `type`, and taken apart with `match`, which the checker forces to be considered case by case.

Affine ownership. Every value may be used *at most once* unless its type implements the `Copy` trait. This makes resource discipline a type-level property: an `IO` handle cannot be used twice, and the order of effects is visible in the code (Chapter 5).

Traits. Ad-hoc polymorphism without inheritance: a `trait` names a set of operations, and an `impl` provides them for a type.

Compiled to native code. The same language that the CEK machine interprets (Chapter 6) is lowered through three-address code (Chapter 7) to RISC-V and runs on a Raspberry Pi Pico 2/2W.

Its nearest relatives are OCaml (the functional core and inference), Rust (the ownership discipline, simplified to "use at most once"), and Haskell (purity and type classes, without laziness or monads—`IO` is threaded as an explicit token rather than hidden in a monad). The research precedent is Alms, OCaml extended with affine types; Lark is approximately Alms made compilable, with traits in place of a module system.

A.2 What Lark is not

Lark is an *illustration*, and its boundaries are chosen, not accidental. Naming them is the honest way to describe what the language is.

It is not a production language. The omissions are deliberate, and each follows from a principle rather than a lack of time:

- *No mutable state*—no variables that change, no references, no arrays of cells. Purity is total, which is what makes the type system's guarantees absolute.
- *No exceptions.* Failure is an ordinary `Result` value, matched like any other.
- *No garbage collector.* Affine ownership plus a bump-pointer arena means memory is never reclaimed per value; the whole arena is released when the program ends. Affine types are a safety guarantee, not a storage manager.
- *No concurrency, no foreign-function interface, no separate compilation.* Imports are inlined; the whole program is one unit.
- *Minimal `IO`*—`print` and `read` on one standard stream. No files, no network.
- *Fixed-width numbers*—`Int` is 32-bit, `Float` is 32-bit IEEE 754, on every backend.
- *A small standard library*, no subtyping, no inheritance, no higher-kinded or dependent types.

It is not an encyclopedia of compiler techniques. At each layer the book surveys the alternatives, and Lark then commits to *one*: hand-written recursive descent, not LR or PEG (Chapter 4); Algorithm W, not bidirectional or dependent checking (Chapter 5); the CEK machine, three-address code, and linear-scan register allocation, not their many rivals (Chapters 6–7). The roads not taken are described as theory; the language embodies a single coherent path, so that a reader can follow one route from source text to silicon without ever losing the thread.

What it is, then, is a member of an old tradition: the teaching language built to be understood completely—Wirth's PL/0, the Pascal subset whose compiler fits in a chapter; Appel's Tiger; Nystrom's Lox. What sets Lark apart within that tradition is that it carries a genuinely modern type system—inference, affine ownership, traits—and that it does not stop at an interpreter: it compiles to native code and runs on real hardware. It is neither a toy nor a product. It is an illustration sized to be held whole in the mind, and run.

A.3 The language at a glance

A single program exercises most of the surface. It declares an algebraic data type, a trait and its implementation, a higher-order function, and a `main` that threads the affine `IO` token through two prints.

Listing A.1: A complete Lark program (verified against `lark/07`)

```
module Shapes

(* an algebraic data type: a sum of two constructors *)
type Shape =
  | Circle of Float
  | Rect of Float, Float

(* a trait names shared behaviour; impl provides it *)
trait HasArea a = {
  fn area : a -> Float
}

impl HasArea for Shape = {
  fn area(s) =
    match s with
    | Circle(r)  => 3.14159 * r * r
    | Rect(w, h) => w * h
    end
}

(* higher-order function: takes a function as argument *)
fn describe(f : Shape -> Float, s : Shape) : String =
```

```
  "area = " + show(f(s))

(* main threads the affine IO token through each print *)
fn main(io : IO) : IO =
  let c = Circle(2.0) in
  let r = Rect(3.0, 4.0) in
  let io = print(io, describe(area, c)) in
  print(io, describe(area, r))
```

It prints

```
area = 12.56636
area = 12.0
```

Every construct here is introduced in a chapter: lexical form in Chapter 3, the grammar that parses it in Chapter 4, the types and the affine and trait rules in Chapter 5, and the evaluation that produces the output in Chapter 6.

A.4 Grammar

The surface grammar in EBNF. Lowercase `names` denote variables, function names, and type variables; capitalised `Names` denote types and constructors. Reproduced from `lark/01/docs/grammar.ebnf` (the lexical enumerations of digits and letters are elided).

Listing A.2: Lark surface grammar (EBNF)

```
program       = module_decl { import_decl } { top_decl } ;
module_decl   = "module" Name ;
import_decl   = "import" Name [ "exposing"
                  "(" name_list ")" ] ;
name_list     = ( name | Name ) { "," ( name | Name ) } ;

top_decl      = [ "export" ] decl ;
decl          = fn_decl | let_decl | type_decl
              | trait_decl | impl_decl ;

fn_decl       = "fn" name [ "[" bounds "]" ]
                 "(" [ params ] ")"
                  [ ":" type ] "=" expr ;
let_decl      = "let" name [ ":" type ] "=" expr ;
type_decl     = "type" Name { name } "=" type_body ;
trait_decl    = "trait" Name { name } "="
```

```
                 "{" { trait_method } "}" ;
impl_decl     = "impl" Name { atom_type } "for" atom_type "="
                 "{" { impl_method } "}" ;

params        = param { "," param } ;
param         = name [ ":" type ] ;
bounds        = bound { "," bound } ;
bound         = Name name ;
trait_method = "fn" name ":" type ;
impl_method  = "fn" name "(" [ params ] ")" "=" expr ;

expr          = let_expr | if_expr | match_expr
              | lambda_expr | infix_expr ;
let_expr      = "let" name [ ":" type ] "=" expr "in" expr ;
if_expr       = "if" expr "then" expr "else" expr ;
match_expr    = "match" expr "with"
                 { "|" pattern "=>" expr } "end" ;
lambda_expr   = "fn" "(" [ params ] ")" "=>" expr ;

infix_expr    = unary_expr { op unary_expr } ;
unary_expr    = unary_op unary_expr | apply_expr ;
unary_op      = "-" | "not" ;
apply_expr    = atom { "(" [ args ] ")" } ;
args          = expr { "," expr } ;
atom          = literal | name | Name | "(" expr ")"
              | "(" expr "," expr { "," expr } ")" ;

type          = fn_type ;
fn_type       = atom_type "->" fn_type | atom_type ;
atom_type     = Name | Name "(" type { "," type } ")"
              | name
              | "()" | "(" type ")"
              | "(" type "," type { "," type } ")" ;
type_body     = type
              | "|" Name [ "of" type ]
                { "|" Name [ "of" type ] } ;

pattern       = "_" | literal | name
              | Name [ "(" pattern { "," pattern } ")" ]
              | "(" pattern "," pattern { "," pattern } ")" ;

op            = "+" | "-" | "*" | "/" | "==" | "!="
              | "<" | "<=" | ">" | ">=" | "and" | "or" ;
literal       = integer | float | string
              | "true" | "false" | "()" ;
```

Three points the grammar leaves implicit. Application is always parenthesised (f(x), never juxtaposition f x); -> in a type is right-associative; and trait bounds are written in square brackets after the function name—[Copy a] or [Show a, Show b]—each bound of the form Name name.

A.5 Quick reference

Reserved words. and, else, end, export, false, fn, if, impl, import, in, let, match, module, not, of, or, then, trait, true, type, where, with. None may be used as an identifier.

Built-in types. Int (32-bit), Float (32-bit IEEE 754), Bool, String, IO, and () (unit). Compound forms: function types a -> b, tuple types (a, b), and applied types such as Result(a, b). The primitive types implement Copy; IO and user types do not, unless declared.

Operator precedence, lowest to highest:

Level	Operators	Associativity
1 (lowest)	or	left
2	and	left
3	== != < <= > >=	left
4	+ -	left
5	* /	left
6	- (negation), not	prefix
7 (highest)	f(x) application	—

Built-in functions (always in scope, no import needed):

Function	Type	Description
`print`	`IO -> String -> IO`	print a line to stdout
`read`	`IO -> (IO, String)`	read a line; `IO` returned first
`show`	`a -> String`	convert to string
`string_length`	`String -> Int`	length in characters
`int_abs`	`Int -> Int`	absolute value
`float_abs`	`Float -> Float`	absolute value
`float_sqrt`	`Float -> Float`	square root
`float_floor`	`Float -> Float`	floor
`float_ceil`	`Float -> Float`	ceiling
`int_to_float`	`Int -> Float`	widen to float
`float_to_int`	`Float -> Int`	truncate to integer
`int_to_string`	`Int -> String`	format integer
`float_to_string`	`Float -> String`	format float

A small `Stdlib` module adds integer, float, string, and `Option` utilities, brought in with `import Stdlib exposing (...)`. The `samples/` directory of the companion code holds nine complete programs; the repository's `tutorial.md` is a longer, worked tour of the language.

Chapter B

The Decision Record

Lark was not designed all at once. It was built in *phases*, each sealed as a snapshot in `lark/0N/`, and each phase records its design decisions in `lark/0N/docs/decisions.md`. Those files are cumulative: every phase restates the decisions of the phases before it and appends its own, so the last phase's file is the whole ledger and the diff between two phases is exactly what that step added. This appendix is that ledger, read in phase order—the language shown as the sum of its choices, accumulating the way it was actually built.

The point of reading it this way is the book's central claim, made scannable: a decision taken in one phase constrains the next. `Copy`-as-a-trait, fixed in Phase 0, is what makes the affine `IO` token of Phase 4 enforceable; the affine token is what lets the Phase 5 code generator emit no ownership checks; the flat IR of Phase 5 is what turns a tail call into a jump. Each entry names the decision, gives the reason in a line, and, where the choice was contested, names the alternative rejected. Phase numbers skip from 0 to 2: Phase 1 is the machine-checked soundness proof (`lark/formal/proof/`), completed between the interpreter and the compiler. The chapter where each phase is discussed is noted in its heading, and the foreword tabulates the folder-to-chapter map of the phases. The full prose rationale, including the implementation-level decisions omitted here, is in the `decisions.md` files themselves.

B.1 Phase 0 — Language design and the lexer (`lark/01`)

Discussed in Chapter 3; the language-wide choices recur through Chapters 4–6. The first phase fixes what the language *is* and builds the scanner.

Delimiter-based syntax. `in` closes `let`, `end` closes `match`; there is no significant whitespace. This keeps the grammar LL(1) and the lexer stateless.

Instead of Python-style indentation, whose synthetic INDENT/DEDENT tokens make the grammar context-sensitive at the lexical level.

`Copy` **as a trait.** All types are affine by default—used at most once; a type opts into free copying by implementing the `Copy` marker trait. Resources are safe by default, as in Rust. *Instead of* treating data as copyable and requiring resources to be declared specially.

`Result` **for errors.** Errors are ordinary `Result a b` values, handled by `match`. There are no exceptions.

File-level modules. One `.lark` file is one module; `import Name exposing (…)` brings names in.

Affine `IO` by resource threading. `IO` is an affine resource that each operation consumes and returns, so it can never be duplicated or used out of order. *Instead of* a monad or unrestricted side effects.

`name` / `Name` **convention.** A lowercase initial marks a variable or type variable; an uppercase initial marks a type or constructor. The lexer classifies on the first letter.

`()` **as a single token.** An open parenthesis immediately followed by a close lexes as one UNIT token—so a zero-argument thunk cannot be written, and unit is one value.

Nested block comments. `(* … *)` may nest; the lexer tracks depth with a counter. A deliberately non-regular feature kept inside the lexer rather than the grammar.

B.2 Phase 2 — The parser (`lark/02`)

Discussed in Chapter 4.

Hand-written recursive descent. One function per grammar rule. *Instead of* a parser generator or a combinator library.

Precedence by level-chain. Operator precedence is encoded as a chain of functions, one per level, each calling the next.

Separate syntactic and typed ASTs. The parser produces a syntactic tree (`tree.py`); the checker will produce a distinct typed tree (`typed_tree.py`).

`_` in parameter position. The wildcard token is accepted as an unnamed parameter, not only as a pattern.

B.3 Phase 3 — The type checker (`lark/03`)

Discussed in Chapter 5.

Hindley-Milner inference. Algorithm W in a single synthesis pass over the tree; the bidirectional refinement is described but deliberately not taken (Chapter 5).

A separate internal type representation. `ty.py` uses integer-identified type variables, distinct from the surface types in the parse tree.

Affine tracking by an explicit set. The checker tracks only locally-bound non-`Copy` names, not the affinity of every type.

Function types are `Copy`. A function value may be referenced any number of times without being consumed.

Let-recursion via a fresh variable. A declaration's own name is bound to a fresh type variable before its body is checked, so it may call itself.

ADT constructor types. Each variant becomes a function in the type environment—nullary constructors get the datatype directly, others a function into it.

B.4 Phase 4 — The interpreter: the CEK machine (`lark/04`)

Discussed in Chapter 6.

A small-step iterative loop. The machine is one `while` loop; `step` produces the next state until a value meets an empty continuation.

Continuation as a list of frames. The continuation is a plain list, pushed and popped at the front—the call stack made into data.

`VPartialCon` for constructors. Constructors are curried in the value domain, applied one field at a time.

`VDispatch` for trait methods. Trait resolution is deferred to run time; a trait method is a value that selects an implementation by the runtime type of its argument.

`is_copy(TVar)` is `True`. An unresolved type variable is treated as copyable, so polymorphic code raises no spurious affine error. *Instead of* a conservative `False`.

Phase 1, the soundness proof (`lark/formal/proof/`, discussed in Chapter 11), is completed here—between the interpreter and the compiler—which is why the phase numbers resume at 2 for the snapshots and the proof carries the out-of-sequence number 1.

B.5 Phase 5 – The compiler and its analyses (`lark/05`)

Discussed in Chapter 7 (the IR) and Chapter 9 (code generation). The largest phase: typed tree to TAC to RISC-V, with the analysis pipeline that register allocation needs.

Three-address code as the IR. The compiler lowers to flat TAC and then to assembly; flatness makes liveness, reachability, and dominance properties of a sequence rather than a tree. *Instead of* direct tree-walking code generation, a bytecode, or continuation-passing style.

Lambda lifting and closure conversion. Nested lambdas are lifted to top-level functions that carry their captured values in an explicit environment record.

Curried multi-parameter lambdas. A multi-argument function is desugared into a chain of one-argument functions, so application has a single rule.

A uniform closure calling convention. Every lifted function takes `(env, arg)`, whether or not it captures anything.

String tags in TAC, integer tags in assembly. Constructor tags are readable names in the IR and compact integers in the backend.

A TAC VM before RISC-V. A TAC interpreter validates the lowering against the CEK oracle before any native code is emitted.

The CFG as the unit of analysis. Liveness is a property of control flow, so the flat code is first recovered as a graph of basic blocks.

Backward dataflow for liveness. Live sets are computed by an iterative fixpoint over the CFG, running backward from uses to definitions.

Interference by clique per block. The interference graph adds a clique over the variables live at each point (Appel's build).

Move coalescing on copy edges. Variables related by a copy are placed in the same register where the interference graph allows, removing the copy.

Linear scan over graph colouring. Registers are assigned by linear scan over live intervals. *Instead of* graph colouring—simpler, and enough for this target.

Callee-saved registers as the pool. Allocation draws from `s1–s11`, so allocated values survive calls without save and restore at every call site.

Self-tail-call optimisation. A function whose last act is to call itself reuses its own frame—the jump-back edge the IR chapter deferred, turning a tail call into a loop.

Floats via runtime stubs. `RV32I` has no floating-point instructions, so float arithmetic and comparison call software routines.

`True`/`False` as integer constants. Booleans are unboxed integers, not heap records, even though they are nullary constructors elsewhere.

Mutual recursion by backpatch. All top-level names are registered before any body is processed, and closures are backpatched so they can refer to each other.

B.6 Phase 6 — Hardening (`lark/06`)

Discussed in Chapter 8 (optimisation and testing) and Chapter 11 (correctness).

32-bit float semantics on every backend. `Float` is IEEE 754 single precision everywhere, so the interpreter, the TAC VM, and native code agree to the bit.

Differential testing. Every acceptance test runs through all three backends and the outputs must be byte-identical—the cross-backend agreement oracle.

Property tests over source strings. Generated test programs are Lark *source*, exercised through the whole pipeline. *Instead of* generating typed AST nodes and skipping the front end.

Affinity checks both `if` branches. A resource used in both branches of an `if` is rejected, even though only one branch runs—the type discipline is about the program text, not the execution.

B.7 Phase 7 — Native runtime and REPL (`lark/07`)

Discussed in Chapter 10.

`TraitBoundError` by post-pass. Trait bounds are checked in a pass after inference. *Instead of* threading a constraint set through the inference algorithm.

Static `show` routing. A call to `show` is resolved at compile time from the argument's static type, not by a runtime lookup.

A Python interpreter for the REPL. The REPL evaluates on the Python CEK, not the compiled C runtime, so each line runs without a build step.

Re-checking the accumulated source. On every input the REPL re-typechecks all prior declarations, then evaluates only the new ones.

B.8 Phase 8 — Rigour: exhaustiveness, totality, defined `Int` (`lark/08`)

Discussed in Chapter 13.

`Int` wraps, and division follows RISC-V. A 32-bit two's-complement integer that wraps on overflow, with the M extension's division rules (`x/0 = -1`, `x%0 = x`, `INT_MIN/-1 = INT_MIN`) on every backend; the C runtime computes in `uint32_t`, since unsigned overflow is defined in C and signed is not. *Instead of* trapping or arbitrary precision, which no backend implements at zero cost—the hardware wraps for free, so wrap is the one semantics all four runtimes can share. Every overflow escape hatch in the test suites is deleted with it.

Exhaustiveness as a post-pass over the typed AST. Maranget's usefulness algorithm runs after inference and substitution, beside the `Show`-bound check, where column types are final; the witness pattern the recursion constructs becomes the error message. *Instead of* a check inside `infer()`, where the scrutinee may still be a type variable and Algorithm W stops being recognisable.

The match-fail trap stays in the IR. Statically unreachable once the check exists, still emitted: the lowered code remains well-formed without trusting the frontend.

`total` is a contextual modifier, not a keyword. Parsed by lookahead after `fn`, so a function named `total` still parses. *Instead of* a reserved word that breaks existing programs.

No integer descent in the totality checker. Because `Int` wraps, `n - 1` is not well-founded—the checker accepts only structural descent into constructors. Two features designed separately forcing each other's hand; the interaction is the design.

B.9 Phase 9 — The adversary: generation, certificates, discharge (`lark/09`)

Discussed in Chapter 13.

Generate programs by inverting the typing rules. Goal-first generation (pick a type, pick a rule concluding it, recurse into the premises) yields whole well-typed programs, concentrating the fuzzing budget on code that reaches lowering, allocation, and codegen. *Instead of* random text or AST mutation, which mostly exercises the parser's error paths.

Ambiguous operators are a type error. An operator whose operand type is still a type variable when its declaration is generalised is rejected—the monomorphism restriction that ended the RV32 miscompilation, on SML's precedent for overloaded arithmetic. *Instead of* runtime dispatch on RV32 (values are raw 32-bit words, no tags) or whole-program monomorphisation.

Affine variables may not be captured. Closures are `Copy`, so a single capture is a potential duplication; resources enter a lambda as parameters, at the call site where the tracker can count them. *Instead of* counting closure applications, which no static pass can do.

A certificate on every compilation, not a verified allocator. `regcheck.py` re-derives liveness independently, on the flat instruction list, and `asm.gen()` refuses any allocation that fails it; a failure is an internal compiler error, deliberately outside the user diagnostics. *Instead of* the old `verify()`, which shared its analyses with the allocator it judged, and instead of proving linear scan correct once—the certificate survives an allocator rewrite.

The kernel checks everything, and `fix` is gated out. Bare terms are type-checked before normalisation, any failed line fails the run, and general recursion sits behind `core_allow_fix`—off for the proof kernel, on for the `llang` runner, because consistency is exactly the totality of the total layer. *Instead of* soundness by discipline, which Chapter 13 shows had already failed three ways.

`Float` **stays out of the generator.** The TAC machine computes in double precision while the CEK rounds through single, so random float programs diverge by design; the debt is documented rather than papered over.

Chapter C

Reading the Formalism

This appendix is a decoder, not a mathematics course. The book's formal notation—the $\Gamma \vdash e : T$ of Chapter 5, the horizontal bars of the typing rules, the "proof by induction" of Chapter 11, the Π and Σ of Chapter 12, the graded judgements of Chapter 13—is compact, and compactness is exactly its point and exactly its cost. For a reader trained in mathematical logic the notation is transparent; this book does not assume that reader. It assumes a programmer, and it makes that programmer one promise here: *every piece of formal notation in this book is a compressed description of code you have already seen.* A judgement is the signature of a function in `infer.py`. An inference rule is one clause of that function. A derivation is its call tree. A proof by induction is a recursive function. None of these is an analogy; each is, as this appendix shows, the literal content of the notation.

Read this appendix in either of two ways. Straight through before Chapter 5, as a fifteen-minute inoculation; or on demand, when a chapter's notation outruns you, using the table in Section C.4 as the entry point. Nothing here is new material—it is the book's existing content, read at half speed.

C.1 A Judgement Is a Question

The workhorse notation of Chapters 5 through 12 is the *typing judgement*:

$$\Gamma \vdash e : T$$

Read it aloud, right to left of the turnstile first: "the expression e has type T, under the assumptions Γ." Three parts, each with an exact counterpart in the type checker:

- Γ (capital gamma) is the *type environment*: the record of what is currently in scope and at what type. In `infer.py` it is the parameter named `env`—

a dictionary from names to types. When the notation writes $\Gamma,\ x : T$ ("Γ extended with x at type T"), the code copies `env` and adds one entry before recursing into a binder's body.

- $\vdash$ (the *turnstile*) is punctuation, not an operation. It separates the assumptions from the claim, the way a colon separates a Python signature from its body. There is nothing to compute in a turnstile; it marks where the "given" ends and the "then" begins.
- $e : T$ is the claim itself: this expression, that type.

Put together, the judgement is not a statement of fact but a *question that the checker answers*: given `env`, does `e` have type `T`? Which is to say, the judgement is the type signature of the checker itself:

Listing C.1: The judgement $\Gamma \vdash e : T$, as a signature (from `infer.py`, simplified)

```
def infer(env, expr):        # Gamma |- e : ?
    ...
    return typ               # ... : T
```

A valid judgement is one the function returns successfully; an invalid one raises a type error. Everything else in the formal chapters is built from this one reading, so it is worth pausing until it feels obvious: $\Gamma \vdash e : T$ *is* `infer(env, e) == T`, written in a notation five decades older than Python.

C.2 An Inference Rule Is a Clause of a Recursive Function

The horizontal bar is where most readers stall, and the decoding is one sentence: *above the bar are the recursive calls; below the bar is the return value.* An inference rule

$$\frac{\textit{premise}_1 \qquad \textit{premise}_2 \qquad \cdots}{\textit{conclusion}}$$

says: to establish the conclusion, establish each premise. As code: to return the value below the line, first make the calls above it. A rule with *nothing* above the bar is an *axiom*—a judgement that holds with no subgoals—and its code reading is just as direct: it is a base case, a clause that returns without recursing.

Here is the correspondence at full length, on the rule for `if`. The rule (Chapter 5 style):

$$\frac{\Gamma \vdash e_c : \mathrm{Bool} \qquad \Gamma \vdash e_1 : T \qquad \Gamma \vdash e_2 : T}{\Gamma \vdash \texttt{if}\ e_c\ \texttt{then}\ e_1\ \texttt{else}\ e_2\ :\ T}$$

Three premises: the condition is a `Bool`, and the two branches have the same type T, which is then the type of the whole expression. Now the clause of `infer` that implements it (simplified from `infer.py`—the substitution plumbing that Hindley–Milner threads through every call is elided, since it is bookkeeping for unification, not part of the rule's shape):

Listing C.2: The same rule as code: the `IfExpr` case of `infer` (simplified from `infer.py`)

```
case IfExpr(cond=cond, then_=then_, else_=else_):
    ct = infer(env, cond)        # premise 1: G |- e_c : ...
    unify(ct, T_BOOL)            #    ... and it must be Bool
    tt = infer(env, then_)       # premise 2: G |- e_1 : T
    et = infer(env, else_)       # premise 3: G |- e_2 : T
    unify(tt, et)                #    ... the same T
    return tt                    # conclusion: whole if : T
```

Read them side by side and the mapping is total. Each premise above the bar is one recursive call to `infer`. A *side condition*—the requirement that the condition's type be `Bool`, that the branches agree—is a `unify` (in a checker without inference, it would be a plain equality test). The conclusion below the bar is the `return`. The metavariables e_c, e_1, e_2, T are the local variables of the clause. There is no residue: nothing in the rule fails to appear in the code, and nothing in the code (once unification's plumbing is set aside) fails to appear in the rule.

Derivations are call trees. Chapter 5 says a proof of $\Gamma \vdash e : T$ is a *tree* of rule applications. The code reading: it is the *call tree* of `infer`—the trace a debugger would show, with one stack frame per rule application. For a concrete instance, here is the full derivation that `if true then 1 else 2` has type `Int`, first as the formal tree,

$$\frac{\vdash \texttt{true} : \mathrm{Bool} \qquad \vdash \texttt{1} : \mathrm{Int} \qquad \vdash \texttt{2} : \mathrm{Int}}{\vdash \texttt{if true then 1 else 2} : \mathrm{Int}}$$

whose three leaves are axioms (a literal has its type, with nothing to check above the bar), and then as the trace:

Listing C.3: The same derivation, as the checker's call tree

```
infer({}, IfExpr(...))                   # the root of the tree
  infer({}, Lit(true))   -> Bool    # leaf: axiom for literals
  infer({}, Lit(1))      -> Int     # leaf
  infer({}, Lit(2))      -> Int     # leaf
                         -> Int     # the conclusion
```

When a formal chapter says "by the derivation of $\Gamma \vdash e : T$" it means: by the structure of this call tree, which exists exactly when the checker succeeds. And when Chapter 11 builds a value of the dependent type `Expr g t`, it is building this same tree as a *data structure*—the call tree reified, so that a later proof can recurse over it.

C.3 A Proof by Induction Is a Recursive Function

"We proceed by induction on the structure of e" is the sentence that most often loses the reader untrained in proof, and it should not, because the reader of this book has been *writing* structural inductions since Chapter 4. Every function in this book that recurses over the AST—the parser's printer, `infer`, the lowerer, the CEK machine's dispatch—has the same shape: one case per node kind, each case handling its node by calling the function on the node's children and combining the results. Structural induction is that shape, used to establish a property rather than compute a value.

The dictionary is three entries long:

- *The property $P(e)$ to prove* is the function's return type: the evidence the function delivers for its argument.
- *The induction hypothesis* is the recursive call's return value: the evidence, already in hand, for the children. Nothing more mysterious than trusting your own recursion—which is exactly what every recursive function does.
- *One case per rule (or constructor)* is the `match`: the proof must handle every way an e can be built, just as a total function must handle every constructor—the same exhaustiveness the checker enforces on Lark programs.

The book contains a perfect specimen, and it is only three lines. The main theorem of Chapter 11—evaluation soundness—is proved "by induction on the evaluation." Here is that proof, as it actually appears in `lark-preservation.lcore`:

Listing C.4: Induction as recursion (`lark-preservation.lcore`)

```
eval_produces_val : Eval t e v -> IsVal t v
eval_produces_val = indrec Eval
   (\t e v _. IsVal t v)      -- the property P
   (\t v iv. iv)              -- base case: evidence in hand
   (\t e e' v s ev ih. ih)    -- inductive case: use the IH
```

The motive is the property; the two cases match the two constructors of `Eval`; and the induction hypothesis is literally an argument named `ih`, delivered by the recursion and passed along. When Chapter 12 says that under Curry–Howard, induction and recursion "are one operation," this is the cash value: the proof *is* the recursive function, checked for the same two things any total recursive function needs—that every case is covered, and that the recursion is on something smaller.

C.4 The Symbols, in One Table

Each row gives the notation, how to say it aloud, and its counterpart in the book's code. The last column is where the book first leans on it.

Notation	Say it as	In code	From
$e ::= x \mid \lambda x.e \mid \ldots$	"an e is one of ..."	the AST node classes	Ch. 4
Γ	"the environment"	the `env` dict	Ch. 5
$\Gamma,\ x : T$	"Γ, with x at T"	`env` plus one entry	Ch. 5
$(x : T) \in \Gamma$	"Γ maps x to T"	`env[x] == T`	Ch. 5
$\Gamma \vdash e : T$	"under Γ, e has type T"	`infer(env, e) == T`	Ch. 5
$\frac{P_1 \quad P_2}{C}$	"from P_1 and P_2, get C"	recursive calls, then return	Ch. 5
$T_1 \to T_2$	"function from T_1 to T_2"	`TFn` in `ty.py`	Ch. 5
$e \to e'$	"e steps to e'"	one CEK transition	Ch. 10
$e[x := v]$	"e with v for x"	the CEK machine's env	Ch. 10
$\{P\}\ c\ \{Q\}$	"if P before c, then Q after"	pre/post contract	Ch. 11
$\forall x.P(x), \Pi(x{:}A).B(x)$	"for every x ..."	a (dependent) function	Ch. 12
$\exists x.P(x), \Sigma(x{:}A).B(x)$	"some x such that ..."	a (dependent) pair	Ch. 12
$\bot$, `Empty`	"false; the type with no value"	an uninhabited type	Ch. 12
`Expr g t`	"derivations of g $\vdash$ _ : t"	the call tree, as data	Ch. 11
$0, 1, \omega$ (grades)	"unusable; at most once; freely"	`is_copy`, the `tracked` dict	Ch. 13
`GExpr g t g'`	"from g, $e : t$, leaving `g'`"	`tracked`, before and after	Ch. 13

Table C.1: The book's formal notation, decoded. The two arrows are unrelated despite the shared glyph: between *types*, $\to$ builds a function type; between *expressions*, $\to$ is one step of evaluation. Context always disambiguates, but the collision is worth knowing about in advance.

C.5 How to Read a Formal Statement

Decoding symbols is necessary but not sufficient; a dense formal display must also be read *slowly*, and slowness has a technique. Four moves, in order, work on every formal statement in this book:

1. Name the judgement forms. Find the shapes: is this about typing ($\Gamma \vdash e : T$), stepping ($e \to e'$), or both? A theorem like preservation—if $e : \tau$ and $e \to e'$, then $e' : \tau$—is one sentence *relating* two judgements, and seeing that is most of reading it.

2. Read each rule as a clause. Above the bar, recursive calls; below, the return; side conditions, `if`-guards (Section C.2). If a rule resists, find its code twin: the formal specification (`lark-formal.tex`) keeps a correspondence table mapping every formal construct to the Lark source line that implements it, and the chapters cite files throughout.

3. Feed it the smallest program you can. Metavariables invite vagueness; kill it with an instance. For anything about typing, try `if true then 1 else 2`; for anything about stepping, try $(\lambda x.\, x)$ `1`. One concrete derivation, worked with a pencil, is worth three readings of the general rule—and the exercises in Chapters 5, 11 and 12 are built to force exactly this move.

4. Ask what would break it. Every rule earns its keep by *rejecting* something. For each rule, construct the smallest program that violates it (`if 1 then 2 else 3`; a branch mismatch; a variable used after it is consumed) and check that the rule, read as code, throws. A rule understood only by its acceptances is half understood—the book's whole final act, from the differential tests of Chapter 11 to the planted-bug validations of its proofs, runs on this move.

None of this makes the formal chapters easy; it makes them readable, which is the correct ambition. The notation is five decades of compression applied to ideas this book spends four hundred pages decompressing—and the code, which the reader can always run, was inside it all along. When a display stalls you, come back to the table, take the four moves in order, and trust the promise this appendix opened with: it is all code you have already seen.

Bibliography

[Abelson et al., 1996] Abelson, H., Sussman, G. J., and Sussman, J. (1996). *Structure and Interpretation of Computer Programs.* MIT Press, Cambridge, MA, 2nd edition.

[Ager et al., 2003] Ager, M. S., Biernacki, D., Danvy, O., and Midtgaard, J. (2003). A functional correspondence between evaluators and abstract machines. In *Proceedings of the 5th ACM SIGPLAN International Conference on Principles and Practice of Declarative Programming (PPDP)*, pages 8–19, New York, NY. ACM.

[Aho et al., 2006] Aho, A. V., Lam, M. S., Sethi, R., and Ullman, J. D. (2006). *Compilers: Principles, Techniques, and Tools.* Addison-Wesley, 2nd edition. The Dragon Book.

[Appel, 1998] Appel, A. W. (1998). *Modern Compiler Implementation in ML.* Cambridge University Press.

[Atkey, 2018] Atkey, R. (2018). The syntax and semantics of quantitative type theory. In *Proceedings of the 33rd Annual ACM/IEEE Symposium on Logic in Computer Science (LICS)*, pages 56–65. ACM.

[Barendregt, 1984] Barendregt, H. P. (1984). *The Lambda Calculus: Its Syntax and Semantics*, volume 103 of *Studies in Logic and the Foundations of Mathematics.* North-Holland, Amsterdam, revised edition.

[Berger and Schwichtenberg, 1991] Berger, U. and Schwichtenberg, H. (1991). An inverse of the evaluation functional for typed λ-calculus. In *Proceedings of the 6th Annual IEEE Symposium on Logic in Computer Science (LICS)*, pages 203–211. IEEE.

[Chaitin, 1982] Chaitin, G. J. (1982). Register allocation & spilling via graph coloring. In *Proceedings of the SIGPLAN Symposium on Compiler Construction*, pages 98–101, New York, NY. ACM.

[Claessen and Hughes, 2000] Claessen, K. and Hughes, J. (2000). QuickCheck: A lightweight tool for random testing of Haskell programs. In *Proceedings of the 5th ACM SIGPLAN International Conference on Functional Programming (ICFP)*, pages 268–279, New York, NY. ACM.

[Cooper and Torczon, 2022] Cooper, K. D. and Torczon, L. (2022). *Engineering a Compiler.* Morgan Kaufmann, 3rd edition.

[Damas and Milner, 1982] Damas, L. and Milner, R. (1982). Principal type-schemes for functional programs. In *Proceedings of the 9th ACM SIGPLAN-SIGACT Symposium on Principles of Programming Languages (POPL)*, pages 207–212, New York, NY. ACM.

[DeMillo et al., 1978] DeMillo, R. A., Lipton, R. J., and Sayward, F. G. (1978). Hints on test data selection: Help for the practicing programmer. *Computer*, 11(4):34–41.

[Hindley, 1969] Hindley, R. (1969). The principal type-scheme of an object in combinatory logic. *Transactions of the American Mathematical Society*, 146:29–60.

[Howard, 1980] Howard, W. A. (1980). The formulae-as-types notion of construction. In Seldin, J. P. and Hindley, J. R., editors, *To H. B. Curry: Essays on Combinatory Logic, Lambda Calculus and Formalism*, pages 479–490. Academic Press, London. Original manuscript circulated 1969.

[Kildall, 1973] Kildall, G. A. (1973). A unified approach to global program optimization. In *Proceedings of the 1st Annual ACM SIGACT-SIGPLAN Symposium on Principles of Programming Languages (POPL)*, pages 194–206, New York, NY. ACM.

[Lonnert, 2026] Lonnert, S. (2026). *From Code to Computation: A Modern Guide to Programming and Theory.* BoD.

[Maranget, 2007] Maranget, L. (2007). Warnings for pattern matching. *Journal of Functional Programming*, 17(3):387–421.

[Martin-Löf, 1984] Martin-Löf, P. (1984). *Intuitionistic Type Theory.* Studies in Proof Theory. Bibliopolis, Naples. Notes by Giovanni Sambin of lectures given in Padua, 1980.

[McBride, 2016] McBride, C. (2016). I got plenty o' nuttin'. In *A List of Successes That Can Change the World: Essays Dedicated to Philip Wadler*, volume 9600 of *Lecture Notes in Computer Science*, pages 207–233. Springer.

[McKeeman, 1998] McKeeman, W. M. (1998). Differential testing for software. *Digital Technical Journal*, 10(1):100–107.

[Milner, 1978] Milner, R. (1978). A theory of type polymorphism in programming. *Journal of Computer and System Sciences*, 17(3):348–375.

[Necula, 2000] Necula, G. C. (2000). Translation validation for an optimizing compiler. In *Proceedings of the ACM SIGPLAN 2000 Conference on Programming Language Design and Implementation (PLDI)*, pages 83–94, New York, NY. ACM.

[Nielson and Nielson, 2007] Nielson, H. R. and Nielson, F. (2007). *Semantics with Applications: An Appetizer*. Undergraduate Topics in Computer Science. Springer, London.

[Nystrom, 2021] Nystrom, R. (2021). *Crafting Interpreters*. Genever Benning. Also freely available at `https://craftinginterpreters.com`.

[Pałka et al., 2011] Pałka, M. H., Claessen, K., Russo, A., and Hughes, J. (2011). Testing an optimising compiler by generating random lambda terms. In *Proceedings of the 6th International Workshop on Automation of Software Test (AST)*, pages 91–97, New York, NY. ACM.

[Patterson and Waterman, 2017] Patterson, D. A. and Waterman, A. (2017). *The RISC-V Reader: An Open Architecture Atlas*. Strawberry Canyon, Berkeley, CA, 1st edition.

[Plotkin, 1981] Plotkin, G. D. (1981). A structural approach to operational semantics. Technical Report DAIMI FN-19, Computer Science Department, Aarhus University.

[Pnueli et al., 1998] Pnueli, A., Siegel, M., and Singerman, E. (1998). Translation validation. In *Proceedings of the 4th International Conference on Tools and Algorithms for the Construction and Analysis of Systems (TACAS)*, volume 1384 of *Lecture Notes in Computer Science*, pages 151–166. Springer.

[Poletto and Sarkar, 1999] Poletto, M. and Sarkar, V. (1999). Linear scan register allocation. *ACM Transactions on Programming Languages and Systems*, 21(5):895–913.

[Pollack, 1998] Pollack, R. (1998). How to believe a machine-checked proof. In *Twenty-Five Years of Constructive Type Theory*, pages 205–220. Oxford University Press.

[Reynolds, 1972] Reynolds, J. C. (1972). Definitional interpreters for higher-order programming languages. In *Proceedings of the ACM Annual Conference*, pages 717–740, New York, NY. ACM.

[Serebryany et al., 2012] Serebryany, K., Bruening, D., Potapenko, A., and Vyukov, D. (2012). AddressSanitizer: A fast address sanity checker. In *Proceedings of the 2012 USENIX Annual Technical Conference*, pages 309–318. USENIX Association.

[Thompson, 1968] Thompson, K. (1968). Programming techniques: Regular expression search algorithm. *Communications of the ACM*, 11(6):419–422.

[Thompson, 1984] Thompson, K. (1984). Reflections on trusting trust. *Communications of the ACM*, 27(8):761–763.

[Tov and Pucella, 2011] Tov, J. A. and Pucella, R. (2011). Practical affine types. In *Proceedings of the 38th Annual ACM SIGPLAN-SIGACT Symposium on Principles of Programming Languages (POPL)*, pages 447–458. ACM.

[Wadler, 2015] Wadler, P. (2015). Propositions as types. *Communications of the ACM*, 58(12):75–84.

[Waterman and Asanović, 2019] Waterman, A. and Asanović, K. (2019). The RISC-V instruction set manual, volume I: Unprivileged ISA. Technical report, RISC-V Foundation.

[Wright and Felleisen, 1994] Wright, A. K. and Felleisen, M. (1994). A syntactic approach to type soundness. *Information and Computation*, 115(1):38–94.

[Yang et al., 2011] Yang, X., Chen, Y., Eide, E., and Regehr, J. (2011). Finding and understanding bugs in C compilers. In *Proceedings of the 32nd ACM SIGPLAN Conference on Programming Language Design and Implementation (PLDI)*, pages 283–294, New York, NY. ACM.

Index

6502, 14
  register scarcity, 159

abstract machine, 110, 175
  as semantic claim, 180
abstract syntax tree, 68
adversarial testing, 205
affine type, 18, 93, 225
  as correctness, 189
  soundness hole, 212
Agda, 200
algebraic data type, 89, 225
algebraic simplification, 147
Algorithm W, 85, 99
assembler, 33
AST, *see* abstract syntax tree
attribute grammar, 109

backpatching, 237
backtracking, 179
bare metal, 161
basic block, 128
beta reduction, 178
bidirectional type checking, 99, 200
binding, 79
bottom-up parsing, 66
bytecode, 32

call-by-value, 178
calling convention, 17, 157
CEK machine, 105, 110, 177
certifying compilation, 211
Clean, 93
closure, 82, 107, 177
closure conversion, 131
code generation, 153
Cogent, 93
coherence, 96
common subexpression elimination, 130
concrete syntax tree, 68
consistency
  logical, 214
constant folding, 144
constant pool, 32
constant propagation, 144
constructor, 89
context-free grammar, 60
continuation, 110, 177
contraction, 93
control-flow graph, 128
correctness, 183
  three meanings, 183
Curry-Howard correspondence, 83, 193, 194
currying, 107
cut, 179

de Bruijn index, 198
dead code elimination, 145
decidability, 201
demotion

of graded contexts, 214
dependent types, 189, 193, 196
derivation, 60
as call tree, 243
design decisions, 233
DFA, 44
differential testing, 136, 188
and generated code, 188
directed acyclic graph, 130
dispatch
computed goto, 31
interpreter, 30
switch, 30
dynamic scope, 82

eliminator, 196
embedded systems, 19
environment, 79, 107
erasure functor, 214
error handling
parser, 72
error recovery, 72
error reporting
lexical, 55
type checker, 99
evaluation, 105
evaluation context, 178
exhaustiveness, 89
exhaustiveness checking, 206

Felleisen, Matthias, 177
fetch-decode-execute, 12
finite automaton, 44
First set, 64
`fix`
and consistency, 214
Follow set, 64
formal specification, 187
formalism
reading, 241
reading method, 245
Frege, Gottlob, 83
fuzzing, 188
differential, 205

generalisation, 85
graded types, 212
graph colouring, 155

heap, 17, 18
Hindley-Milner inference, 85, 225
Hoare logic, 184

identity element, 147
Idris, 200
impl block, 96
induction
as recursion, 244
structural, 244
inference rule
how to read, 242
inherited attribute, 109
instantiation, 85
instruction selection, 154
instruction set, 11
instruction set design, 32
interference graph, 236
intermediate representation, 123
motivation, 124
interpreter, 105
limits, 117
IR, *see* intermediate representation
ISWIM, 176

judgement
how to read, 241

Kleene's theorem, 46

lambda calculus, 84
lambda lifting, 236
Landin, Peter, 176
large language model
checking output of, 188
Lark, 3
build phases, 233

reference, 225
scanner, 47
`lcore`, 196
leader, 128
Lean, 200
left recursion, 61
leftover typing, 213
let-polymorphism, 85
LexError, 55
lexical analysis, 41
lexical scope, 82, 107
linear scan, 155
linear type, 93
live interval, 155
liveness, 145
LL(1) parsing, 64
load-store, 16
load-store architecture, 16, 157
logic programming, 179
loop optimization, 147
loop-invariant code motion, 147
lowering, 131
LR parsing, 66

Martin-Löf type theory, 196
maximal munch, 154
measurement, 148
memory model, 17
monomorphism restriction, 207, 209
MOS Technology 6502, *see* 6502
move coalescing, 236
mutation testing, 209

name resolution, 79
NFA, 44
nonterminal, 60
normalisation by evaluation, 196
notation
how to read, 241
table of, 245

occurs check, 85
ontology, 83
opcode, 23
operand encoding, 32
operational semantics, 175
operator precedence, 230
optimization, 143
diminishing returns, 148
meaning preservation, 143
oracle
differential, 136
orphan rule, 96
ownership, 93, 225

panic mode, 72
parse table, 64
parse tree, 68
ParseError, 72
parser, 59
recursive descent, 61
strategy, 67
parsing, 59
pattern matching, 89
ϕ-function, 129
Π-type, 196
planted bugs, 209
polymorphism
ad-hoc, 96
postcondition, 184
precondition, 184
premature optimization, 148
preservation, 185
production rule, 60
profiling, 32
program generation
well-typed, 207
progress, 185
Prolog, 179
proof burden, 201
proof checker, 193
proof kernel
bugs in, 214

proofs as programs, 194
property-based testing, 188
    generative, 207
propositions as types, 194
pumping lemma, 46

quantitative type theory, 212

Raspberry Pi Pico, 161
reachability analysis, 145
recursive descent, 61
register, 16
register allocation, 15, 155
    certified, 211
register machine, 13
    implementation, 27
regular expression, 46
resolution, 179
resource discipline, 93
resource safety, 189
resource threading, 234
RISC-V, 16
    calling convention, 157
    code generation, 153
Russell, Bertrand, 83
Rust, 93

sanitizers, 209
scanner, 41
    contract, 41
    hand-written, 47
scope, 82
search tree, 179
SECD machine, 176
semantics
    defined, 206
    denotational, 176
    operational, 176
semantics-preserving transformation, 143
semiring
    usage, 212
sense and reference, 83
shift-reduce parsing, 66
Σ-type, 196
simply typed lambda calculus, 84
SLD resolution, 179
soundness proof, 198
specification, 187
spilling, 155
SSA, *see* static single assignment
stack
    call stack, 17
    memory region, 17
stack frame, 157
stack machine, 13
    implementation, 23
static memory, 17, 18
static single assignment, 129
strength reduction, 147
structural operational semantics, 178
subject reduction, 185
subset construction, 46
sum type, 89
symbol table, 79
synthesised attribute, 109

TAC VM, 136
tail call, 110
    elimination, 159
tail-call optimization, 159
temporary, 125
terminal, 60
Thompson, Ken, 214
three-address code, 123, 125
token, 41
totality checking, 206
trait, 96, 226
trait resolution, 96
transition system, 176
translation validation, 211, 212
tree-walking, 105

trusted computing base, 205
  of Lark, 217
type
  philosophical, 83
type checker, 79
type class, 96
type environment, 84
type error, 99
type judgement, 84, 241
type safety, 183
type scheme, 79
type system, 79
  expressiveness ladder, 200
type variable, 85
typing rules, 84, 242

undecidability
  of type checking, 201
unification, 85, 179
uniqueness type, 93

value
  domain, 105
value numbering, 130
vector type, 196
verification condition, 184
virtual machine, 21
  motivation, 22
  performance, 35
virtual register, 125

WAM, *see* Warren Abstract Machine
Warren Abstract Machine, 179
weakening, 93, 198
  discharged, 214
well-typed programs do not go wrong, 185
witness
  non-exhaustiveness, 206

zero page, 159

Colophon

Produced with LaTeX compiled by Tectonic (XeTeX),
normalised for print with Ghostscript.

Typeset in Linux Libertine.
Printed on 90 gsm FSC-certified matte paper
sourced from responsibly managed forests.

Written with the assistance of large language models—
tools subordinate to judgment, not a replacement for it.

The continuation is empty; the machine halts.